The Modern Portrait Poem

The Modern Portrait Poem

FROM DANTE GABRIEL ROSSETTI TO EZRA POUND

FRANCES DICKEY

University of Virginia Press · Charlottesville and London

University of Virginia Press
© 2012 by the Rector and Visitors of the University of Virginia
All rights reserved
Printed in the United States of America on acid-free paper

First published 2012

1 3 5 7 9 8 6 4 2

LIBRARY OF CONGRESS CATALOGING-IN-PUBLICATION DATA

Dickey, Frances, 1970–
The modern portrait poem : from Dante Gabriel Rossetti
to Ezra Pound / Frances Dickey.
p. cm.
Includes bibliographical references and index.
ISBN 978–0–8139–3263–7 (cloth : acid-free paper) —
ISBN 978–0–8139–3269–9 (e-book)
1. Poetry, Modern—History and criticism. 2. Portraits—History.
3. Art, Modern—Influence. I. Title.
PN1069.D53 2012
809.1′03—dc23
2011044937

Contents

Illustrations

Acknowledgments

The poets discussed in the following pages drew from and collaborated with each other to an extent that belies traditional ideas of originality. On a more modest scale, the same is true of this book, built from the contributions of other scholars, shaped by the suggestions and ideas of my teachers, colleagues, and students, and most of all founded on the loving support of my husband, Matthew McGrath, and my sons Thomas and Charles. Without their sacrifices, encouragement, and belief that I would finish, I never could have done so. I dedicate this book to them.

I would like to thank my colleagues at the University of Missouri, especially Timothy Materer, for his encyclopedic knowledge of modern poetry and patient reading of the whole manuscript. In many late night sessions, Alexandra Socarides and Anne Myers also beat and coaxed shapeless writing into argument, vagueness into clarity (but any vagueness that remains is mine). I am grateful to the University of Missouri Research Board, Research Council, and the Center for Arts and Humanities for research leave and funding support. Conversations with members of my 2006 portraiture seminar shaped my initial perceptions of the genre and have fruitfully continued over the years; Peter Monacell and Stefanie Wortman edited and commented on portions of the manuscript; and the students in my 2011 genre seminar helped me work out some final knots as I was finishing.

Special gratitude is due to Jahan Ramazani, who selected my article "Parrot's Eye: A Portrait by Manet and Two by T. S. Eliot" for the Kappel Prize at *Twentieth-Century Literature* in 2006, a vote of confidence that inspired the writing of this book. Thanks also to the journal for permission to reprint portions of that article here. Christopher Ricks, Eliot scholar extraordinaire, contributed essential guidance and leavening to my project. Members of the T. S. Eliot Society also made this book possible by their generous reception of my papers, perceptive comments and corrections, and enthusiasm for the poetry of St. Louis's native son. I would especially like to thank Anthony Cuda, David Chinitz, Michael Coyle, Benjamin Lockerd, Cyrena Pondrom, and Melanie and Tony Fathman. Although this book is not based on my dissertation, I have continued to draw on what I learned from my advisors, Allen Grossman and Walter Benn Michaels. My friends Dan Gil and Faye Halpern also helpfully commented on early versions of chapters in this book. Advice from anonymous referees on grant proposals and on my manuscript at the University of Virginia Press helped organize the book and make it more readable. Thanks also to editors Cathie Brettschneider, Ellen Satrom, and Mark Mones for their expert guidance.

Finally, I wish to thank family members and friends who assisted in countless ways with the work of caring for my children during six years of research and writing, especially their three grandparents, Barbara Dickey and Fran and Gary McGrath, and my friend Rebecca Senzer, who helped out in New Haven so that I could look at manuscripts. I remember with gratitude Thomas Dickey and Franklin Allen, whose kindness continues to sustain life and work.

Thanks to the librarians at the Yale Beinecke Rare Book Library for access to the manuscripts of "To La Mère Inconnue" and "Moeurs Contemporaines." Unpublished material by Ezra Pound: Copyright © 2012 by Mary de Rachewiltz and the Estate of Omar S. Pound. Used by permission of New Directions Publishing Corporation. Thanks also to the owners of Charles Demuth's A Prince of Court Painters for permission to reproduce this painting, and to the Wyndham Lewis Memorial Trust for permission to reproduce The Dancers.

The Modern Portrait Poem

❦

Introduction

IN 1908, T. S. ELIOT saw a painting by Manet and described it in one of his first poems, "On a Portrait." A year and a half later, he began "Portrait of a Lady" in his rooms at Harvard, finishing it in Paris in November, but keeping it to himself until he met Ezra Pound in London four years later. In the meantime, Pound had written several of his own portraits, including "Portrait d'une femme" (1912), and went on to develop the genre in the sequences "Moeurs Contemporaines" and *Hugh Selwyn Mauberley*. Pound's college friend William Carlos Williams wrote a "Self-Portrait" series in 1914, followed by "Portrait of a Woman in Bed," "Portrait in Greys," his own "Portrait of a Lady," and other poems with similar titles. Back from the war, E. E. Cummings assembled a sequence of portraits in his manuscript *Tulips and Chimneys* (1922). This flowering of the portrait poem was not a case of mutual influence, for in most cases the poets were drawn to it before they knew each other's writing. Yet the appearance of these works at the very moment of modernization in poetry was also not exactly spontaneous or unprecedented: the portrait poem was a familiar nineteenth-century genre. In the 1860s Dante Gabriel Rossetti and members of his circle had transformed the Victorian portrait poem by bringing it into conversation with new techniques in figure painting. In their exchanges they explored the relations between surface and depth, exterior and interior, as aspects of both art and persons. Around 1908 a new generation of American poets began writing under the sign of Aestheticism and adopted its characteristic genre, making the portrait a vessel for similar questions about identity, interiority, and the relationship between images and words.

Why did the portrait appeal to these young poets at the outset of their careers? Calling a poem "Portrait" in 1912 identified the work with a set of well-established conventions and precedents. Like other generic titles, such as "Elegy" or "Song," "Portrait" oriented the reader's expectations, making the poem legible even if it went on to disrupt those expectations. While the Modernist portrait poem belongs in a lineage of Victorian poems of the same kind, it also reaches out across the boundaries of media, hailing the visual arts as a point of reference. This combination of generic connectedness and intermedial flexibility made the portrait an ideal vehicle for early Modernist experimentation. The interconnection of the arts in Modernism is well known; indeed, the spontaneous self-modernization that occurred in Anglo-American literature around the time of World War I is often attributed to the influence of the visual arts, in particular Futurism and Cubism. When Virginia Woolf claimed that "on or about December, 1910, human character changed," she may have been referring to the impact of the first Post-Impressionist exhibition, which introduced the work of Cézanne, Matisse, and Picasso to London and, along with the 1910 lectures of Futurist F. T. Marinetti, created an avant-garde sensibility overnight. Our current understanding of the relationship of visual art and poetry in Modernism still hinges on this event, viewed as a break with the past. It is standard to credit Futurism and Cubism with ushering in poetic Modernism by creating the visual sensibility that ruptured the traditions of genre and representation.[1] Nineteen-ten to 1913 was unquestionably a period of intense exchange between the arts that led to radical changes in the practice of poetry. Yet that narrative of Modernism ignores the significance of visual art in Victorian culture, including poetry.[2] In this book I argue that an earlier moment of exchange and collaboration between art and poetry in the Rossetti circle fostered the visual sensibility and interest in issues of portraiture that became central to American Modernist poetry.

In the 1860s, Dante Gabriel Rossetti, James McNeill Whistler, and Algernon Swinburne explored the possibilities of portraiture in a rapid exchange of related works. In a series of paintings of women, Rossetti and Whistler shifted their emphasis from the illusion of depth (both as a visual quality and a trait of the portrait subject) to an aesthetic of surface and pattern. At the same time, Rossetti and Swinburne composed ekphrastic poems about these paintings, poems that called into question the conventions of the Victorian portrait poem. The Rossetti circle thus used the portrait to raise questions that would again preoccupy Modernist poets around 1910. Does the self consist of a soul or interior, and if so, can we know it from appearances? What constitutes a person, if not an inside and an outside? In view of these questions, what should a portrait represent, and how? These questions bespeak uncertainty about what a person is, about the reliability of vision as a guide to knowing others, and about the role of artistic representation. If these questions seem familiar, it is because they are also core concerns of modern poets, who imitated, responded to, and revised Rossetti's portraiture. In this book I trace the reception, adaptation, and modulation of the portrait from Rossetti and Swinburne to Ezra Pound, T. S. Eliot, and William Carlos Williams, as well as E. A. Robinson, Edgar Lee Masters, H.D., Amy Lowell, E. E. Cummings, and the authors of the "Spectra" literary hoax, Arthur Davison Ficke and Witter Bynner. Through the portrait poem, modern poets absorbed and transmitted the literary and visual culture of the nineteenth century in which they learned to write.

Rossetti was still "king," as Whistler called him, until 1912.[3] In the year 1900 alone, more than 140 books by and about Rossetti were published in England and the United States; a show of his paintings at the Pennsylvania Academy of the Fine Arts in 1892 brought this painter to American consciousness for the first time.[4] Eliot and Pound began their careers with portrait poems in the style of Rossetti and Swinburne, responding to paintings by Rossetti, Whistler, Edward Burne-Jones, and their contemporary across the Channel, Édouard Manet. Cummings began writing sonnets when he was introduced to Rossetti's *House of Life* sequence, and the sonnet and the portrait became his two most favored genres. The Modernist poets' visual sensibility and preference for the portrait as a poetic genre reflect the late reception of Aestheticism into American culture. Yet they defined their poetic maturity as a correction of Rossetti's influence, which Pound called "Rossetti-itis." Eliot wrote in his 1929 essay on Dante, "Rossetti's *Blessed Damozel,* first by my rapture and next by my revolt, held up my appreciation of Beatrice by many years."[5] Apart from such remarks, both poets maintained a deafening silence about Rossetti. The Modernist publicity campaign against Rossetti and Aestheticism resulted in decades of critical neglect, a trend that has been reversed only recently.[6]

When Modernist poets did acknowledge their debt to the Victorians, it was to Browning they nodded ("Hang it all, Robert Browning, / there can be but the one 'Sordello,'" begins Pound's Canto II), and his impact has loomed large in Modernist scholarship.[7] Consequently, the dramatic monologue has eclipsed the portrait in our understanding of Modernist poetry. Indeed, dramatic monologue and its offshoot, the persona poem, are exceptional in being recognized as genres at all in Modernism, a period when genre itself is said to disappear (although this is a myth, as I hope to convince readers).[8] In 1920, however, when Ezra Pound listed the "Main outline of E.P.'s work to date" on the last page of *Umbra*, he divided this list into "Personae and Portraits," no doubt relying on his audience's familiarity with portraiture to help explain his oeuvre. Similarly, the subtitle of his *Poems 1918–1920* is *Three Portraits and Four Cantos*, where the "three portraits" are "Langue d'Oc"/"Moeurs Contemporaines" (combined in one sequence), "Homage to Sextus Propertius" and *Hugh Selwyn Mauberley*. Not until Pound issued *Personae* in 1926, the definitive selection of his short works including *Mauberley*, did he establish "persona" as the generic name for most of these poems.

Pound's choice to go with "persona" rather than "portrait" was likely motivated, at least in part, by the desire to conceal his ties with Aestheticism and instead claim affiliation with Browning. This choice was gendered: Pound's portraits typically represent women, while his persona poems represent male figures. His retroactive preference for the latter corresponds to the male Modernists' suppression of the feminine that Cassandra Laity diagnoses.[9] Yet this suppression is only part of the story, for the Aesthetic portrait poem contained an important element of self-reflection. As they turned from representing female to male figures, Eliot and Pound both internalized qualities of the Rossettian woman by reproducing her mirror image in what were loosely disguised self-portraits, such as Eliot's "Portrait of a Lady" and Pound's *Mauberley*. As one critic has written, in Modernism "the distinction between self-portraiture and portraiture becomes more and more blurred," or at least the possibility of self-representation lurks in every portrait of another.[10] This blending of selves also extended beyond the mirror-image portrait to group portraits that spread interiority out over multiple figures.

The Victorian portrait poem was the vehicle for a traditional Cartesian view of the self as comprising an interior, the soul, and an exterior, the body. The female portrait poem—more common than the male—typically interpreted the subject's character on the basis of her appearance, applying a clichéd set of symbolic equivalences. Thus, blue eyes signified innocence, blushes implied modesty, an upturned face could signify religious faith, good posture indicated an upright character, and so on. These equivalences were not unique to poetry, but pervaded the sentimental literature and art of the time.[11] The portrait poems of Browning, Rossetti, and Swinburne were unusual in this context, for they questioned the simplistic equivalence of inside and outside (although they were not, of course, the only authors to challenge sentimental stereotypes). Each of these poets offered different ways of imagining what a person is and what we can know of others. Browning proposed substituting speech for appearance as the index of character, and this contribution ultimately shaped the many dramatic voices of Modernist writing, including the persona poem. Rossetti rejected the Cartesian division of body and soul altogether, writing in the sonnet "Heart's Hope," "Thy soul I know not from thy body, nor / Thee from myself."[12] Many of Rossetti's paintings and poems privilege the physical body and particularly its surface, suggesting a materialism that Modernist poets found both compelling and disturbing. Yet these lines also imply a mingling of self and other that has quite different consequences. Both Rossetti and Swinburne experimented with eliminating the traditional limits imposed by body, feelings, identity, and memory. Following their lead, Modernist poets also sought to undo the limits (and capacities) of the liberal subject, often imagining consciousness and selfhood as shared rather than individual.

When Eliot and Pound began writing poetry, they inherited Rossetti and Swinburne's project of revising the portrait so that it offered a more nuanced conception of what a person is: less sentimental, less dualist, less committed to the existence of a soul. This project was not limited to portraiture, of course; it was going on in all the arts and sciences. Psychology and anthropology, which interested Eliot deeply, also had their part to play, as did philosophy, medicine, and other disciplines.[13] As poets, however, they directed their energies to the genres that investigated the constitution of the self in poetic form.[14] Modernist poetic portraiture roughly follows two divergent but complementary paths that correspond to possibilities explored in Aestheticism. Connecting with a familiar strain of Modernism, one group of portraits emphasizes the surface and materiality of the person, who is compared to things both natural and manmade.[15] Including poems by Eliot, Pound, Williams, Robinson, Masters, Lowell, and H.D., these portraits particularly exhibit verbal condensation, brevity, self-reference, and fascination for concrete objects and visual images. Such poems have little room for interiority, for they invest surface with all the significance once reserved for the invisible aspects of the self. In a move that by no means cancels out the insight of these works yet has quite different implications, a second group of portraits explores interiority as a quality shared among and between figures, or between figures and objects. While the figures may be individually represented as solid or diaphanous, they are typically not given substantial depth; rather, depth occurs between and among them. This kind of portrait represents what I am calling, after Charles Taylor, an "interspatial self."

In *Sources of the Self: The Making of the Modern Identity*, Taylor traces the emergence of inwardness from Augustine through Descartes, Locke, and Montaigne, into the twentieth century, connecting this idea with developments in philosophy, politics, and the arts. He analyzes how the emergence of interiority went hand-in-hand with the objectification of aspects of human life, including the physical body. Interiority was necessary to this development because it became the place, the control center, from which objectifications and decisions occurred. Yet, as Taylor writes, "the perfectly detachable consciousness is an illusion," if a necessary one.[16] Romantics and Modernists challenged and offered adjustments to the essentially imaginary distinction between inside and outside. Taking Pound as an example, Taylor sees the Modernist dislocating the self from its traditional interior place and representing it instead in between persons, and between persons and things.[17] His term for this dislocated sense of interiority is the "interspatial epiphany."[18] I see a similar move occurring earlier in the work of authors who profoundly shaped Pound's practice as a poet, particularly Swinburne and Henry James. Taylor is not the only one to identify this phenomenon in Modernism, but he usefully makes it available in the context of a longer history of the self.[19]

❧

Portraiture has played an important role in the evolving conception of interiority.[20] Painted portraits, even self-portraits, represent an individual figure from the exterior and dramatize the distinction between exterior and interior. This "basic dichotomy" is widely recognized as a feature of portraiture, described as a "*décalage* between surface (that which is visible, or the physical aspect) and interior (that which is hidden, or the psychological aspect)," or "the *difference* between an inner, abstract subjectivity and an objectivised, material body."[21] Though the meaning of portraiture in earlier centuries is contested, historians agree on a general trend toward emphasizing moral character and spiritual traits in addition to physiognomic characteristics and wealth.[22] The "heroic era" of portraiture in the fifteenth and sixteenth centuries coincided with the development of a humanistic conception of identity as inward and conscious.[23] The development of this idea of inwardness challenged the portraitist to represent aspects of the individual that were not visible to the eye. In practice, many character traits were conveyed by a system of conventional symbols, including pose and lighting as well as accessories and clothing. Even in the mid-nineteenth century it was an article of faith that the portraitist's task was to plumb the depths of the sitter's soul.

My book begins at the point where the longstanding tradition of interiority—whether articulated in philosophy, poetry, or art—comes under sustained pressure from modernity. One of the first places to register this pressure was painting, and here my understanding of what happened to the portrait is guided by Michael Fried's theorization of flatness in modern painting. *Manet's Modernism or, The Face of Painting in the 1860s* is about Manet's technique as a painter and the qualities that distinguished him, in the long run, as the "father of Modernism." Fried examines the compositional arrangements, colors, and brushstrokes that contributed to an overall appearance of flatness or depthlessness in Manet's paintings of the 1860s and 1870s. Fried claims that Manet sought to explore the formal qualities of his medium, drawing attention to the canvas and the application of paint, rather than offering an illusion of three-dimensional space. This project stands in contrast to the development of perspective in the Renaissance, when "Instead of being an opaque and impervious surface, [the painting] becomes like a window through which we see reality as it appears from that perspective."[24] For Taylor, the opening out of the painting into three-dimensional space is an important moment in the emergence of interiority. By the same token, the flattening of the painting to a two-dimensional surface also marks a change in the conception and representation of selfhood.

Fried sets Manet's flatness in opposition to a quality that he calls "absorption."[25] Absorptive paintings aim to draw the viewer into the imaginary three-dimensional space represented, making him or her unconscious of looking at a canvas. Typically this effect is achieved by representing a figure absorbed in an activity involving silent concentration, such as reading, writing, sewing, listening to music, or praying. Absorptive compositions offer easy entry into the work and intimacy with the subjects. Although Fried does not expressly say so, these works also suggest that the figure possesses the quality of inwardness. "Theatrical" paintings, by contrast, make the beholder conscious of facing the painting. Although a single painting may employ both effects, Fried claims that the absorptive mode became popular during the eighteenth century and persisted as a norm to the middle of the nineteenth century, while becoming increasingly difficult to execute successfully.[26] Manet was one of the first painters of his generation to abandon absorption for the theatrical effects of flatness and frontal poses.[27] In a frontally posed work, the figure looks out at the viewer, staging a confrontation. Portraits tend to be frontal, and thus many of Manet's figure paintings have the appearance of portraits, although the generic identity of the work and the social identity of the subject are often ambiguous.

Manet was not the only artist to experiment with an aesthetic of flatness: in England in the 1860s, both Rossetti and Whistler emphasized the flat painted surfaces of their decorative portraits. As in Manet's disconcerting single-figure paintings, Rossetti and Whistler's women do not seem to be doing anything, yet at the same time they do not seem to be looking at us. They inhabit a strange state in between absorption and engagement, and it is often said of them that they are absorbed with themselves. When there is no visible object of absorption or clues indicated by the painting, their attitude is ambiguous. That ambiguity raises a series of increasingly disturbing questions beginning with "what is she thinking about?" and moving on to the more skeptical, "is it possible to know her mind?" "Does she have a mind?" and finally, "What is a mind? What is a person?" Many examples of these expressions may be found in the portrait-like female figure paintings of the 1860s, which is the starting place for the modern portrait poem. In particular, I locate this starting place in Rossetti's ekphrastic sonnet "The Portrait" (1869) and Swinburne's "Before the Mirror" (1865), a response to Whistler's *The Little White Girl* of 1865 (later *Symphony in White, No. 2*). These poems consider the figure's thoughtful gaze and ask where we are to find her self or soul: not inside the figure, but rather on the surface of the canvas (in Rossetti's case), or in the interstices and reflections of the painting, and between painting and viewer (in Swinburne's case). Their interpretations of flatness underwrite the variations and transformations of the Modernist portrait poem.

Some of the portrait poems discussed in this book are ekphrases, verbal representations of visual representations.[28] Yet portraiture's relationship to ekphrasis is complex, and I argue that at least in the period under consideration, the two kinds pull apart. Poems about painted portraits date back at least to the seventeenth century in English and earlier in Italian; this type of poem describes an actual or imagined picture of a person and interprets the sitter's character on the basis of the picture.[29] This subgenre continued to flourish in the nineteenth century, even as poets from Browning to Rossetti subjected it to a searching revaluation. The poem that calls itself a portrait, without reference to a specific work of art, actual or imagined, is of more recent date. Thus, although the twentieth century saw the rapid expansion of ekphrasis per se, within the genre of portraiture the primacy of the work of art seems to have diminished, at least in the early and "high" stages of Modernism.[30] This change can be seen in a shift in the style of naming such poems, from "On a Portrait," or "Lines on a Portrait" to the claim of self-sufficiency implied by the title "Portrait of so-and-so." The Modernist withdrawal from explicit ekphrasis reflects a reorientation of the conception of the subject away from a dualistic inside/outside model, in which appearances are understood to signal specific character traits. Instead, the modern portrait poem investigates a variety of possibilities about the self, whether viewing persons as discrete and thing-like, or exploring the way that selves blend and intersect. These explorations continue to draw on visual portraiture as a source of ideas, but not necessarily by interpreting the meaning of specific paintings.

In using the term "portrait" in the title of a poem, the poet signals that he is engaging with visual art at some level. The engagement may be negative, such as claiming that words represent people better than images, or it may be superficial, simply signaling that, like a visual portrait, the following poem represents a single figure. In more substantial engagements, the poem may draw on formal qualities of painting, such as the flatness discussed above, or in later works, the techniques of abstraction, Cubism, and collage. Formal qualities from painting are not necessarily absorbed *as form* into poetry—they may also appear as motifs, themes, or style of language. Indeed, a portrait poem may respond to painting in an uncountable number of ways. Yet, all these poems have one feature in common: they are intermedial.[31] The portrait poem communicates with visual and other media. Although the specifically ekphrastic trait of the portrait poem diminishes in the Modernist era, the intermedial aspect of the genre continues to shape it. In particular, the relationship between poetry and painting becomes a model for exchanges between poetry and music, opera, dance, and film. Also, and more fundamentally, intermediality becomes a model for the interspatial self: a self constituted by exchanges between and among sources (other people's ideas, works of art, objects), in contrast to the traditional concept of the free-standing individual constituted and governed by an interior soul or mind. Historically, the genre of the portrait poem is sensitive to other media, and perhaps for this reason it became an ideally flexible vehicle between 1908 and 1922 for exploring ideas about the self and the relationship of the different arts.

The consistent naming of poems as "portrait" in this period signifies a relationship among the arts but also a claim that the portrait is a poetic genre. There are many poems that could be described as portraits based on their content, but title is one of the best indications of genre.[32] In this book I focus primarily on portraits so designated by their authors, whether in the title of the work, or in the title of a sequence or list in which the poem appears. Beyond these definite cases I also consider a penumbra of related works written by the same author in a similar manner as those he or she called "portrait." This rather pedestrian reliance on titles and headings restricts the scope of the study, and it would be possible to argue that every poem about a single figure is a portrait. Under this broader definition, a large percentage of Modernist poems would belong to the genre, a fact that is itself significant but would render the object of study too vague. Rather, I have chosen to examine the clear cases more closely and hope that these will ultimately shed light on the more broadly defined portrait poem of the twentieth century.

My understanding of the portrait poem is guided by Alastair Fowler's definition of genre as a loose "repertoire of traits" that change over time and can be combined with traits from other genres, rather than as an exclusive category from which a work can be ruled out if it is missing a certain trait.[33] Fowler's work has been especially helpful in clarifying how poetic genres, including the many subdivisions of the vast category of "lyric," are poetically viable and critically useful even though such classes are fundamentally vague. A reliable picture of a genre emerges only from exploring both its diachronic and synchronic dimensions: tracing its development over time, and comparing a cross-section of related works composed at the same time.[34] My book attempts to combine these two kinds of analysis, observing changes to the portrait across two main episodes separated by forty years (the Rossetti-Swinburne exchange, and the Pound-Eliot-Williams exchange), and noting differences of approach within each of these groups. In particular, I draw on Fowler's taxonomy of generic modulations and transformations, such as contraction, expansion, aggregation, and combination with traits of other genres.[35] The time period is ultimately too short to say which changes should be viewed as transformations (in which one genre turns into another) and which merely as modulations (the genre develops another branch but retains its "family resemblance"), and I do not distinguish rigorously between these two kinds of change. In the hands of these Modernist poets, the portrait changed rapidly and in different directions, but susceptibility to change is the nature of genre. It is a commonplace of art criticism that portraiture "dies" in the twentieth century, despite the portrait's healthy afterlife in Modernism and Postmodernism.[36] In the period of this study, however, the portrait does not disappear; rather, it undergoes a fascinating renewal that illuminates the workings of modern poetry.

The poems examined in this book belong together in the sense that they descend in different directions from a popular kind of Victorian lyric poem. Conspicuous by their absence are the prose portraits of Gertrude Stein, perhaps the most prolific and inventive of all Modernist portrait-writers. Like the poets in this study, Stein also reappraises the subject-sitter relation and pushes the limits of representation, but distinguishes herself by pushing those limits further and more systematically than the poets. According to Wendy Steiner's profound analysis of Stein's literary portraiture, she aimed to imitate her subject without symbolic mediation, thus "overturning the norms of her medium, in which a portrait can be effected, at best, through indexical-symbolical means."[37] While Pound, Eliot, and Williams certainly played with the conventions of the nineteenth-century portrait poem, dropping some and reversing others, their aim was not to overturn but to modify the existing genre and its means for representing an individual. These means were squarely symbolic, insofar as they sought to represent what the subject was "like," often through elaborate metaphors. It is precisely my contention that these modern poets were not doing anything radically new, but rather adjusting and rearranging the traits of the Aesthetic portrait poem to their own purposes. Their constant reference to Aesthetic precursors suggests that they viewed their own experimentation in this way, as interventions within an existing poetic tradition. Although some critics refer to Stein's portraits as poetry, Steiner treats them as prose (in the tradition of the seventeenth-century prose "character" and its successor, biography). It is not surprising that the most radically avant-garde portraiture found its place in prose, a medium historically more amenable to risk and novelty than poetry. Stein's portraiture and its "failure," as Steiner finds it ultimately to be, has encouraged the idea that portraiture became so unmoored by Modernist experimentation that it lost touch entirely with its traditional aim of representing an individual. I aspire to complement Steiner's work by tracing the process of generic change in a medium more tied to tradition than prose.

That change varied from poet to poet and from year to year. To reflect their heterogeneous approaches to the portrait poem, this book is organized around specific moments in individual poets' careers, with a distinct shift marked at the year 1912. The first three chapters examine the features of the Aesthetic portrait, both painted and poetic, and trace the way that Pound and Eliot received features of this genre from both media into their own early work. The second half of the book examines the modulation of the portrait poem by contraction, expansion, and adopting traits from other art forms and literary genres.

Chapter 1, "Portraiture in the Rossetti Circle: Window, Object, or Mirror," examines three approaches to portraiture available in the 1860s. The first is a traditional conception of the portrait as a window revealing the sitter's interior qualities. William Cowper's ekphrastic portrait "On the Receipt of My Mother's Picture" (1798) became canonical in the Victorian era and established the conventions for this genre. In 1859, Dante Gabriel Rossetti's painting *Bocca Baciata* inaugurated a new style of flat, decorative female portraiture challenging the assumption that appearance should or could reveal the sitter's soul. Rossetti explored the implications of his new painting in two poems entitled "The Portrait." One, a sonnet, treats the portrait as a self-sufficient object of beauty, assimilating the soul of the sitter to her body and both to the material artwork, emphasizing surface and formal condensation. The other, a dramatic monologue, responds to a painted portrait as an uncanny mirror in which past and present, Beloved and self mingle, undermining the traditional dualism of portraiture. James McNeill Whistler's *The Little White Girl* and Algernon Swinburne's "Before the Mirror" also experiment with this third possibility, reintroducing the quality of interiority as a space shared between individuals and over time. The Modernist portrait poem takes up, develops, and combines these two models of Aesthetic portraiture, with their attributes of pictorial concreteness and fluid interspace.

Chapter 2, "Ezra Pound: Portraiture and Originality," concerns the most prolific portrait-writer among the Modernist poets, who was also the most profoundly shaped by his early immersion in the work of Rossetti, Swinburne, Whistler, and Yeats. During the years of his apprenticeship and modernization from 1905 to 1913, Pound used portraiture—traditionally one of the most mimetic art forms—to find his way into a poetic tradition that he deeply venerated, as well as to deflect anxiety about the originality of his contributions. These early portraits negotiate between Rossetti's visual, concrete, embodied poetics and a negative or apparitional aesthetic derived from Swinburne, Whistler, and Yeats. Drawing on early writings that show Pound's fascination with Rossetti (especially his *Blessed Damozel*) and the manuscript of his unpublished ode "To La Mère Inconnue," this chapter charts the multiple threads of Aestheticism that contributed to his early portraiture and his developing conception of interspace.

Chapter 3, "T. S. Eliot: Getting Out of the Picture," reads Eliot's portraits from 1908 to 1922 in light of his youthful fascination with Aestheticism and Rossetti's picture sonnets in particular. Eliot's early ekphrastic sonnets "Circe's Palace" and "On a Portrait" engage with works by Rossetti, Edward Burne-Jones, Swinburne, and surprisingly, Édouard Manet. In describing the mysteriously inaccessible, dreamlike, flattened subject of Manet's *Young Lady in 1866,* Eliot begins to frame the questions about interiority and knowledge of other minds that motivate his portraits of 1910–11, including the "Mandarins" sequence, "La Figlia Che Piange," and "Portrait of a Lady." These poems increasingly detach themselves from ekphrasis and imagine a new standing-point for the poet/viewer, who resists the power of visual absorption and the model of interiority it implies. Instead, "Portrait of a Lady" develops a model of self not predicated on an interior source of thought and feeling. To get away from the seductive Aesthetic image, Eliot incorporated traits from 1860s painting, and even the portrait genre itself, into works that contest the power of the image.

Chapter 4, "Contraction: From Picture Sonnet to Epigram" examines a phase between 1912 and 1916 when the portrait poem became shorter in length. In this process of contraction, the portrait poem gradually shifted its allegiance from the Rossettian picture sonnet to the classical epigram and epitaph. While shortening from fourteen to two or three lines, the contracted portrait kept many traits of the Rossettian sonnet, especially its verbal condensation and orientation toward visual artifacts and images. At the same time, this reduction in scale corresponded to a shrinking conception of the individual subject. Not interiority, but an almost thing-like quality in the subject characterizes these portraits. This chapter looks at a range of poets who experimented with reducing the size and scope of the portrait: E. A. Robinson, Pound, H.D., Amy Lowell, Eliot, Edgar Lee Masters, and Arthur Davison Ficke and Witter Bynner, whose 1916 "Spectra Hoax" parodied Imagism and testified to the perception that the quintessential Imagist poem compared people to things in epigrammatic form.

Chapter 5, "Expansion: Ezra Pound and Avant-Garde Portraiture," examines Pound's expansion of the portrait after 1916 to accommodate multiple figures, in the context of avant-garde movements that privileged intersection and multiplicity over the individual figure. Pound drew on a variety of art forms as he updated the portrait, including paintings and designs by Wyndham Lewis, Futurist artwork, the sculptures of Henri Gaudier-Brzeska, Diaghilev's Ballets Russes, novels by Henry James, Gustave Flaubert, and James Joyce, and even the moving panorama, a precursor to film. The chapter focuses on Pound's short poem "Les Millwins," his prose memoir *Gaudier-Brzeska*, the portrait sequence "Moeurs Contemporaines" (drawing on portions of this sequence that Pound later deleted), and *Hugh Selwyn Mauberley*. These works translate nineteenth-century concepts of portraiture into a Modernist idiom that reflects the impact of avant-garde art in several media. Pound's multifigure portraits build on the Swinburnian idea of interspace, first elaborated in "Portrait d'une femme" of 1912, to imagine interiority as an effect experienced amongst the figures in the composition and across time, rather than located in a single individual.

Chapter 6, "Pastoral Mode: William Carlos Williams and Nativist Portraiture," turns to Williams, whose portraits from 1912 to 1920 reflect his struggle to establish an authentically American poetics without European influence. Williams shared this project with a circle of New York artists, including his friends Marsden Hartley and Charles Demuth. This chapter connects Williams's knowledge of modern art with his use of the portrait genre, examining his portraiture in the context of the contemporary Nativist movement in art. Nativist painting likened the American-born body to the American landscape, often in eroticized terms. Williams used the pastoral mode to shift the orientation of his poetry from literary tradition to the Nativist ideal of representation without received conventions. From his "Pastorals and Self-Portraits" sequence of 1914 through the portraits of *Al Que Quiere!* and his "Portrait of a Lady" of 1920, Williams developed a series of pastoral contrasts that increasingly privileged the physical body and the American landscape. Though Williams's goal is independence from the European tradition, his ideal of portraiture as pure body also recapitulates the Rossettian project of joining body and soul in the portrait and extends what Jerome McGann calls the "materialist 'thing tradition'" originating with Rossetti.[38]

The book ends with a short Coda discussing the portrait poems of E. E. Cummings. His *Tulips and Chimneys* (1922) is one of the most experimental works of "high" Modernism yet surprisingly exhibits key traits of the Rossettian portrait, from flower motifs to a programmatic insistence on the unity of body and soul. These poems show the vitality and flexibility of the portrait poem and Rossetti's contribution to this genre as it began a new life in the twentieth century.

PART ONE

The Portrait Poem to 1912

❧

ONE

Portraiture in the Rossetti Circle

WINDOW, OBJECT, OR MIRROR

T HE ARTIST ENGAGED on a portrait, is to inscribe the character and not the features," instructed an 1861 article on portraiture. The artist "must 'esteem the man who sits to him as himself only an imperfect picture or likeness of the aspiring original within.'"[1] According to this view of portraiture, the artist's job is to make the sitter's hidden interior visible, to interpret the sitter's soul on the basis of his or her physical appearance. While the ideas about portrait-painting expressed in this article from *Bentley's Miscellany* remained more or less consistent in the popular imagination through the nineteenth century, they were already being challenged by Dante Gabriel Rossetti in a series of new paintings of women begun in 1859. In the decade that followed, Rossetti, James McNeill Whistler, and Algernon Swinburne built on each other's insights as all three sought to decouple the portrait's significance from the sitter's interiority.

In this chapter I map out the conventions of the Victorian portrait poem and examine the changes that Rossetti and his circle wrought on this genre. I focus on three models of portraiture found in poetry around 1860–1870: the portrait as window, object, or mirror. William Cowper's 1798 "On the Receipt of My Mother's Picture" was much admired throughout the nineteenth century and set the model for many portrait poems about women. Cowper leads the reader through a series of "faithful" representations, from the expression on the sitter's face, to her soul, to the God that authorizes both her being and her portrait. The portrait assures the legibility of appearances as a sign of interiority, treating the face as the window to the soul. Consistent with Victorian sentimentalism, this approach remained popular through 1900.

At the same time, however, portrait poems by Wordsworth, Tennyson, and Browning introduced doubts about the legibility of appearances, challenging the idea that one can see "through" a portrait (or a face) to the subject's soul. In the 1860s, Rossetti developed a style of female portraiture that extended these challenges by privileging the physical beauty of the sitter and the decorative surface of the painting at the expense of messages about her soul or character. His emphasis on surface marked the modernity of Rossetti's painting in a way that was immediately recognized by his circle of fellow artists and writers. In this respect Rossetti also anticipated and prepared the way for developments in modern painting that privileged flatness over depth, and design over narrative.

Rossetti composed two portrait poems that offer quite different interpretations of his new style of painting. Both entitled "The Portrait," one is a sonnet that forms part of the *House of Life* sequence, and the other is a dramatic monologue. The sonnet considers the status of the portrait as a self-sufficient aesthetic object, showing how the value of the portrait can be seen to reside on the surface of the painting. Image-laden and condensed, the sonnet draws attention to itself and the painting as material objects that require no referent other than themselves. The approach mapped out by this sonnet descends into Modernism via Imagism and "the materialist 'thing-tradition.'"[2] Modernist portrait poems equating people with things such as Ezra Pound's "An Object" can be traced back to this materialist interpretation of Rossetti's surfaces.

Rossetti's other poem called "The Portrait" explores portraiture as reflection and doubling. Though a mirror is a material object, it reflects the insubstantial image of the space before it. A mirror creates a space that is neither *on* nor *behind* its surface, but rather exists *in between* itself and the objects it reflects. Rossetti shared his lifelong interest in reflections and doubles with both Swinburne and Whistler, who also developed this idea of an in-between space, or "interspace" as Swinburne called it. Swinburne's "Before the Mirror" of 1865 describes Whistler's painting *The Little White Girl* (later titled *Symphony in White, No. 2*), thinking through the significance of the flattened picture plane in this painting and in Rossetti's recent portraits. Instead of locating the girl's meaning on the surface of her body or on the canvas, Swinburne imagines a kind of interiority that exists in between reflecting surfaces, such as between the girl and her image in the mirror (in Whistler's painting) and between the viewer and the girl in the picture (in the poem itself). Interiority is shifted from the individual subject to the relation between herself and objects in the painting, her reflection, and ourselves. The differing modes of portraiture received from Rossetti and his circle—condensed and material vs.

expansive and interspatial—underwrite the genre as it developed in the Modernist era.

Window: Cowper's Legacy

Reflecting mainstream views about portraiture, the author of the *Bentley's Miscellany* article quoted above affirms the portraitist's role as an interpreter of the soul. The painter discovers "the permanent, the essential, the ideal," in the subject; he chooses the "noblest moment of the sitter, when the 'God within him lights his face.'"[3] The most famous exposition of the relationship between portraiture and the sitter's eternal soul is, as the author explains, William Cowper's "On the Receipt of My Mother's Picture out of Norfolk, the Gift of My Cousin Ann Bodham": "of all benedictions . . . with which English poetry has hailed the portrait-painter, there is none, probably, that speaks so home to the common heart, as that by Cowper, in the familiar instance (familiar in all our mouths as household words—for a household word it is, in itself) of his Mother's Picture."[4] The language of "home," "heart," and "household" emphasizes the poem's status as an anchor both of its genre and the traditional values it articulates. Probably the best-known portrait poem of the first half of the nineteenth century, Cowper's "On the Receipt of My Mother's Picture" also extended its influence well into the second half.[5] This poem was identified as the "best poem for class study" of Cowper in an 1878 literature textbook.[6] Another critic declared in 1880, "There is nothing more pathetic yet more simple in English poetry than [Cowper's] lines on his mother's picture."[7] This famous poem exemplifies a popular strain of nineteenth-century poetic portraiture whose purpose was to affirm the intelligibility of the sitter's expression and guide its audience through the sitter to a transcendental source variously identified as God or the soul.

Cowper's poem is occasioned by seeing his mother's portrait, leading the poet to recall her and tell the story of her death when he was only six years old. As is conventional in nineteenth-century ekphrastic portraits, the poem begins by describing the subject's appearance in the painting and associating her character with her facial features:

> Those lips are thine—thy own sweet smile I see,
> The same that oft in childhood solaced me . . .
> The meek intelligence of those dear eyes
> . . . here shines on me still the same.[8]

His mother's "power to soothe" is her chief character trait in the poem. In the same opening lines, the poet credits the portrait with "baffl[ing]

Time's tyrannic claim," in immortalizing her through her image. The portrait is an agent of connection, linking her appearance to her character, and the son to his deceased mother.

The meaning and efficacy of the portrait is guaranteed by a strong chain of fidelities reaching from the poet, through the painting, to his mother, and on up through her to God. Cowper addresses the picture as "Faithful remembrancer of one so dear." This term "faithful" comes to cover every relationship invoked in the poem: the accuracy of the painting to the sitter, the quality of his mother's affection toward him ("Thy constant flow of love, that knew no fall"), his memory of her ("All this still legible in memory's page, / And still to be so to my latest age"), the sincerity of his tribute to her ("Perhaps a frail memorial, but sincere"), and the quality of her own religious faith. Grounded in filial love and religious belief, the poet's faith also operates to guarantee his account of his mother's character, as interpreted and elaborated from the painting. Cowper in turn attributes his faithfulness to hers. He ends by asserting that her love remains faithful to him even long after death: "Time has but half succeeded in his theft,— / Thyself remov'd, thy power to soothe me left."[9] Cowper thus positions her as the origin of both portraits, the painted and the ekphrastic, and of the fidelity that guarantees their legibility and meaning.

Cowper's mother in a sense presides over other nineteenth-century portrait poems. Cowper's filial relationship with the subject of the portrait not only justifies his assertions about her character, it also authorizes his poem and the very genre to which it belongs. The figure of the mother permits the poet to step over the evidential gap between appearances and interiority—indeed, to deny any evidential gap whatsoever. Cowper's confidence in the fidelity of exterior appearances to interior states makes his poem a touchstone for the author of the *Bentley's* essay on portraiture. For many Victorian readers in 1861, this poem written at the outset of the social, economic, and intellectual upheavals of the nineteenth century must have had the reassuring air of an elderly mother, still capable of affirming values and beliefs that had been undermined by science and the fraying of traditional communal ties.

"On the Receipt of My Mother's Picture" also exemplifies the typical gendering of such poems: Cowper's subject is female, as it is in the majority of nineteenth-century ekphrastic portraits. Male portraits do exist, but they are less common, and follow different conventions. In the male portrait, the subject is typically identified by name and is more likely to be a historical figure than a family member. Thus the standards for knowledge about him are different from those governing female por-traits: evidence for his character is drawn from his public deeds and fame, rather than from interpretation of his face and figure. While dramatizing the double standards governing social value for men and women in the nineteenth century, this difference also perhaps explains why the female portrait might have been a more interesting genre for poetic experimen-tation: it engages with fundamental philosophical and religious questions about what a person is and how we know each other. Looking ahead, one of the contributions of the twentieth-century portrait poem is to transfer the conventions and questions associated with female portraiture to male subjects.

⚘

Cowper's legacy was a tradition of portrait poems emphasizing the trans-parency of the sitter. The Quaker poet Bernard Barton (1784–1849) wrote a large number of such poems, including "Emma: Verses Suggested by a Portrait" (1845), in which he ascribes "maidenly" qualities to his sitter on the basis of her facial features:

> Eyes of mild and thoughtful tone,
> Forehead—where no care is shown,
> Cheeks just tinted from the rose,
> Lips where lurking smiles repose![10]

Each feature of the girl's appearance is linked to a standard character trait that such a person might be expected to have. He hastens to assure us that she not only *looks* this way, but everyone who knows her swears it's so: "Fancy deems the likeness true, / Those who know thee vouch it, too." Barton specifically links Emma's "simple loveliness" with her "guileless heart," combining outside with inside in a single quality: "innocence."[11] Innocence is an ideal trait for the portrait subject; by contrast, a guileful person creates a gap between his true feelings and a deceitful appear-ance. Thus Barton calls his portrayal of Emma a "blissful task" because he can easily describe her character and "soul" in terms of her looks. Like Cowper's mother, Emma exhibits a seamless continuity between inside and outside.

Elizabeth Barrett Browning's 1844 "A Portrait" begins, "I will paint her as I see her." The poet describes the subject's face as "lily-clear," an expres-sion that implies both white skin and a clear conscience. As in Barton's poems, the forehead and eyes tend to be the focal point of the connec-tion between interior and exterior: "a forehead fair and saintly, / Which two blue eyes undershine, / Like meek prayers before a shrine."[12] Similarly, Frederick Locker-Lampson's 1857 "On 'A Portrait of a Lady' By the Painter" begins,

> She is good, for she must have a guileless mind
>   With that noble, trusting air. . . .
> She is lovely and good; she has frank blue eyes . . .
> With her wistful mouth, and her candid brow.[13]

Each of the sitter's features—posture, brow, eyes—is described as the outward expression of an inner trait. The same trope is repeated in John Stuart Blackie's 1886 "Portrait of a Lady": "every feature tells / A treasured sweetness in the soul within, / That beats like music through the lucid skin."[14] As in Cowper's "On the Receipt of My Mother's Picture," the chief virtue of Blackie's subject is her fidelity: "Her skill is to be true and natural . . . / She knows no falseness . . . truth flows from her deep blue eye."[15] Her fidelity grounds the correspondence between interior and exterior, just as Barton emphasizes Emma's innocence for the same reason. This convention may be found as late as Francis Palgrave's 1892 "Portrait of a Child of Seven": "Fair shrine!—yet of a fairer far within / Thou art but outward mask and symbol weak . . . we seek / The soul beneath the skin."[16] In this case, the reliability of appearances to "tell" the interior is secured by the youth of the subject, who, at seven, would be less likely to dissemble than an adult. The choice to portray a child might suggest that by the 1890s special measures were necessary to prop up the presumption of transparency.

From Cowper through Palgrave it is thus possible to trace a consistent repertoire of traits for a popular version of the female portrait poem. Such a poem typically presents an image of the woman, whether in a painting or as visualized by the poet; describes a conventional set of physical traits, such as blue eyes, high forehead, fair skin, and graceful carriage, each of which is linked by the poet to an interior quality, such as piety, truthfulness, innocence, and loyalty; and affirms these virtues on the basis of the poet's personal acquaintance with the sitter. The poem often develops a theme of fidelity that applies to the accuracy of the representation, the sitter's character, and the poet or painter's loyalty to the sitter. A typical portrait poem closes affirmatively, tying the poet's well-being to the fidelity of the portrait and the sitter's character. This type of portrait poem naturalizes many assumptions: appearances reflect character, the stereotyped traits of female beauty are linked to stereotyped female virtues, and such a formula for female subjectivity has a basis in social reality. Ultimately this type of poem aims to "soothe" as the portrait of Cowper's mother does, by affirming a set of conventions for female appearance and behavior and tying emotional and social well-being to the validity of these conventions.

❧

While these examples typify the Victorian portrait poem, the genre also exhibits variations, reversals, and new branches throughout the century. Bolder poets explore more openly the tension or incompatibility between exterior and interior, still image and uttered description. Wordsworth's 1834 "Lines Suggested by a Portrait from the Pencil of F. Stone" recapitulates many of Cowper's themes, while introducing a new element of doubt that becomes increasingly prominent in poems by Browning, Tennyson, and Rossetti.[17] Wordsworth's "Lines" describe a picture of his god-daughter Jemima Quillinan, who is depicted looking down "in quiet pensiveness." The sitter's pose and facial expression lead Wordsworth to meditate on her thoughts, and he raises doubts about whether we can know what she is thinking from observing the painting:

> Offspring of soul-bewitching art, make me
> Thy confidant! say, whence derived that air
> Of calm abstraction? Can the ruling thought
> Be with some lover far away, or one
> Crossed by misfortune, or of doubted faith?[18]

This meditation contains the seeds of later paintings and ekphrases in which the sitter's blank expression suggests either a failure of access to her mind, or no mind to access at all. Wordsworth curtails these disturbing possibilities, however, by pointing to the blue cornflower she holds in her hands, as an indication of what she is thinking. Flowers play an important role in Victorian female portraiture, including Rossetti's and Whistler's, as a symbolic language that elucidates the sitter's character and state of mind. In Wordsworth's poem, the cornflower (associated with bachelorhood) signifies the girl's virtue; by an elaborate reference to Ceres, who mourned for her daughter Proserpine, the flower also suggests Jemima's filial grief. She is not thinking of a lover but of her deceased mother. Wordsworth uses the cornflower to dispel doubts raised by the girl's ambiguous expression, yet the effort of doing so, requiring both classical lore and personal knowledge of the sitter, predicts the future dilemma of portraiture: a loss of faith in the correspondence between exterior and interior.

More famous than Wordsworth's "Lines" are Tennyson's "The Gardener's Daughter" and Browning's "My Last Duchess." These two ekphrastic portraits published in 1842 effectively break with the genre by shifting the orientation of the poem—indeed, wresting it—away from the image of a woman to the male speaker who presents her portrait.[19] In both poems a visual portrait of a woman becomes a mere prop for revealing the character of a male dramatic speaker. The speaker in "The Gardener's Daughter" narrates the story of meeting a girl named "Rose," but devotes only eighteen lines (out of 285) to describing her and none at all to the painting he reveals at the end of the poem. In "My Last Duchess," the Duke's description of the Duchess famously reveals more about his character than hers. As the male speaker becomes a character with a past, secrets, and flaws, the importance of the woman in the painting shrinks. To put the change another way, these poems reveal and examine the masculine privilege entailed in describing the picture of a woman. The speaker's words, and not the woman's appearance, become the index of character. The date of publication of these poems is regarded as the start date of the dramatic monologue, but in another sense it is also the moment in which dramatic speaking and the question of perspective enter the generic repertoire of the ekphrastic portrait. An attentive reader of Browning, Rossetti began his career writing dramatic monologues driven by questions of perspective, as in "The Blessed Damozel," which alternates among three voices representing different points of view. The Modernist persona poem descended from Browning and the portrait poem descended from Rossetti have intertwined histories and share many traits.

Object: Rossetti's Aesthetic Portraiture

The nineteenth-century portrait poem received its most extensive development in the hands of the poet, translator, and painter Dante Gabriel Rossetti (1828–1882). Rossetti explored portraiture in oils and watercolors, sketches, translations, short fiction, dramatic monologues, ballads, and sonnets. A leading member of the Pre-Raphaelite Brotherhood (1848–1853), Rossetti had already established his authority as an artist by 1850, when he ceased to exhibit his paintings publicly. After the death of his wife, Elizabeth Siddal, in 1862, his lavishly decorated home at Cheyne Walk became a magnet for a younger generation of painters and poets. The "Rossetti circle" of the 1860s and 1870s included Rossetti and his brother William; the visual artists William Morris, Frederick Sandys, Simeon Solomon, Edward Burne-Jones, and (for a time) James McNeill Whistler; and the writers William Meredith and Algernon Swinburne.[20] In 1859, Rossetti turned from illustration and narrative painting to a series of highly decorative portraits of beautiful women with faraway, vacant expressions. His new style of portraiture sparked a creative exchange among these artists and writers that affected the development of the genre in both painting and poetry. Their exchange primarily concerned *surface,* as a quality of both artworks and persons.

While the Victorian portrait poem conventionally regarded both the subject's face and her painted image as a window to the soul, Rossetti and his friends experimented with privileging face and image not as windows but as flat surfaces endowed with aesthetic value. The consequences of this move were initially more evident in painting than in poetry. Modernism in painting has long been associated with a shift from illusionism that offered a three-dimensional view of the world as seen "through" the painted picture to a self-conscious cultivation of the two-dimensional properties of the material canvas. Clement Greenberg identified Édouard Manet in particular as the "father of Modernism" for making flatness a central attribute of his paintings—meaning that they appear depthless, as the application of paint on a piece of cloth.[21] Manet and later painters drew attention to the surface of the painting by loosening or ignoring the rules of perspective and rejecting the use of chiaroscuro. Rossetti used the same techniques at the same time, painting scenes with multiple vanishing points and actively working against the viewer's disposition to look for a world behind the painting. Rossetti was particularly attentive to the metaphorical relationship between painted surfaces and the surface of the human body, which was his primary subject matter. In his painted and poetic portraits, Rossetti explored this relationship, raising questions about the meaning of the surface of the body, especially in view of the possibility that it does not provide a window to the soul, any more than the painting can be viewed as a window to nature.

The meaning of Rossetti's contributions can be better understood in contrast to the contemporary work of George Frederic Watts, friend of Rossetti and center of another circle that was also associated with the Aesthetic movement.[22] In 1851, Watts had begun painting a series of portraits of the distinguished men of his age, which he called his *Hall of Fame;* he bequeathed the collection to the National Portrait Gallery in 1895.[23] One of the most distinguished portraitists of his era, Watts believed that a portrait should be "a summary of the life of a person, not the record of an accidental position, or arrangement of light and shadow."[24] According to David Peters Corbett, "Watts's aspirations exemplify the claims made for the visual in the second half of the nineteenth century, opaque depth translated into clearly read surface, the mysteries of identity made transparent."[25] These claims were perhaps easier to sustain in male than in female portraiture. Watts's work, which emerged from the same artistic milieu as that of his friends Rossetti and Millais, demonstrates the continuing viability of the "window" theory of portraiture.

At the same time, however, belief in the legibility of personal appearances was exposed to challenges on many fronts. These challenges were modernity itself: the rise of urban centers where individuals passed on the street without recognizing or greeting one another, the growth of print media that spread information but reduced the role of personal acquaintance in daily life, the weakening of religious beliefs assuring the existence and immortality of the soul. Dorothy Ross identifies the second half of the nineteenth century as a period of increasing skepticism in all areas of life and intellectual disciplines.[26] In 1865, John Stuart Mill was the first modern philosopher to raise the question about our knowledge of others on the basis of appearances: "By what evidence do I know, or by what considerations am I led to believe, that there exist other sentient creatures; that the walking and speaking figures which I see and hear, have sensations and thought, or in other words, possess Minds?"[27] We can observe the appearance and behavior of others, but we can never directly experience their experience (thoughts, feelings, sense of self). Thus we forever lack direct evidence of the existence of their minds. Though Mill ultimately argues against skepticism about other minds, he grasps the problem of knowing others. If it cannot be solved, he writes, then "I am alone in the universe." Skepticism about interiority presented both a challenge for portrait painting and also, as Rossetti discovered, an opportunity to explore new approaches. Whereas the portraitist had traditionally been tasked with overcoming the distinction between interior and exterior by making character evident from appearances, beginning in 1859 Rossetti experimented with portraits that elevate appearances and surface (both canvas and the sitter's exterior) to the value previously reserved for character or spirit.

In the 1850s, Rossetti painted mainly Arthurian and Dantean scenes in watercolor. Like his youthful dramatic monologues and ballads, these visual works told stories, in keeping with the narrative tradition in painting. In 1859, however, Rossetti turned his hand to oil portraits, a genre that had long fascinated him but that ranked low in the academic hierarchy of painting for being imitative and commercial.[28] The first of a series of small portraits of beautiful women was *Bocca Baciata,* commissioned by his patron George Boyce, depicting the head and shoulders of the model Fanny Cornforth set against a flat floral background (fig. 1). Rossetti identified the work to Boyce specifically as "Fanny's portrait," proudly declaring that "the head . . . is more like, I think, than any I have done."[29] Rossetti's circle reacted passionately to the work. It was reported that Boyce was likely to "kiss the dear thing's lips away."[30] Swinburne enthused that it was "more stunning than can be decently expressed."[31] William Holman Hunt (a member of the original Pre-Raphaelite Brotherhood) commented that "it impresses me as very remarkable in power of execution—but still more remarkable for gross sensuality of a revolting kind . . . I see Rossetti is advocating a principle the mere gratification of the eye and if any passion at all—the animal passion to be the aim of art."[32] These strong reactions indicate the significance attached to Rossetti's new practice of the portrait as a source of pleasure in itself.

Rather than telling a story or pointing to an invisible quality of the sitter, the new portraiture was "aesthetic" in the sense that its purpose or end was its own beauty. This approach proved profitable to Rossetti, whose wealthy male patrons were eager to decorate the walls of their

FIG. 1. Dante Gabriel Rossetti (1828–1882), *Bocca Baciata* (*Lips That Have Been Kissed*), 1859. Oil on panel, 32.1 x 27 cm. (12⅝ x 10⅝ in.). (Museum of Fine Arts, Boston; Gift of James Lawrence, 1980.261; Photography © 2012 Museum of Fine Arts, Boston)

lavish homes with the images of beautiful women. If commodification is one meaning of these portraits, however, it is not the only meaning. Rossetti's aesthetic portraits self-consciously offer a compensation for the lack of access to the sitter's soul by elevating beauty to the significance once reserved for the soul. Objectification of the female body is hardly a new strategy in art, to be sure, but Rossetti was responding to the narrative and moralizing tendencies of nineteenth-century English art, in which female beauty was typically served up as part of a lesson or story that superficially justified the existence of the painting. Committed in his own way to truth-telling, Rossetti both exposed the fundamentally material condition of painting (made of paint and canvas, and sold for money), and tried to imagine a new basis for justifying its existence apart from an educational, moral, or religious significance.

The appearance of the model and the whole impression of *Bocca Baciata* emphasize its status as an aesthetic object. The sitter's beauty is indistinguishable from the richness of the painting.[33] The decorative quality extends from the model's face and pose to her golden hair, each strand of which is visible. It extends to the adornments in her hair and on her person, the gold braid in her dress, and the flowers floating in the space behind her head, emphasizing the flatness of the picture and its nonnarrativity. The gold coins that the model wears as earrings associate visual beauty with material value. A window ledge or parapet in the foreground cuts sharply across the picture plane, rendering the space "flat, two-dimensional."[34] This compositional feature, which Rossetti would repeat in many future portraits, creates continuity between the painting and its frame, as if to suggest that we are not looking through a window at the scene, but rather that the picture and its frame are of the same kind, that is, a pretty thing hanging on the wall. Rossetti typically designed his own frames and oversaw their production carefully, linking canvas and frame with shared motifs and color schemes. The design of the frames emphasized the decorativeness and flatness of the canvases they contained.[35]

Just as the composition and framing devices of Rossetti's new portraits emphasized the flatness of the pictures—their status as paint—the expressions on his sitters' faces emphasized their mental blankness. *Bocca Baciata* shares her mysteriously inexpressive look with most of Rossetti's future portraits. Critics describe the look of Rossetti's female sitters as "inscrutable," "with near neutrality of facial expression," and "[staring] out into space for no apparent reason."[36] Her expression combines elements of absorption—absorbed in her own mental state, she does not seem conscious of being looked at—with a distinctly theatrical pose of gazing straight out of the canvas. In paintings of the 1860s by Whistler and the French artists Alphonse Legros and Henri Fantin-Latour, Michael Fried identifies a "divided or double structure" that similarly combines absorptive techniques with theatrical devices. These canvases show female figures absorbed in thought, yet placed in a shallow, decorative space that pushes back against the beholder's gaze. Fried writes that such effects struck contemporary audiences as both *excessive* and *intense*—just as Rossetti's associates found *Bocca Baciata* either "revolting" or "stunning." Fried interprets the divided structure of 1860s painting as a way of recuperating the exhausted absorptive tradition while establishing a new relationship with the viewer on the basis of what he calls "facingness": not the melodramatic overkill associated with theatrical (rhetorical) painting, but rather an embrace of the abstract quality of being in front of the viewer.[37] Rossetti's Aesthetic portraiture cultivates "facingness" at several levels, for the value of the painting explicitly resides on its "face"—both the face of the model and the surface of the canvas, which are, of course, the same thing.

Seeming "determined to pursue forbidden or contradictory intellectual limits," *Bocca Baciata*'s pictorial flatness and expressionless face disrupted the Victorian representational hierarchy of body and soul.[38] Most critics agree that Rossetti's religious skepticism drove his many different artistic projects.[39] Opposed to traditional body-soul dualism, Rossetti sought to unite the two principles under the sign of the visible, material realm. As Helsinger notes, Rossetti's ambitions imply "a strong reaction against conceptions of interiority."[40] His elevation of surface was fundamentally connected to his doubt about what might lie beyond appearances and after the life of the body. While Rossetti's watercolors of the 1850s still employed religious imagery, albeit in a strangely decorative way, the new portraits shed religious iconography and transferred the halo of value to the canvas and the body of the sitter. This strategy appealed to Rossetti's circle, while its final meaning remained open, and a variety of interpretations were, and are, possible. In what follows, I develop two interpretations of Rossetti's decorative portraits based on his two poems entitled "The Portrait," one a sonnet and the other a dramatic monologue. These two interpretations descend into Modernism as two different strains of the portrait poem: one emphasizes its status as a thing and end in itself, and the other frames the portrait as a site of reflection where the portraitist encounters himself in the guise of another, leading to a multiplication of images and echoes in the interspace between painting and viewer.

Perhaps the most common interpretation of the Rossettian portrait is to understand it as an end in itself. Rather than giving us access "through" the painting to the sitter, it offers itself as an autotelic, self-sufficient object of beauty. The idea of the artwork-for-itself is a central tenet of Aestheticism and a theme of many Modernist works. Rossetti's painting *Lady Lilith* and its accompanying sonnet "Body's Beauty" probably did the most of all his works to encourage this idea (fig. 2). *Lady Lilith* represents a voluptuous woman in white at her dressing table, combing her hair as she looks in a hand mirror; another mirror on the bureau reflects a wild-looking tree presumably suggesting Eden, Lilith's first home before she fled from Adam.

"Body's Beauty" emphasizes Lilith's self-absorption, indifference to others, and magnetic powers:

> And still she sits, young while the earth is old,
>> And, subtly of herself contemplative,
>> Draws men to watch the bright web she can weave,
> Till heart and body and life are in its hold.[41]

Lilith concentrates value and attention in herself, or rather *on* herself, for it is specifically her "body's beauty" that matters to her and others. Rossetti wrote in a letter about his new picture that Lilith is "gazing on herself in the glass with that self-absorption by whose strange fascination such natures draw others within their own circle."[42] Swinburne similarly commented in his "Notes on Some Pictures of 1868," "she charms and draws down the souls of men by pure force of absorption, in no wise willful or malignant; outside herself she cannot live, she cannot even see: and because of this she attracts and subdues all men at once in body and in spirit."[43] The self-absorbed figure of beauty passed into Modernism via Walter Pater, who recast Swinburne's interpretation of *Lilith* for his ekphrasis of *La Gioconda* in *The Renaissance*:

> She is older than the rocks among which she sits; like the vampire, she has been dead many times, and learned the secrets of the grave; and has been a diver in deep seas, and keeps their fallen day about her; and trafficked for strange webs with Eastern merchants: and, as Leda, was the mother of Helen of Troy, and, as Saint Anne, the mother of Mary; and all this has been to her but as the sound of lyres and flutes, and lives only in the delicacy with which it has moulded the changing lineaments, and tinged the eyelids and the hands.[44]

This passage became a touchstone for Aestheticism and was canonized by Yeats in the *Oxford Book of Modern Verse* as the first modern prose poem. Frank Kermode links the "inward-looking countenance" of Rossetti's *Lilith* with Yeats's self-contained, "self-begotten" dancer.[45] While the meaning and value of Aesthetic self-absorption have been much contested, critics from Kermode to McGann and Douglas Mao identify it as one source of the autotelic, object-like quality of some Modernist writing—the writing that "should not mean but be."[46]

Rossetti's sonnet "The Portrait" articulates the idea of aesthetic self-absorption in portraiture, likening the physical portrait to a shrine and

FIG. 2. Dante Gabriel Rossetti (1828–1882), *Lady Lilith*, 1868 (altered 1872–73). Oil on canvas, 95.3 x 81.3 cm. (Delaware Art Museum, Samuel and Mary R. Bancroft Memorial, The Bridgeman Art Library)

ultimately substituting it for the living subject. The poem compactly deploys the conventions of ekphrastic portraiture. Gesturing to the painting in question, the speaker affirms its likeness to the original:

> O Lord of all compassionate control,
>> O Love! let this my lady's picture glow
>> Under my hand to praise her name, and show
>> Even of her inner self the perfect whole.

He then proceeds to link the sitter's visible features to invisible ones: her glances and smile to "the very sky and sea-line of her soul," the mouth to her "voice and kiss," the "shadowed eyes" to her memory and consciousness. The sonnet ends ("Lo! it is done") by hailing the painting's capacity to immortalize the sitter.

> Her face is made her shrine. Let all men note
>> That in all years (O Love, thy gift is this!)
>> They that would look on her must come to me.[47]

Yet even as Rossetti affirms the transparency of the beloved's face and her image, he also pursues the seemingly incompatible goal of making the portrait independent from the sitter.

At first, the poem seems to emphasize the portrait's traditional role as a guide to the sitter's character. Helsinger argues that in his picture sonnets, including this one, Rossetti aimed to "return a primarily decorative, aesthetic art to portraiture: the visionary portrayals of psychic and moral states."[48] The multiplying pronouns, pronominal adjectives, and demonstratives build a sense of referentiality into the poem by constantly drawing our attention to what is anterior to it. Yet the references to the lady's invisible aspects compete with references to the portrait itself, following the speaker's gesture in the second line, "let this my lady's picture glow," and his stated purpose of making the "perfect" whole visible to those who would "seek . . . her beauty's furthest goal." What is our "goal," then, to know her "inner self" or to see his portrait of her?

Rossetti eliminates the need for an independently existing sitter by attributing subject-like capacities to the painting itself. The idea that a portrait promises to speak, or seems as if it could speak, is a common conceit both in ekphrastic portraiture and gothic tales about portraits, such as Poe's "The Oval Portrait." In Rossetti's sonnet, "the mouth's mould testifies of voice and kiss": rather than proving the limit of visual representation, the image of the beloved's lips satisfies the desire for speech and living presence. Though testimony is typically verbal, here the image of the lips alone seems to substitute for anything they could say. Why would speech be necessary if the image can testify? Rossetti further claims, "the shadowed eyes remember and foresee." Playing on the trope of eyes as windows to the soul, Rossetti here attributes consciousness to the eyes *in the painting*. "Shadowing" is a technique of painting as well as an effect of light. The shadows under her eyes give the effect of thoughtfulness and recollection, but the painter's use of shading is responsible for her look. Now it is the painted eyes that seem to remember. The capacities of speech (to "testify"), memory (to "remember"), and intention (to "foresee") are given to the artwork itself.

The speaker seems to boast when he concludes, "They that would look on her must come to me." Yet the "me" at this point no longer clearly refers to the painter/poet, but rather to the object he has created—both the painting and the text of the poem. The final word "me" identifies the poet with his sonnet, the painter with his painting, and substitutes the artifact for its maker. This substitution parallels the speaker's identification of the sitter with her portrait in the previous lines. The finished work thus embodies both the sitter and the painter, converting their time-bound love into a timeless icon authorized by Love. The portrait-shrine becomes the goal of our seeking; we need look no farther. This sonnet exemplifies the traits that compose the Modernist "object" poem identified in different ways by Kermode, McGann, and Mao: brevity, verbal condensation, the use of highly symbolic images, and a circuit of identifications that equate the sitter and the poem itself with one or more material objects.

Yet the close of the poem also suggests a different interpretation that Rossetti would develop in his dramatic monologue "The Portrait." When he says "me," does the painter/poet identify himself with the subject of the painting at a deeper level? The painting is not only a highly decorated surface but a mirror whose significance has less to do with its intrinsic material or aesthetic value than with what it reflects. Mirrors and doubles fascinated Rossetti throughout his career, and his oeuvre contains many works that "double up" with other works: translations, picture sonnets, portraits, and illustrations. This interest sprang not only from the artist's fascination with representation; it was a way of exploring the meaning of the soul in a secular world. The mirror, the double, and the portrait represent a separable aspect of the person that, like the soul, is both self and not self. Yet, unlike the soul, a reflection or even a ghostly double seems limited to the earthly world of humans and does not refer upwards to transcendental realms.

Rossetti explored the motif of doubles and uncannily lifelike portraits in a series of early works including the stories "Hand and Soul" and "Saint Agnes of Intercession," the drawing "How They Met Themselves," and the poems "Sister Helen," "The Bride's Prelude," and "On Mary's Portrait, Which I Painted Six Years Ago," which became the basis for his dramatic monologue "The Portrait." In his use of the doubling motif, Rossetti combined the Neoplatonic ideal of love as the union of body and soul with the spirit of Gothicism, particularly the gothic portrait tale.[49] Rossetti's "Hand and Soul" (1849) tells the story of a Renaissance painter who becomes disenchanted with painting religious art, has a vision of a woman who claims to be his soul, and paints her portrait. This tale, which Rossetti later described as an "artistic *confessio fidei*," appears to confirm the Romantic injunction to compose from the heart; yet, at the same time, the painter cannot recognize or represent his soul until it appears to him in a visible, exterior manifestation.[50] The vision of his soul in the form of a woman underwrites much of Rossetti's later portraiture. Rossetti's "Saint Agnes of Intercession" (1850) tells a darker version of this narrative. A contemporary painter discovers the exact image of his own face and that of his beloved in a pair of fourteenth-century portraits, leading to the disturbing realization that he may share his identity with two other people who lived long before. These works explore "how to dismantle the subject's presumptive privilege of self-identity."[51]

In his dramatic monologue "The Portrait," Rossetti recast and intensified much of his earlier writing on doubles, reflection, and portraiture, especially the unpublished text of "On Mary's Portrait, Which I Painted Six Years Ago." Elizabeth Siddal's death had made this early work autobiographical in a way that Rossetti could not have imagined when he wrote it, and he threw it in her grave along with other manuscripts at her burial. After the poems were "exhumed" in 1868, Rossetti revised "On Mary's Portrait" in light of his experience as a painter and a bereaved and guilt-stricken husband. Whereas his sonnet "The Portrait" works to close the distance between the sitter and her portrait, ultimately by claiming to substitute the artifact for the woman, his dramatic monologue by the same title insistently explores the gaps between portrait and original. It opens with the conventional gesture of ekphrastic portraiture—"This is her picture as she was"—vouching for the painting's likeness to the sitter. Yet in contrast to the reassurance that Cowper and Wordsworth receive from a similar experience, and even the perverted glee of Browning's duke, Rossetti's speaker is disturbed by the picture and finds its likeness unnatural:

> It seems a thing to wonder on,
> As though mine image in the glass
>   Should tarry when myself am gone.
> I gaze until she seems to stir,—

Confirming the sitter's likeness to her image leads not to affirmation of her immortal soul, but a mise-en-abîme of analogies: he compares her portrait to his own reflection lingering in a mirror, imagines that it might speak (two stock gothic fantasies), and then contrasts her portrait with her corpse in the ground ("And yet the earth is over her"). Whereas Cowper follows a chain of fidelities leading from his mother's portrait to her immortal soul in heaven, Rossetti's speaker expresses uncertainty and anguish, religious skepticism and superstitious yearnings.

> Yet only this, of love's whole prize,
> Remains; save what in mournful guise
>   Takes counsel with my soul alone,—
>   Save what is secret and unknown,
> Below the earth, above the skies.[52]

Rossetti's sonnet "The Portrait" offers one response to the problem of the "unknown" soul: to make it known and visible in the material artwork. But here in the dramatic monologue, the painting as an end is not sufficient; it is "*only* this."

Finding no clear solution to the problem of the evanescent soul, Rossetti keeps the problem in play, and the speaker talking, by a cascade of images and reflections. The speaker compares the beloved's portrait to "her shadow on the grass," "her image in the stream," and the echo of her song. He recalls the many doublings of their initial meeting: they stooped together to drink water; he repeated his words of love to her; he prepared to paint her portrait by arranging her in a setting of "plants in bloom . . . To feign the shadow of the trees." Now, after her death, the reflections continue: his memory "echoes" the events of their courtship by perpetually replaying them in his mind; walking by himself he revisits the places where they walked together; and he imagines his own "hopes and aims" standing about her image. These reflections issue from her portrait, itself an eerie meeting place of doubles:

> In painting her I shrined her face
>   Mid mystic trees, where light falls in
> Hardly at all; a covert place
>   Where you might think to find a din

Of doubtful talk, and a live flame
Wandering, and many a shape whose name
Not itself knoweth, and old dew,
And your own footsteps meeting you,
And all things going as they came.[53]

To paint the beloved is to "shrine" her in a series of multiplied reflections and echoes. The word "shrine" also appears in the sonnet "The Portrait," where it means an icon of beauty that stops time by substituting itself for the beloved. In the dramatic monologue, by contrast, "shrining" is an act that can go on indefinitely as a series of repetitions, and indeed *must* go on in order to perpetuate the memory of the deceased subject.

The difference between the two poems that Rossetti called "The Portrait" has much to do with their forms. The verbal condensation imposed by the sonnet's length restrictions and the Petrarchan conventions of itemization and self-reference push Rossetti's shorter poem toward its thing-like self-absorption. By contrast, the measure of the poet's success in dramatic monologue is to sustain the utterance and make it plausible as speech, rather than to keep it within a prescribed length. The dramatic monologue remains constantly aware of its own status as a speech act in a social context, constructing a self and negotiating with the expectations and beliefs of an imagined auditor. The form entails not brevity and closure but a messy realism and proliferating points of view. Rossetti's choice to call two poems "The Portrait"—articulating divergent concepts of the genre—signifies the opening out of portraiture in two different directions. One avenue leads toward contraction, condensation, and a materialist conception of the subject, developed in Imagism and its offshoots such as the Spectra Hoax and Williams's portraits of the physical body. Another avenue leads toward expansion, use of multiple voices and points of view, and an interspatial conception of self, hovering in the spaces between one speaker and another, and between images and their reflections. "Reflection," writes McGann, is the "presiding deity" of Rossetti's work, and reflection also presides over this latter kind of portraiture extending forward into the twentieth century.[54] The lineage of this motif descends not from Rossetti alone but rather from his circle, for Swinburne had already written one of the best-known ekphrastic portraits about reflection in 1865, when "On Mary's Portrait" was still lying in Siddal's grave. As in many aspects of the two poets' relationship, it was hard to say who influenced whom; rather, their insights into the future of portraiture took place more or less in concert during the 1860s.

Mirror: Between Whistler and Swinburne

The decade between *Bocca Baciata* and Rossetti's *Poems* of 1870 saw the emergence of the "art for art's sake" theory and movement in England and the creation of many of its most important works, including Swinburne's *Poems and Ballads* (1866) and *William Blake* (1868). While Rossetti's early poetry and his paintings shaped Swinburne, it was the younger poet who published his book of poems first. Swinburne's "Before the Mirror," written about Whistler's *The Little White Girl* and affixed to the frame of the painting when it was first exhibited in 1865, captures the intensity of the exchange among Rossetti, Whistler, and Swinburne. It is not surprising in this context that the poem is concerned with reflections and echoes. Indeed, the concept of interspace articulated in the poem could be interpreted as a theory of artistic creativity in a "circle" such as Rossetti's. More specifically, Whistler's painting and Swinburne's ekphrasis build on Rossetti's sumptuous, flattened paintings to propose that a portrait's meaning resides not *on,* but *between* surfaces. In their different media, both Whistler and Swinburne disperse the portrait subject's consciousness, if it can be called that, between herself and her reflection and throughout compositional elements of the work.

The American-born and Paris-trained painter James McNeill Whistler entered Rossetti's circle around 1862. Over the next four years, Whistler painted a number of pictures of single female figures, "versions of the Rossettian type," clearly showing the influence of his artistic associations.[55] Whistler's *The Little White Girl* of 1864 (fig. 3) hits hard the theme of reflection, which Rossetti had explored the year before in *Fazio's Mistress.* The White Girl's long hair and flowing dress, her reflective or absorbed expression, and the accessories decorating the picture are also in dialogue with Rossetti. Whistler's play on shades of white echoes Rossetti's bold use of this color in *Ecce Ancilla Domini!* (1850). Like *Bocca Baciata, The Little White Girl* is a portrait of a woman intimate with the painter—Joanna Hiffernan—though not specifically identified as a portrait in the title. Whistler affixed the text of Swinburne's poem to the frame of his painting when exhibiting it in 1865, much in the way Rossetti had inscribed his picture sonnets for *The Girlhood of Mary Virgin* on the frame of his painting in 1849. The exchange between Swinburne and Whistler shows both men imitating Rossetti at some level, and yet also taking his suggestions farther and introducing changes to the genre.

The prominence of a large mirror in *The Little White Girl* alludes to and contrasts with the use of mirrors in recent paintings by Rossetti and Holman Hunt. In Hunt's *Awakening Conscience* (1854), a mirror on the wall behind the fallen woman reflects the garden outside her house, suggesting that as she turns away from her seducer, she will seek moral guidance in nature. The mirror opens out to a better world, and to the moral of this narrative painting. Rossetti's *Fazio's Mistress* of 1863 employs the mirror to turn our attention in the opposite direction: inward to the female figure's beauty. She looks with languorous fascination at her own reflection, which we cannot see. The mirror is a device for focusing attention on

FIG. 3. James McNeill Whistler (1834–1903), *Symphony in White, No. 2: The Little White Girl*, 1864. Oil on canvas, 76.5 x 51.1 cm. (Tate Gallery; Digital Image © Tate, London 2011)

the self-absorption and physical beauty of the sitter. Rossetti employed the hand mirror again in *Lady Lilith* (conceived around the same time as *The Little White Girl* but not completed until 1868), while adding a standing mirror on the bureau that reflects an optically impossible scene of nature, making reference to Lilith's origins in Eden. Rossetti uses mirrors in both paintings to emphasize the figures' amoral self-absorption in their own beauty.

In taking up the mirror motif, *The Little White Girl* departed both from Hunt's use of reflection to convey a religious message and from Rossetti's emphasis on embodied beauty. Throughout his career, writes Fried, Whistler "was drawn by an ideal of painting as absence," leading him "to evoke virtuality or apparitionality through the motif of an image in a mirror" in several important works of the 1860s, including this painting and *The Artist in His Studio* (fig. 6, discussed in chapter 2). Such paintings seem to depict "not material beings and objects but mere apparitions (i.e. reflections)," with the goal of making the painting "seem almost immaterial."[56] While Fazio's Mistress and Lilith see themselves in their mirrors, the White Girl seems not to see anything (in this respect the figure is absorptive); rather, we see her face from two angles, one turned away from and one turned toward the viewer. A series of doubles radiates out from her reflected image. The mirror also reflects two paintings hanging on the wall, one obscured except for the frame, and one showing a seaside or river scene. This painting is echoed in the seaside scene painted on the girl's fan. The right angles of the frames of the paintings double each other, and are in turn visually echoed by the right angles of the fireplace and mantelpiece. Two Chinese pots stand on the mantelpiece, one red and one blue-and-white, their colors reflected in the girl's fan. These doubles emphasize the design aspects of the painting, its paintedness, suggesting not source and copy, but a mise-en-abîme of immaterial visions.[57]

The picture reflected behind the girl's head in the mirror is similar to many that Whistler would paint in the later 1860s and 1870s, made famous under the title of "Nocturnes." Though it has not been identified, this canvas may be Whistler's *Brown and Silver: Old Battersea Bridge*, dated 1859–63 but probably no earlier than 1862, which he exhibited with *The Little White Girl* at the Royal Academy in 1865.[58] Whistler's cataloguers Dorment and MacDonald propose that *Brown and Silver* shows the view out of the painter's window on Queen's Row in Chelsea, where he lived briefly beginning around December 1862, a few months after meeting Swinburne and Rossetti.[59] In March, he moved to Lindsey Row, where *The Little White Girl* was painted.[60] Whistler's apparent choice to show the reflection of *Brown and Silver* thus significantly revises the convention of including a window or the reflection of one (as in Hunt's *The Awakening Conscience*). Rather than showing us the view out of an existing window, Whistler gives us a reflection of a painting of the view out of his old window, in a sense recalling the past (Swinburne was conscious of this) but rendering it so blurry as to be illegible. The painting suggests an analogy between two meanings of reflection: meditation, suggested by the girl's pose, and mirroring. Surrounded with optical reflections, the figure of the girl is absorbed into this matrix as an aspect of light and design.

Swinburne's response to Whistler's painting was immediate. "Here are the verses, written the first thing after breakfast and brought off at once," he wrote on April 2, 1865, suggesting that Whistler affix his poem to *The Little White Girl*'s frame in the upcoming Royal Academy Exhibition. The verses contained in the letter—"Before the Mirror"—register a gradually dawning realization that meaning is not located in the usual places in the painting. The poem tracks a shift from looking at the painting as if it were one of Rossetti's, to looking at it on its own terms. This shift is expressed in the letter to Whistler: "I found [in the picture] at once the metaphor of the rose and the notion of sad and glad mystery in the face languidly contemplative of its own phantom and all other things seen by their phantoms. I wanted to work this out more fully and clearly, and insert the reflection of the picture and the room; but Gabriel says it is full long for its purpose already, and there is nothing I can supplant."[61] A difference of opinion between the two poets has arisen: Swinburne wants to add the reflection of the picture on the wall, thereby doing justice to the full range of Whistler's echoes and doublings, but Rossetti thinks the poem is too long and he needs to stop. Their difference suggests Swinburne's eagerness to explore the possibilities of reflection and mise-en-abîme as far as he can take them; the elder poet urges concision. As we shall see, the poem tracks the gradual opening of this difference between them concerning what the subject of female portraiture is or should be.

"Before the Mirror" consists of three sections of three stanzas apiece, each section taking a different approach to the painting. In the first section, the viewer looks for a conventional narrative meaning; in the second, the girl speaks to her reflection in the mirror, vocalizing what self-sufficient beauty is like as a conscious state; and in the third section, the viewer seems able to flow into her consciousness himself. What he discovers in the process is that there is no specific knowledge or feeling that belongs to her and distinguishes her as herself; rather, as the subject of the painting, "she" is a "formless" place through which "old loves and faded fears"—not necessarily hers—float and flow away. The poem thus expands its own consciousness from the narrow question of what the girl feels to "the flowing of all men's tears beneath the sky."[62] Formally, the alternation between speakers and changing points of view, which would become a fundamental feature of Modernist portrait poems, also sets up a series of reflections similar to the repetitions and mirrorings in Whistler's painting, a seemingly infinite multiplication of frames.

In the first section, the viewer responds to the painting in a conventional way, asking what feelings the girl is concealing:

> Behind the veil, forbidden,
>   Shut up from sight,
> Love, is there sorrow hidden,
>   Is there delight?[63]

This section views the painting with the standard nineteenth-century approach of looking for a narrative, usually concerning love.[64] Swinburne's question about the meaning of the girl's expression is in keeping with the ekphrastic convention of reading appearances for what they can reveal of the interior ("behind the veil," "shut up from sight," "hidden"). In deploying this convention as a question rather than an answer, however, Swinburne leaves open whether there *can* be an answer.

In the second section of the poem, the girl answers the poet's question while addressing her own reflection. What Swinburne gives her to say could be attributed to any of Rossetti's female portraits, perhaps better than to Whistler's *The Little White Girl:*

> I watch my face, and wonder
>   At my bright hair;
> Nought else exalts or grieves
>   The rose at heart, that heaves
> With love of her own leaves and lips that pair.[65]

Swinburne's chosen motif of white and red roses—introduced in the first stanza of the poem—has less in common with Whistler's ethereal azaleas and more with Tennyson's "The Gardener's Daughter" and Rossetti's symbolically charged uses of the rose, especially in *Venus Verticordia,* begun in 1864 and brought near completion in 1865. In his "Notes on Some Pictures of 1868," Swinburne would write of this picture, "her glorious bosom seems to exult and expand as the roses on each side of it. The painting of leaf and fruit and flower in this picture is beyond my praise or any man's."[66] Similarly, the hair in Whistler's work is not bright, nor is it conceivably the object of the girl's interest, whereas it is the visual and thematic focus of several major paintings by Rossetti from the same time: *Fazio's Mistress* (1863), *Morning Music* (1864), and *Woman Combing Her Hair* (1864), as well as *Lady Lilith*. Swinburne's implication that the girl may be thinking about her own beauty and past kisses ("She knows not loves that kissed her / She knows not where") also connects the poem more closely with the eroticized bodies in Rossetti's paintings, and specifically to *Bocca Baciata*. Whistler's dark-haired girl, by contrast, is modestly dressed with her hair pulled back, as she looks at her wedding ring in a subdued way, a detail that suggests quite different thoughts for her than for Rossetti's sensuous beauties.

In the second section, then, the poem responds to Whistler's painting much as one accustomed to looking at Rossetti's portraits might. Swinburne interprets the look on Joanna Hiffernan's face as if she were Fanny Cornforth, absorbed in her own beauty. For Rossetti, the blank looks on his sitter's faces draw attention to themselves and the paintings as autotelic aesthetic objects. Here, Swinburne imagines what state of consciousness such an aesthetic object might experience. The girl is conscious of two things: her own beauty, and the limits on her knowledge of what that beauty means. When she says, "I watch my face, and wonder[,]" we expect to learn what she wonders (her thoughts and feelings), but her wonder turns out to be a state of passive amazement "At my bright hair." Her intransitive use of "wonder" demarcates the limits of her consciousness, encompassing her own beauty but excluding an investigation of its significance or source. Beyond her awareness of her face, hair, lips, and hand, all the girl knows is that she *doesn't know*: "Art thou the ghost, my sister . . . / Am I the ghost, who knows?" Swinburne imagines what it is like to be an aesthetic object, whether as a person, a flower, or a painting. It is to have no past or future, no feelings, but nevertheless a consciousness of beauty: "But one thing knows the flower, the flower is fair."[67]

In a sense, the girl's utterance in "Before the Mirror" simply explains the implications of Rossetti's portraits: autotelic beauty that has no referent or origin, and needs none. Yet, in attributing consciousness and speech to the girl, Swinburne necessarily reintroduces a kind of interiority to Rossetti's aesthetic of surface. This interiority is not exactly inside the girl, still less "behind" the picture, but rather exists in the space between the girl and her reflection, defined by the interaction between herself and her "ghost," and between the girl's voice and the poet's. This disembodied interiority is not unlike the divided structure of Whistler's painting, which uses "an absorptive matrix to give affective 'depth' to a highly decorative gestalt."[68] The in-between space Swinburne evokes is also what he terms an "interspace." In "A Ballad of Death" (1866), Swinburne refers to the region between a woman's breasts as a "tender interspace."[69] In "Tristram of Lyonesse" (1882), he uses the term to designate the space between two lovers and an interval of time between one kiss and the next.[70] As an accomplished classicist, Swinburne would have been aware that the comparative form of the Latin adjective "inter" is "interior," and that the superlative form is "intimus." "Interspace" thus draws on the closely related English words "interior" and "intimate," to suggest a relation between things, particularly between two people, that shares or verges on the quality of interiority.

As discussed earlier, Charles Taylor employs the term "interspace" to refer to an interiority situated between people or between people and things. He describes the Modernist concept of self as an epiphany that occurs "not so much in the work as in a space that the work sets up; not in the words or images or objects evoked, but between them. Instead of an epiphany of being, we have something like an epiphany of interspaces."[71] Taylor specifically finds this interspatial mode in the poetry of Ezra Pound, and although Taylor probably did not have Swinburne in mind as its source, the connection is no coincidence, for Swinburne, like Rossetti, had an early and deep influence on Pound. In particular, "A Ballad of Death" was one of Pound's favorite poems by Swinburne.[72]

Swinburne's title, "Before the Mirror / (Verses written under a Picture) / Inscribed to J. A. Whistler," places the poem in relation to the mirror in the painting, to the painting itself, and to the painter, in that order. The prepositions "before," "under," and "to" indicate that the poem is concerned with relations in space and time ("before" can mean previous in time, or spatially in front of) as well as between persons. As an ekphrastic work, the poem itself is another instance of such relationality. Swinburne creates Baudelairean "correspondences" between the arts, and between time and space, while specifically trying to imagine how these correspondences generate a kind of interiority detached from individual consciousness. The poem's exploration of interspace responds to and correlates with the reflections and repetitions in Whistler's picture. The two faces of the figure, two porcelain jars, two azalea sprays, two riverscapes, two paintings reflected in the mirror, and so on, are "in" the painting, but do not signify what is "in" the girl, neither her emotions nor memories of the past. Although her reflection is at the center of the picture, both visually and thematically, her personal identity is not: neither her thoughts, nor her character and past, nor even her social status are clearly indicated in the painting. To the extent that the painting stops short of portraiture, it also defers or transfers interiority from the figure to the canvas itself.

Similarly, the interspace in Swinburne's poem generates an interiority that is not constituted by the girl's personal history of loves and disappointments or her intentions for the future, yet still has a temporal dimension. Typically, an ekphrastic portrait narrates some portion of the sitter's history in order to interpret her appearance. The temporal dimension provides the sitter with psychological "depth" by explaining how she came to be where she is and secures one of the key aspects of identity, which is continuity over time through memory. Swinburne explicitly refuses to represent the girl's temporal aspect, raising the question of personal memory in the first section ("Love, is there sorrow hidden, / Is there delight?") and negating it in the second, where she denies knowledge of past or future. Instead, the third section of the poem offers a generalized conception of time without personal memory. This variation contributes to Swinburne's development of an interspace not tied to or located in individual interiority.

Section III describes temporality as a general condition of flow and drift that cancels out the importance of an individual past and future. Swinburne had already explored this condition in "The Triumph of Time" (1863–64), a dramatic utterance by a disappointed lover who bitterly addresses his departing beloved as they stand by the edge of the sea. The lover declares that since he has been denied union with his beloved, he will join his life to that of "the great sweet mother, / Mother and lover of men, the sea," where he may find sleep and oblivion. He imagines himself as a "stream, / One loose thin pulseless tremulous vein," flowing to the sea, where he will become "A pulse of the life of thy straits and bays, / A vein in the heart of the streams of the sea."[73] This metaphor effectively refigures time from a linear progression (flowing in a single direction, like the stream) to a diffuse, ancient, encompassing medium:

> But thou, thou art sure, thou art older than earth;
> Thou art strong for death and fruitful of birth;
> Thy depths conceal and thy gulfs discover;
> From the first thou wert; in the end thou art.[74]

Swinburne plays on the difference between individual memory, as a painful consciousness of previous losses and might-have-beens, and natural or geological time, in which a single human life is proportionally insignificant and quickly forgotten—a mere raindrop on the undulating surface of the sea.

To be conscious of the second kind of time is to lose sense of the significance of individual memory. At the close of each of the three stanzas in section III of "Before the Mirror," the girl's seeing of her reflection is absorbed into the vastness of time: "Deep in the gleaming glass / She sees all past things pass, / And all sweet life that was lie down and lie," and most explicitly in the closing lines,

> She sees old loves that drifted,
>   She knew not why,
> Old loves and faded fears
> Float down a stream that hears
>   The flowing of all men's tears beneath the sky.[75]

Each stanza closes with reference to the universality of sorrow and death, expressed by the "dead mouths of many dreams" and the sound of "all men's tears."

The first two sections seem to struggle with the limits on individual human consciousness: in the first, the viewer doesn't know what the girl is thinking; in the second, the girl doesn't remember her past. By contrast, the last section vastly expands the consciousness of the poem.[76] Not only does the girl now have access to "all past things" and "all men's tears," but the viewer has access to her thoughts as well. Consciousness, which proceeds by "formless gleams," seems to have no individual boundaries. Her memories, thoughts, and even feelings are passing states, not possessions: "Glad, but not flushed with gladness." The noun "gladness" is a possession, but the adjective "glad" is simply a state that one passes through, or rather, it passes through her. Her consciousness is open to "all men's tears" and yet does not own any of its own states. She is—and the painting is—a place through which thoughts, feelings, and memories pass: an interspace.

Swinburne's expansion of temporality in the third section accompanies the introduction of sound, a motif of great importance to him.[77] While "seeing" is the theme of much of the poem, ultimately it is hearing that reveals the meaning of the image: the sound of singing, sighing, and tears. Swinburne's emphasis on sound (not only here but in all his work) was reflected in Pater's assessment that "all art constantly aspires to the condition of music."[78] For Whistler, Swinburne, Pater, and others, the analogy with music provided an important strategy for justifying nonnarrative, nonmoralizing artworks. Instrumental music offered the best model of an art that could be enjoyed and judged on purely formal grounds. As Prettejohn notes, music had emerged by 1867 as a theme in paintings by Frederick Leighton and Albert Moore—as well as in Whistler's new titles—that drew on the analogy between form in music and in visual art.[79] In "Before the Mirror," music emerges as a theme at the moment when the poem realizes the significance of Whistler's method of echoes. Swinburne's recognition in turn may have affected Whistler's decision to retitle the work *Symphony in White, No. 2* in 1867.[80]

Swinburne's "Before the Mirror" introduces new traits to the portrait poem that are important to its development in the twentieth century: multivocality, nonnarrativity, and a system of surface reflections that replaces a traditional conception of interiority. Yet the poem also poses a fundamental challenge to portraiture, first by presenting a figure with no past or future and knowing nothing, and then by invoking the entire history of man's sorrows as the meaning of this figure. Indeed, in giving his poem three titles, Swinburne had plenty of chances to call it a portrait and did not. (In comparison, Whistler's original title with its determinate article "the" suggests a portrait of a specific person.) Although it takes its cue from a lineage of portrait poems and shares many traits with these precursors, "Before the Mirror" self-consciously branches off in the final section, away from portraiture. As well, the priorities established by music do not favor portraiture. Unlike instrumental music, portraiture is fundamentally referential. Its scale is individual rather than universal, and though a portrait could easily be imagined to have a dramatic dimension (as in "My Last Duchess," or even in section II of "Before the Mirror"), it can less easily be imagined to have a musical one. In its commitment to art for art's sake, "Before the Mirror" quickly departs from the core requirement of the visual and verbal portrait: that it represent a specific individual.

"Before the Mirror" thus points toward a Modernist conception of a disaggregated, decentered self while also suggesting the difficulty of representing such a self in the genre dedicated to picturing the freestanding individual. Perhaps for this reason Rossetti wanted Swinburne to finish the poem where it was and not to pursue the reflections any further. While Rossetti himself had explored the multiplication of selves in his dramatic monologue "The Portrait," this is a deeply personal and troubled poem; his sonnet by the same name is more typical, especially of the output of his later years. Indeed, *Lady Lilith* and its accompanying sonnet "Body's Beauty" may also be read as Rossetti's response to the unnerving multiplication of reflections and echoes in Whistler's painting and Swin-burne's poem. "Body's Beauty" emphasizes Lilith's sameness over time, her magnetic power over others, and her concentration on her own body. Like Swinburne, Rossetti theorizes beauty for beauty's sake, but with a very different conclusion about where this beauty is to be found and what it means.

When a new generation of American poets nurtured on Aestheticism turned their hand to portraiture around 1908, they found these two distinct approaches available: on the one hand, Rossetti's condensed, image-laden, autotelic picture-sonnet; on the other, the expansive, multivocal, outward-flowing dramatic portrait to which Browning, Rossetti, and Swinburne had each contributed their part. The challenge for these poets who sought to write portraits—a genre with intuitive appeal for inhabitants of a land preoccupied with individuality—was to find a way to use these different models to suit their poetic needs in the twentieth century.

❧

TWO

Ezra Pound

PORTRAITURE AND ORIGINALITY

O F THE AMERICAN MODERNIST poets, Ezra Pound entered the twenti-eth century most openly under the sign of Rossetti and English Aes-theticism; he was also the most prolific writer of portrait poems. Before the publication of his collected *Personae* in 1926 officially brought his entire oeuvre of short poems under this generic label, Pound treated the portrait as one of his major genres. On the last page of *Umbra*, Pound listed his pre-1918 works as "Personae and Portraits," and a year later, gathered his more recent work under the title *Poems 1918–1920, Including Three Portraits and Four Cantos.* From these rubrics, it is clear that to the end of his career as a writer of short poems—he turned perma-nently to epic in 1920—the portrait constituted a major generic cate-gory for Pound. His portraits fall roughly into three generations. Exam-ined in this chapter, the first and most self-consciously Aesthetic group stretches from *Hilda's Book* of 1906 to the pastiches of *Canzoni* (1911) and some poems of *Ripostes;* the second group consists of epigrammatic and epitaphic portraits in *Lustra,* discussed in chapter 4; and finally, the sequences "Moeurs Contemporaines" and *Hugh Selwyn Mauberley* (in chapter 5) expand the genre while combining and modulating it with other avant-garde art forms. Most of these works seem far removed from Pound's early hero-worship of Rossetti, Whistler, Swinburne, and Yeats. Yet they build on the submerged foundations of Aestheticism in ways that run deeper than style. Pound's youthful admiration of Rossetti and the Aesthetic movement drew him to portraiture; under his hand the genre and its associated questions became quintessentially "Modernist" topics.

In this chapter I examine a series of poems that Pound wrote from 1908 to 1912 portraying female figures. These poems experiment with two contrasting versions of Aestheticism: the concrete and the "apparitional." A concrete, material, and visual mode of portraiture derived from Rossetti appears in "La Donzella Beata," "House of Splendour," and other poems of *Hilda's Book* and *Canzoni*. Published between these two books, *Exultations* displays a contrasting aesthetic of disembodiment, incorporating elements from Whistler, Swinburne, and Yeats. Pound's process of sifting through competing Aesthetic influences is dramatically displayed in his unpublished manuscript "To La Mère Inconnue" and its revision in "Portrait: from 'La Mère Inconnue'" of *Exultations*. This previously undescribed work shows both Pound's anxiety about his imitative styles and how he used portraiture to move the subject of the poem away from himself—indeed, to negate the idea of interiority altogether. After examining this draft and its revision in detail, I turn to Pound's most anthologized work of portraiture, his "Portrait d'une femme" of *Ripostes*, which successfully integrates concrete and disembodied aesthetics in a single extended simile and articulates his concept of an interspatial self. I conclude with "To Whistler, American," a mirror-portrait of Whistler and Pound himself that rewrites Aestheticism as an "American Risorgimento." Rather than rejecting and freeing himself from Aestheticism during these early years, as is usually claimed, Pound was sorting through its features and seeking a way to frame his own sense of belated reception as a positive quality rather than a weakness. A genre dedicated to copying what is already present, portraiture itself became a way for Pound to embrace the idea of imitation.

⁊

Rossetti was among the earliest icons in Pound's religion of beauty for its own sake. Pound modeled his first collection, *Hilda's Book*, on Rossetti's *House of Life*, opening the volume with "La Donzella Beata," a reply to Rossetti's most famous double work, *The Blessed Damozel*. As H.D. later recalled of their courtship: "the early D.G. Rossetti and the *Vita Nuova* translation and pre-Raphaelite pictures that Ezra brought me. Concern with 'The Blessed Damozel'! Surely, Ezra read it to me—yes."[1] Pound first read Villon, Cavalcanti, and Dante in Rossetti's translations; about his own 1910 translations of Cavalcanti he remarked that "Rossetti is my father and my mother."[2] Pound's medievalism and his career-long concern with erotic love as a physical and spiritual experience of transcendence also were set in motion by the early impact of Rossetti. Finally—and this is the aspect I will focus on—Pound's visual sensibility and his affinity for portraiture were very much shaped by Rossetti's painting and his image-laden poetry.[3] In particular, Rossetti's influence accounts for a stylized materialism in Pound's early portraits. From "La Donzella Beata" to "House of Splendour" in *Canzoni,* Pound adopted the painter's motifs of roses and golden frames to symbolize the union of body and soul in the visible, material world. Later on, the condensed Imagistic and satiric portraits of *Lustra* explored this idea in a different key.

Pound also began his career under the spell of his fellow countryman James McNeill Whistler, whose elevation of beauty for its own sake appealed to the young poet as early as 1906.[4] In unpublished articles on art, Pound quoted extensively from Whistler's "Ten O'Clock Lecture."[5] He adopted the dress and attitudes of Whistler, signing his poems with a gadfly in imitation of the painter's famous butterfly. Whistler's public advocacy of form and technique over moral message made a deep impression on Pound, so that as late as 1915 he claimed Whistler as an "ancestor" of Vorticism.[6] In contrast to the polished, luxurious, insistently material surfaces of Rossetti's paintings, Whistler's portraits conveyed evanescence and insubstantiality. His "symphonies" and "nocturnes" emphasized paint as light and harmony rather than as material artifacts, qualities that Pound imitated in poems from 1908 such as "Nel Biancheggiar."[7] The visual indefiniteness of these painterly poems became a feature of his writing in *A Lume Spento* and *Exultations,* such as the poem "'Fair Helena' by Rackham." More generally, a quality of absence or apparitionality in Whistler's work correlates closely with the negations on which Pound's own portraiture is built—such as, most famously, the claim "No! There is nothing" in "Portrait d'une femme."

In Pound's developing style, Whistler's Impressionism blended with similar elements drawn from Swinburne.[8] H.D.'s autobiographical novel *White Rose and the Red,* which pairs members of the Rossetti circle with H.D.'s acquaintances from the war years in London, gives the role of Pound to a character named Swinburne.[9] Pound composed many Swinburnian works in his early years, including "Salve O Pontifex!" (an ode to Swinburne), "Ver Novum" (in *Hilda's Book*), the two "Villonauds," "Aux belles de Londres," "Ballad for Gloom," and "Anima Sola." Pound experimented with the sestina, a form that Swinburne reintroduced to modern poetry, and opened his "Elegia" in *Canzoni* by quoting "The Triumph of Time."[10] In Pound's 1918 essay "Swinburne and His Biographers," he identifies "The Triumph of Time" as one of the poet's three best works, along with "Ballad of Life" and "Ballad of Death," writing that "The two ballads and the *Triumph of Time* are full of sheer Imagism, of passages faultless."[11] One of Swinburne's most famous works, "The Triumph of Time" resonates through Pound's verse in the metaphor of a maternal, echoing sea. His unpublished "Ode," discussed in this chapter, is addressed to such a figure, the "mère inconnue." In contrast to Rossetti's poetics of physical embodiment and visual images, Swinburne evoked a fluid self, connected to remote ages and places through the flow of time and sound. Pound often plays these two modes off against each other, as in "Portrait d'une femme" and later *Mauberley*.

The best known of all Aesthetic influences on Pound was Yeats, whom Pound followed to London in 1908.[12] For Pound in 1908, Yeats was a living monument to the accomplishments of an earlier generation of artists and poets whose work he sought to extend. The poems of *A Lume Spento* and *Exultations* show his apprenticeship most clearly, such as "La Fraisne," which opens Pound's first published volume by paying homage to Yeats's "The Madness of King Goll." Along with many verbal echoes, Pound's developing notion of the persona owed much to Yeats's use of speakers in *The Wind Among the Reeds*.[13] To speak of Yeats's impact on Pound is also to describe another route by which Rossetti's ideas and iconography reached him, for Yeats himself had grown up in the outer orbit of the Rossetti circle and became their ardent supporter when his father, the painter John Yeats, turned against Aestheticism. In the 1880s and 1890s, as Rossetti's reputation was elevated by a stream of publications and exhibitions, the painter-poet became "the specific inspiration for Yeats's immediate intellectual circle. Of the Rhymers Yeats later recalled, 'Rossetti was a subconscious influence, and perhaps the most powerful of all.'"[14] Yeats's symbolism and his idealization of the female figure have much in common with Rossetti's, but without the painter's physical concreteness. While Rossetti laments the passing of earthly love "which blooms and fades, and only leaves at last, / Faint as shed flowers, the attenuated dream," Yeats celebrates this afterglow.[15] The Yeats that most strongly affected Pound is that of the "attenuated dream."

In a reversal central to the history of twentieth-century poetry, Pound later repudiated these influences, dismissing his early "Rossetti-itis" and the "stale creampuffs" of *A Lume Spento*.[16] Hugh Kenner and other critics followed suit, sneering at the "Rossettian tosh" of Pound's early work, and it is a commonplace to explain his modernization as a reaction against Aestheticism.[17] In one of the most extensive studies of Pound's early poetry, Thomas Grieve argues that Pound purged the "voice of self-expression," the obsession with "personality," and the "subjective mode" that he had learned too well from Rossetti, Swinburne, Pater, and Yeats.[18] It is undeniable that Pound moved from expressing his own emotions to exploring a wider range of figures and issues. He sought to reimagine interiority as a shared rather than personal quality. This project arose, however, out of the apprenticeship he was later eager to repudiate. Whether insistently materialistic or apparitional, Aesthetic poetry and painting undermine the very idea of an interiority from which feeling and self-expression issue. In following various threads laid down by the previous generation, Pound too experimented with presenting himself and the sitters of his portraits without invoking the conventional model of interiority. Pound's representation of himself and others as an absence, a "clear space," reflected not only similar ideas found in Whistler, Swinburne, and Yeats, but also the difficulty of defining himself in a field that was at the time so crowded with artistic giants.

❧

Rossetti offered a powerful poetic and visual model for a modern portraiture that dispensed with the traditional dualism of body and soul, and his "pictorial concreteness" showed the way to the development of a visual aesthetic in Modernism, most famously in Imagism.[19] From *Hilda's Book* (1905–7), through the "gold and ivory" of *Canzoni* (1911) to *Ripostes* (1912) and the Imagist portraits of 1913–14, Pound followed Rossetti's example of treating portraits as aesthetic and material objects. Primarily representing female figures, Pound's portraits consistently return to Rossettian motifs, such as flower petals and golden frames, as devices for emphasizing the physical presence of the sitter.

"La Donzella Beata" articulates Pound's complex relationship with Rossetti on the grounds of the painter-poet's most famous pair of works, "The Blessed Damozel" of 1850 and his later painting by the same name, completed in 1878. The reception of this pair of works was long delayed by Rossetti's reluctance to show his paintings publicly. Following the exhibitions of Rossetti's work after his death, his influence spread throughout the European continent and the United States, its full impact not felt until the 1890s, when Pound was just beginning to develop his aesthetic sensibility. A show at the Pennsylvania Academy of the Fine Arts in 1892 (when Pound was seven) was one of the most important events in the "American consciousness of Rossetti's art."[20] *The Blessed Damozel* was thus by no means "old news" at the time that Pound was writing the poems of *Hilda's Book,* but well enough known that images would have been widely available.[21]

Embodiment is the message of Rossetti's ballad and painting and Pound's response to these works. Walter Pater's 1883 "Appreciation" of Rossetti remarked on the "definiteness of sensible imagery, which seemed almost grotesque to some, and was strange, above all, in a theme so profoundly visionary."[22] The opening stanza, which Rossetti affixed to the frame of his painting, expresses the intensely material quality of the damozel and her heavenly environment:

> The blessed damozel leaned out
>   From the gold bar of Heaven;
> Her eyes were deeper than the depth
>   Of waters stilled at even;
> She had three lilies in her hand,
>   And the stars in her hair were seven.[23]

The poem repeatedly collapses the invisible into the visible, and time into space, to emphasize the Damozel's physical presence: "she saw / Time like a pulse shake fierce / Through all the worlds" (lines 49–51). Rossetti has deemphasized the narrative as much as possible, instead presenting a series of static visual scenes. In the much later painting, Rossetti expresses a similar message of embodiment by emphasizing the surface and materiality of the painting itself (fig. 4). A gold bar cuts across the canvas, rendering "the inhabited space flat, two-dimensional."[24] The bar is repeated in the flat gold frame that encases the picture and divides it from the lower half, the predella showing the earthly lover gazing upward. Gold tints also show behind the heads of the lovers above the Damozel, throwing the "background" forward to the picture plane and emphasizing the nonnaturalistic character of the entire representation. The Damozel's gaze also contributes to the flatness of the painting; like many of Rossetti's female figures, she looks out blankly or as if in a trance. Both painting and poem insist on the Damozel's physical presence despite, or to compensate for, the fact that she is dead.

The "sensible" quality of the Damozel's heaven and her vision of the future had a religious significance for Rossetti, who rejected Cartesian and Christian dualism and understood the body as a manifestation of the soul, not as its opposite ("Lady, I fain would tell how evermore / Thy soul I know not from thy body, nor / Thee from myself, neither our love from God."[25]) His vague references to the immortality of the soul conflict, at least in "The Blessed Damozel," with the lover's skepticism about his eventual reunion with his beloved.[26] The poem affirms the significance of erotic love and refuses to countenance a disembodied existence after death. Rossetti returns persistently to the material world as the only reliable object of knowledge, and within this world, the body of the beloved as the source of meaning and value. "O love, my love! if I no more should see / Thyself, nor on the earth the shadow of thee," cries the poet in the sonnet "Lovesight," "How then should sound upon Life's darkening

FIG. 4. Dante Gabriel Rossetti (1828–1882), *The Blessed Damozel*, 1871–78. Oil on canvas, 136.84 x 96.52 cm (53⅞ x 38 in.). (Harvard Art Museums, Fogg Museum of Art, Bequest of Grenville L. Winthrop, 1943.202; Photo: Katya Kallsen © President and Fellows of Harvard College)

slope . . . The wind of Death's imperishable wing?"[27] Poem after poem ends in the shadow of death, or, like "The Blessed Damozel," tries to imagine a world in which the body lives on after death.

In 1871 Robert Buchanan reviewed Rossetti's *Poems* in "The Fleshly School of Poetry," famously attacking the poet for extolling "fleshliness as the distinct and supreme end of poetic and pictorial art" and implying that "the body is greater than the soul, and sound superior to sense."[28] The review described Rossetti's representation of erotic love and the human body as "sickening," "shameless," "nasty," "trash," and so on, frequently misquoting and taking passages out of context. As unfair as the attack was, Buchanan hit on a real quality in Rossetti's work with far-reaching implications: the value he placed on physical presence and his correspondingly deep skepticism about immortality. Buchanan's criticism of the "glassy" quality of Rossetti's mind sounds very much like a description of his painting and, indeed, of Modernist painting in general:

> The mind of Mr. Rossetti is like a glassy mere, broken only by the dive of some water-bird or the hum of winged insects, and brooded over by an atmosphere of insufferable closeness, with a light blue sky above it, sultry depths mirrored within it, and a surface so thickly sown with water-lilies that it retains its glassy smoothness even in the strongest wind.[29]

Buchanan's language of glassiness picks up the qualities of Rossetti's paintings of women—the decorative, flat appearance of the canvases and the figures' "glassy" looks that seem not to express anything. Buchanan deplored Rossetti's privileging of the medium as an end in itself and saw this trait as an expression of materialism, of valuing "body" over "soul." Thus he imagines Rossetti's mind not as an interior or a source of illumination, but as a mirror that reflects an "insufferable" world of physical objects. Buchanan's review recognized aesthetic modernity in Rossetti's work and attacked it as an aspect of the economic and social modernization that threatened to substitute a material definition of the person for the Christian concept of soul. In *Mauberley*, Pound would find himself strangely both decrying and agreeing with Buchanan.

❧

In "La Donzella Beata," however, Pound receives and takes ownership of Rossetti's poetics of physical presence. The fourteen-line unrhymed poem attempts to outdo Rossetti by substituting a more corporeal Hilda for the heavenly Damozel. The poet contrasts his own beloved with one

> That would wait Lily-cinctured
> Star-diademed at the gate
> Of high heaven crying that I should come
> To thee.[30]

Rossetti's Damozel, of course, was uncrowned and unbelted; Pound parodies her to divert attention from the fundamental similarity between the two representations. Like Rossetti, Pound compares the union of soul and body to an erotic union between lover and beloved and challenges conventions of poetic and sexual propriety to elevate the value of erotic love. (Laity writes that Pound's poem exhibits "the Romantic, Dantean conception of the beloved as a twin soul.")[31] Also like Rossetti, Pound pays lip service to the traditional idea of the soul while focusing on the body of the beloved, describing her as "rose hued mesh / Of o'er fair earthly flesh" and "gold white," using two of the painter-poet's favorite metaphors for the unity of body and soul (roses and gold). The grotesque mesh/flesh rhyme underscores how easily a person may become a thing, a consistent theme in Pound's portraiture through *Lustra* and into *Mauberley*. Similarly, "Shadow" praises the beloved's soul as "full of rose / Leaves steeped in / Golden wine," absurdly literalizing Rossetti's claim that the body and soul are one.[32]

Written in the wake of Pound's study of Rossetti's translations of Cavalcanti, *Canzoni* revisits the style of his poetic "father and mother" with a harder and more insistent materialism. "Epigrams" distills the image of the female body to a few lines:

> O ivory, delicate hands!
> O face that hovers
> Between "To-come" and "Was,"
> Ivory thou wast,
> A rose thou wilt be.[33]

In 1908 Pound had referred to Rossetti's poetry as "the intense, surcharged beauty of blood and ivory," a description that closely resembles the "ivory" and "rose" of this poem.[34] In a mode similar to Rossetti's "Rose Mary," *Canzoni* combines exact renderings of medieval objets d'art with a Neoplatonic love religion: "Lo, there are many gods whom we have seen, / Folk of unearthly fashion, places splendid, / Bulwarks of beryl and of chrysophrase."[35] The visible world remains concretely physical, even if the act of vision has metaphysical implications; in "Canzon: The Vision," an "ivory woman with . . . bands of gold" sails a "bark of painted sandal-wood" and "golden sails / That clasped the ribbands of that azure sea."[36]

"The House of Splendour" of *Canzoni* is particularly in communication with Rossetti and his circle, adopting Rossetti's idea of a poetic "House of Life" and the painter's imagery of a golden-haired beloved against a golden background. The poet describes "my Lady in the sun, / Her hair was spread about . . . / And red the sunlight was, behind it all," echoing lines from Rossetti's "The Bride's Prelude": "the sun flooded: it o'er spread / Like flame the hair upon her head / And fringed her face with burning red."[37] Rossetti's paintings often depicted a golden-haired woman in a golden setting, such as in *Helen of Troy* (1863) or *Sancta Lilias* (1874), a study for *The Blessed Damozel* that was given to the Tate Gallery in 1909. Pound could have seen the latter when it was exhibited in its original gold frame in 1911. In this striking, unfinished work, the gilded robe of the Damozel blends almost completely with a golden background, creating the impression that "the modeled head and hair appear to float not so much on as in this flat and shallow gold surface."[38] Pound similarly blends the human figure with her hair, gown, and the wall behind her, describing each aspect in turn as woven gold: "Her gold is spread, above, around, inwoven"; "all her robe was woven of pale gold"; and "woven walls deep patterned, of email."[39] The lady's dress and the interior decoration of her house could have been designed by Morris or Whistler and share the same "definiteness of sensible imagery" that seemed "strange" to Walter Pater in "The Blessed Damozel." "House of Splendour" is nostalgic in style, yet its insistent concreteness also previews such poems as "An Object" of *Ripostes* or "Albâtre" of *Lustra*, which describes a woman in a white bathrobe with a white dog, enthroned in a "great chair" framed by candles. These portraits in effect carry out the implications of Rossetti's aesthetic of physical presence, contracting and hardening the sitter to a single object.

☙

Exultations, published between *Hilda's Book* and *Canzoni*, displays a contrasting aesthetic of absence and insubstantiality. These poems emphasize echoes, rumors, and faint voices, as well as cloud, shadow, twilight, and dimness. Reviewing *Exultations* in 1909, poet Edward Thomas wrote, "having allowed the turbulent opacity of [Pound's] peculiarities to sink down, we believe that we see very nearly nothing at all."[40] Vacuousness—or apparitionality—is not only a style in this volume; it is a central concept. In "Histrion" of 1908 Pound had described the self as a "clear

FIG. 5. Arthur Rackham (1867–1939), *Fair Helena*, 1908. Illustration based on pen and watercolor original; 12.5 x 18.8 cm; from Shakespeare's *A Midsummer Night's Dream: With Illustrations by Arthur Rackham, R. W. S.* (London: William Heinemann, 1908).

space" through which "the souls of great men / At times pass," "a sphere / Translucent, molten gold, that is the 'I' / And into this some form projects itself."[41] This description of himself is similar to Yeats's Fergus, who finds that "I have grown nothing, knowing all."[42] But while Fergus continues to say "I" through a series of transformations, Pound dispenses with the personal pronoun. The "sphere translucent" or "clear space" inside the poet empties out the concept of interiority as the origin of thoughts and feelings. *Exultations,* a volume whose character is usually attributed to Yeats, explores this idea in various domains.[43] "'Fair Helena' by Rackham" and "Portrait: from 'La Mère Inconnue'" portray insubstantial, even absent subjects in the form that Rossetti had devoted to presence, the picture sonnet.

"Fair Helena" methodically works to undo Rossetti's poetics of physical presence even as it retains the shell of the picture sonnet. The image to which Pound's title refers is an illustration in Arthur Rackham's 1908 *Midsummer Night's Dream* (fig. 5). Rackham's detail-packed, flattened picture planes bear a family resemblance to Aesthetic painting; Helena's loosened, wavy hair, bared shoulders, and flowing robes could be taken from one of Rossetti's paintings of Jane Morris such as *Astarte Syriaca* or *Proserpina*. "Fair Helena" is as ethereal as these figures are embodied, however. By 1908, Rackham had already established his reputation as an illustrator of fancy, with editions of Grimm's *Fairy Tales,* Washington Irving's *Rip Van Winkle,* J. M. Barrie's *Peter Pan,* and Lewis Carroll's *Alice's Adventures in Wonderland.* A review of *Alice* in 1906 described the "tender, flickering light of imagination" in his figures, which had added "a wealth of uncanny, dreamlike mystery to the story."[44] As a nighttime frolic populated by fairies, *Midsummer Night's Dream* was suited to Rackham's special talent for depicting a playful world of the not-real. Helena appears translucent, the folds of her dress resembling the trunks of trees around and behind her. White tints on her dress also resemble the reflection of the moon and stars in the water behind her. We might be looking right through her; she seems hardly there.

Helena's spectral appearance may reflect the tenuousness of vision in Shakespeare's play, especially in the scene that her image illustrates. On the page facing the illustration, Hermia makes a case for hearing over seeing: "Dark night, that from the eye his function takes, / The ear more quick of apprehension makes."[45] Pound's picture sonnet also undermines vision, proceeding through a series of reversals that raise and then disappoint our hopes for knowledge of the figure. It begins with a description of

Rackham's image ("When the purple twilight is unbound, / To watch her slow, tall grace"), but quickly obscures her with clouds and shadows. The speaker says he likes "to know her face," but continues, "is in the shadow there" (knowing *that* her face is there is quite different from knowing its lineaments by seeing it). Again, he likes "to think my voice / can reach to her," but this hope is qualified at the turn of the line: "As but the rumour of some tree-bound stream."[46] Calling himself a "stream," Pound hearkens to streams in Swinburne's "The Triumph of Time" and "Before the Mirror," in which "She hears across cold streams, / Dead mouths of many dreams that sing and sigh."[47] The poem states its preference for sound-poetry under the aegis of Shakespeare and Swinburne. It is, after all, a poem about taste, opening with an epigraph from Browning's "De Gustibus": "What I love best in all the world?"

These reversals negate Rossetti's message of visual presence for an aesthetic of sound and physical absence. They also create a structure of reflection, in which the poet adopts the qualities of the half-seen, translucent figure in Rackham's illustration. Just as he knows only "that" her face is in the shadow, he hopes she knows "Naught but my dream's felicity." Pound's sonnet takes a page from Rossetti's book and rewrites it in the "apparitional" style of Whistler, Swinburne, and Yeats. The poem particularly echoes Rossetti's sonnet "Lovesight," but where Rossetti urges physical closeness as a temporary stay against death, Pound substitutes an echo chamber of voices "heard just beyond the forest's edge" of the poem, including Shakespeare, Browning's *Men and Women*, Swinburne's *Poems and Ballads*, Yeats's *Wind Among the Reeds*, and Rossetti's *Poems*.

In its apparent emptiness, "Fair Helena" cultivates a strategy of Aestheticism that became a staple of Pound's avant-garde portraiture in "Moeurs Contemporaines" and *Hugh Selwyn Mauberley*. Though Grieve and others refer to Pound's Aesthetic poems as "subjective," there is little or no subjectivity in them. "Impersonal," once the watchword of Modernism and now its bête noire, better describes the style and aims of "'Fair Helena' by Rackham" and similar poems where Pound places the various "Masters of [his] Soul" in dialogue with each other while negating his own voice and presence. Pound would soon develop this technique—which might seem like a weakness in *Exultations*—as the central compositional principle of his portraiture, representing the subject as an empty space or medium traversed by other voices and figures. Pound's process for arriving at this principle is recorded in the drafts for his first poem to be given the title "portrait": "Portrait: from 'La Mère Inconnue,'" a sonnet placed beside "'Fair Helena' by Rackham" in *Exultations*.

✿

"Portrait: from 'La Mère Inconnue'" seems no more portrait-like than "Fair Helena," insofar as it, too, lacks an identified or individual subject. Yet Pound's choice of title makes a significant statement about the meaning of the genre for him. The work first appeared in Ford Madox Hueffer's *English Review* in 1909 under the title "Un Retrato" ("a portrait"). He went on to compose two other poems with the title of "portrait": "Portrait d'une femme" of 1912 and "Ritratto," a section of "Moeurs Contemporaines" of 1918. All three are metaportraits, in the sense that they reflect on what portraiture is through a self-conscious dialogue with the nineteenth century. The background of the earliest of these—which Pound chose not to include in his 1926 *Personae*—clarifies and illuminates not only his relationship with Aestheticism but also, more concretely, the meaning and purpose of the two later portraits.

Like "Fair Helena," "Portrait: from 'La Mère Inconnue'" engages in a complex dialogue with Rossetti, Yeats, and Swinburne. Again, it presents itself as a picture sonnet although no specific image emerges from his language of dimness, shadows, and echoes. Rather, the poem represents portraiture as a process of inheriting the past, with the poet quite literally serving as a kind of "clear space." Pound achieved this self-effacement through a struggle with himself that is recorded in an earlier version of the poem, a rambling unpublished manuscript at the Yale Beinecke Library entitled "Ode" on one side and "To La Mère Inconnue" on the other.[48] The draft identifies a poetic mother and father and asks how he can be original if his poetry comes from them. The Beinecke manuscript reveals that the addressee of this "Ode" is the subject of Pound's published "Portrait" of 1909. But who is "La Mère Inconnue"? Pound's choice to call this figure "inconnue" or "unknown" is telling, for the poem is precisely about the question of origin.

The manuscript consists of approximately 75 lines in indeterminate meter and rhyme scheme, treating the theme of poetic inspiration. Several passages clearly describe an experience of poetic "birth," as in these lines near the opening:

> But where the stream of silence azure slips
> Into the first salt wave
> Of that melodious great sea and is content
> To be no longer silence but voiced sound;
> There came the purple robed one and he gave
> To me, no thing fore-dreamed

> But some unthought of element
> Proceeded from him.[49]

These lines sketch out a myth of poetic birth or vocation in which a male figure of poetic authority ("the purple robed one") confers an original ("unthought of") idea on the silent poet, while a maternal sea envelops him and gives him voice. This narrative articulates Pound's anxious preoccupation with the question of poetic source, positing at least two principles of inspiration, roughly male and female.

The paternal "purple robed one" who confers originality on the poet is, ironically, a clichéd figure of religious and secular authority often invoked by nineteenth-century poets including Morris, Swinburne, and Yeats. Indeed the word "purple," which appears seven times in the manuscript, has an element of self-reference, as a term that carries over poetic authority from them to himself. As the presiding influence over *Exultations*, Yeats seems like a prime candidate for the role of "purple robed one." "Purple" is an important color in *The Rose* (1893) and other early volumes, from the "purple glow" of "The Lake Isle of Innisfree" to the "purple deeps," "purple sea," "purple hours" and so on in "The Wanderings of Oisin." In particular, "The Ballad of Father Gilligan" hails "He Who is wrapped in purple robes, / With planets in His care."[50] Yeats is "purple-robed" both in the sense of being an authority figure and embodying the mystique of the entire Aesthetic movement, whose mantle he inherited. The purple-robed figure embodies the central conflict that motivates this "Ode," a conflict between two theories of poetry: as original expression, or as an inheritance received from the past. In the drama of origins that Pound narrates here, the purple-robed one and the "melodious sea" contribute everything; the poet himself, nothing.

Pound's reference to himself as a "stream" flowing into "that melodious great sea" is a direct echo of Swinburne's "The Triumph Time," in which the speaker imagines flowing down to the sea to become a "pulse" and a "vein in the heart of the streams of the sea." He proposes union with the sea as a compensation for the loss of his beloved, addressing the sea as both a maternal source and an erotic object: "great sweet mother, / Mother and lover of men, the sea."[51] In his 1908 ode to Swinburne, "Salve O Pontifex," Pound had identified Swinburne with the sea, and this sea as the site of "mingling," "multiplicity," and "unity."[52] In both Swinburne's poem and Pound's homage to the elder poet, the sea thus represents a principle of continuity that "mingles" and "transmutes" separate individuals in an encompassing medium. For Swinburne, the sea represents time itself, and thus to be immersed in it is to come into contact with ancient origins: "thou art older than earth . . . From the first thou wert; in the end thou art."[53] Swinburne associates the sea with the origins of vernacular poetry through the figure of the twelfth-century Provençal poet Jauffre Rudel: "There lived a singer in France of old / By the tideless dolorous midland sea."[54] In linking his own poetic vocation with Rudel's, Swinburne imagines his song as the distant descendant of the first modern vernacular poetry. Swinburne and Rudel meet in a sea of time that connects the Middle Ages with the speaker's present. In comparing Swinburne to a wave in "Salve O Pontifex," Pound alludes to the ancient trope that identifies the rhythm of waves breaking on the shore with poetic meter. The continuity of this rhythm connects the ancient poet with the modern, and the Victorian poet to his twentieth-century disciple, who requests, "Breathe thou upon us!"

The association between the sea and the mother is also archetypal, encoded in the French homonyms "mer" (sea) and "mère" (mother). The English word "mere" (sea), used by Buchanan in describing Rossetti's mind, is a cognate of "la mer." Pound's title "La Mère Inconnue" plays on these words, hailing the maternal figure of the sea as his "mère." The very language that enables him to speak of his poetic origins belongs to Swinburne. The Romantic conception of art as authentic self-expression seems to require that poetic inspiration originate *inside* the poet. But Pound's family model suggests that inspiration comes from outside the poet, from his poetic "mother" and "father." The manuscript is troubled by the discovery that he owes his poetic existence to all-powerful precursors:

> Ode! lest some read thee saying secretly
> "Thou singst the rose as others sing the rose"
> Tell them they lie, for out of purple dreams
> Procedeth all thy substance & thy worth.[55]

In these interesting lines, Pound correctly predicts the future accusation of his critics, who will find *Exultations* and his other early volumes derivative and imitative. Indeed, Pound had been "sing[ing] the rose" in various keys since he opened his career with *Hilda's Book* five years before. The "Ode" wrestles with a contradiction: although Romantic conceptions of the poet presuppose original thought and feeling "proceeding" from somewhere inside, he experiences the sources of poetry as flowing to him from outside, from a remote source. The very idea of originality itself is inherited. Though a poem may originate in "dreams," even those seemingly private or subconscious experiences may be traced to "others." These lines try to make a distinction between mere copying ("Thou singst the rose as others sing the rose") and a state of reception, in which "purple dreams" bring inspiration to the poet. This distinction is one of mood: copying is active; reception is passive. As in "Histrion," Pound tries to theorize himself as a negative state, a "sphere translucent . . . that is the 'I'."

Long associated with lyric self-expression and particularly with Keats's most personal utterances, an ode is a peculiar genre to choose for exploring one's own lack of originality. This incongruity must have struck Pound as well, for when he revised "To La Mère Inconnue," as he had to in order to make it printable, he turned it into a portrait. By contrast to ode, portraiture points away from the writer and toward another figure, the sitter. The primary goal of a portrait is to capture the qualities of someone else, even if the work ultimately reflects the dynamic between the two people and contains an element of self-expression. The portrait is formally oriented away from the speaker and toward another. Thus it was the appropriate vessel for exploring the ways in which the poet is not the source of his poems.

❧

In revising "To La Mère Inconnue" into a portrait, Pound brought the text and its anxieties under control by placing it under the discipline of Rossetti's "The Portrait." This revision located Pound's sonnet at the intersection of three of his most important forebears, with his poetic origins reaching back to "Provence and the far halls of memory." The eminent Victorian critic Arthur Quiller Couch also recognized the Pre-Raphaelite quality of the poem when he selected it for inclusion in the 1912 *Oxford Book of Victorian Verse,* along with Pound's Swinburnian "Ballad of Gloom." Like "Fair Helena," the "Portrait" draws its vocabulary from the region of the "attenuated dream" that was the hallmark of Yeats's fin-de-siècle style: "echoes," "blended bells," "purplest shadows" and "softest voices."[56] Yet structurally, the poem has many similarities with Rossetti's sonnet of 1869, "The Portrait." Both sonnets begin by announcing the intention to portray and praise the beloved; they call on the muse, named "Love" in Rossetti's case and "memory" in Pound's; they treat the beloved as the object of worship, whose face it becomes the goal of many to see; and they pay tribute to her in an itemized list. Rossetti's announcement in the opening of his sestet, "Lo! it is done," is echoed by Pound's "Lo, there come echoes."

Rossetti's stated goal in "The Portrait" is to "show / Even of her inner self the perfect whole," by making the sitter visible and fusing her identity with her image.[57] By contrast, Pound's poem is not about a specific woman; "la mère inconnue" is really a "dream" from "afar."[58] She is "inconnue" in the sense that she is too distant to be known except through "echoes." While Rossetti's "goal" is to make the beloved present, indeed to substitute her painted image in place of the mortal person, Pound represents the "dim splendour" and "tribute" of several centuries of "amour de loin," the poetic tradition of love from afar. Rossetti's portrait describes the beloved's smile as a "refluent wave" that carries the "sea-line" (or horizon) of her soul to the viewer; in Pound's, the "ceaselessly resonant" sea is the medium or vehicle that carries "echoes" to him and "tribute" to the unknown beloved. In Rossetti's portrait, the beloved's eyes are "shadowed," indicating her memory and consciousness; in Pound's, "purplest shadows stand" independently of the beloved, to pay homage to her. In other words, Pound has transferred the attributes of the beloved over to poetry itself, and specifically to the sea that transmits the poetic tradition (that is, memory).

Pound's "Portrait" is thus truly about nothing, as Edward Thomas remarked. At the beginning of Rossetti's sestet, the poet exclaims, "Lo! it is done!" concentrating our attention in his picture and its sonnet. The beginning of Pound's sestet instead cries "Nay!" dismissing the possibility of capturing the subject's "inner self." The poem doesn't have an external referent. The idea of a portrait of "nothing" makes possible a shift from the individual human figure as the subject of portraiture, to the spaces or "distance" between multiple figures. If there is no single subject of "Portrait: from 'La Mère Inconnue,'" certainly there are multiple figures who define the work. The portrait is an intersection among Pound's poetic precursors Rossetti, Swinburne, and Yeats, with "Provence and the far halls of memory" as a distant origin. The "faint diversity" of all these sources creates the vague sense of depth or distance between figures rather than within a single individual.

❧

The portrait of nothing recurs powerfully in "Portrait d'une femme." Long regarded as an important milestone in Pound's modernization, this portrait of 1912 is as famous as "Portrait: from 'La Mère Inconnue'" is obscure.[59] Despite stylistic and formal differences, however, the two poems share the same content and conventions: the portrait subject as muse figure, the sea as her medium, tribute or "payment" to her in the form of "dim" but valuable goods, a catalogue of her attributes, the figure of an admirer, the trope of weaving, and finally the speaker's cry "No!" / "Nay!" that negates the portrait or portrait subject. The final meaning of the two works is quite different; even so, when we place them side by side it is clear that the 1912 portrait in some sense revises that of 1909.

In rewriting "Portrait: from 'La Mère Inconnue'" as "Portrait d'une femme," Pound returned in important respects to his earlier "Ode." He reverted to the blank verse of the "Ode," in which the unrhymed, evenly rhythmic lines imitate the sound of the "melodious great sea." At thirty lines, "Portrait d'une femme" was on the long side for *Ripostes,* over twice the length of the sonnet "Portrait," representing a more expansive form closer to the "Ode." Like the "Ode," "Portrait d'une femme" directly addresses a female figure—called "la mère" in the "Ode," and "une femme" in the 1912 poem. Pound's French title nods to his earlier "La Mère Inconnue" and to the mère/mer pun brought over from Swinburne. Both works are troubled by the question of where ideas come from. The charge Pound tries to refute in the "Ode"—"Thou singst the rose as others sing the rose"—returns in "Portrait d'une femme" as "there is nothing . . . that's quite your own."

Most important, "Portrait d'une femme" focuses its entire energies on developing the metaphor of the sea that also drives the "Ode": "Your mind and you are our Sargasso Sea."[60] The "Sargasso Sea" metaphor connects the 1912 "Portrait" to the maternal sea of the "Ode," the "distant seas" of "Portrait," and Swinburne's "great sweet mother" and "tideless dolorous midland sea." In the background we may also hear Rossetti's "sea-line of her soul" from "The Portrait" and the "purple sea" of Yeats's "Wanderings of Oisin." "Portrait d'une femme" thus returns to the feminine gendering of the sea found in "The Triumph of Time" and Pound's "Ode." The tidelessness of Swinburne's Mediterranean particularly suggests the lazy stillness of the Sargasso Sea, a becalmed area of the Atlantic surrounded by currents, where seaweed collects and ships may be stranded. The stillness of both seas hearkens back to the "Blessed Damozel's" "depth / of waters stilled at even" and Buchanan's "glassy mere." Pound's Sargasso Sea is less like a mirror that reflects impressions, however, and more like Swinburne's sea ("Thy depths conceal and thy gulfs discover") as a medium for flotsam and jetsam, "in the slow float of differing light and deep."[61]

The extended metaphor of "Portrait d'une femme" meditates on the idea that selfhood appears to be received or collected from external sources. This metaphor simultaneously permits two quite different ideas of externality: the self is composed of "things," or of "nothing." Pound had developed these ideas in poems such as "House of Splendour" and "Fair Helena," and "Portrait d'une femme" brings them together in a single extended portrait. In "Portrait d'une femme," the "things" that might constitute the subject include "tarnished, gaudy, wonderful old work; / Idols and ambergris and rare inlays," an appealing catalog leading one to suppose that Pound is describing an antiques collector.[62] These objects have been downgraded from the "dim splendor" of the 1909 "Portrait" to "dimmed wares of price" in 1912.[63] The presence of rare and tarnished things in "Portrait d'une femme" is itself a kind of "fee" or "tribute" paid to Rossetti, whose style is allied with the glitter of gold. Yet, although the poem consists largely of a description of "this sea-hoard of deciduous things," each additional item added to the list is only an elaboration on the opening metaphor, "Your mind and you are our Sargasso Sea." Her "things" are figures for what the woman knows and remembers: "Ideas, old gossip, oddments of all things, / Strange spars of knowledge." She is constituted not out of material objects but from information and testimony, anecdote and memory, much as Pound describes himself as constituted by other people's ideas in "Histrion," "Fair Helena," and "To La Mère Inconnue." Although Pound seems to criticize the "femme" for her lack of originality, in fact this poem elaborates his longstanding theory that thoughts and feelings derive from external sources. "Portrait d'une femme" combines the "distant seas" of "memory" and the remote beloved of "Portrait: from 'La Mère Inconnue'" into one figure whose memory is a medium. This medium—a "clear space," a sea, a "nothing"—collects and gives access to objects and people, and particularly to history. The medium does not confer value on these things nor is she an object in herself, in contrast to the golden women of *Canzoni*. But in losing her own substance, the subject gains a kind of depth. This depth is not the source of her feelings, intentions, and thoughts; rather, it is a space of intersection. And these minds, in turn, give access to others, in a temporal progression leading back in time toward the ever-vanishing origins of culture, in the "tideless dolorous midland sea."

The real-life referent of this portrait is presumably Florence Farr, an accomplished dramatic performer, writer, and leader of the occult order of the Golden Dawn. In a July 1912 letter to Dorothy Shakespear, Pound wrote, "As for F. F. Ceylon ought to suit her. I wonder if she'll see her portrait before she goes." Dorothy's reply: "Just read a new book by 'Florence Farr.' *Such* a Sargasso Sea muddle. Every body divorced several times, & in the end going back to their originals."[64] As a young woman Farr embodied the Pre-Raphaelite feminine ideal, appearing in Burne-Jones's *The Golden Stairs* (1880). She interpreted the work of George Bernard Shaw and W. B. Yeats on stage, as well as conducting close but contentious relationships with both men (the "great minds" Pound refers to). In collaboration with Yeats she developed a form of poetic chanting that she accompanied on a special instrument called the psaltery, made for her by Arnold Dolmetsch.[65] Pound's portrait may combine Farr with Olivia Shakespear, the poet's future mother-in-law, who was a minor novelist and society hostess and also Yeats's former companion and lover. Farr and Shakespear were friends and even collaborated on the composition of several plays. Dorothy reports in a June 1912 letter that "O.S. was pleased with the 'Portrait d'une femme.'"[66]

In different ways, Farr and Shakespear were involved in the transmission of poetic language and heritage that Pound identifies as the poet's work in his 1909 "Portrait." As an actress and singer, Farr brought life to dramatic and poetic compositions, and as a leader of the Golden Dawn she literally was a spiritualistic "medium." Olivia Shakespear was less an artistic medium than a social one, but her role in putting Pound in contact with the poetic world of London was more significant to his life than Farr's. Through cultural events and social gatherings at her house Pound came into contact with many of the artistic figures of the previous generation, most importantly Yeats. This kind of cultural assemblage became an important model for Pound's portraiture as he developed the genre toward multifigure compositions. Even Yeats himself, the "great mind," served Pound as a conduit to the poets of the nineties and to Rossetti. The chain continues back, for Rossetti's translations introduced Pound to Dante and Cavalcanti.

Pound's apparently negative characterization of the "femme" as "nothing" gives the impression that he, or the speaker of the poem, resents her access to the "great minds" and consequently wishes to belittle her accomplishments. In an extensive critical engagement with this poem, Rachel Blau DuPlessis argues that "Pound's poem is a mechanism in the service of one kind of male subjectivity—the active creation of a shallow but provocative female muse for the containment of historical New Woman effervescence and achievement."[67] In this reading, the poem works to still and flatten the historical Florence Farr—an active, creative, unconventional woman—into a passive muse figure. In the context of Pound's previous portraiture, however, "Portrait d'une femme" actually marks a considerable advance in his representation of women. Unlike Pound's previous muse figures, beginning with Hilda, the "femme" seems to have a life of her own. Her portrait does not reduce her to a thing, but rather identifies her with what she knows and remembers. Pound places her in a historical context ("great minds sought you") and gives her biographical background ("you preferred it to the usual thing"). While Pound's earlier portraits place his subjects in a pseudomedieval context or none at all, this poem locates Farr in her own times as an unconventional woman with connections to the artistic giants of her generation. That it is even possible to speak of the identity of the "femme" marks a change in Pound's methods of portraiture, male and female.

The contemporaneity of the "femme" extends beyond her debt to Florence Farr. In her we see a more developed account of interspatial selfhood than in any of his previous poems.[68] Multiple figures intersect in her, extending from Florence Farr, back through Yeats, Swinburne, and Rossetti, to the far reaches of the vernacular poetic tradition. As a muse figure she echoes Rossetti's "Lady," Swinburne's "midland sea," and further back to the "amour de loin" of Provençal poetry. Her identity consists of a series of relations to these near and far figures, who themselves exist in relation to earlier figures. Thus Pound reintroduces a concept of depth as the distance between origins and reception, articulated in the poem as the layering of cultural detritus:

> In the slow float of differing light and deep,
> No! there is nothing! In the whole and all,
> Nothing that's quite your own.
>   Yet this is you.[69]

Pound's "No!" echoes and refuses Rossetti's "Lo" in "The Portrait," moving beyond Rossetti's poetics of presence that elevates the physical body of the subject and the material artifact of her picture. Rather, Pound represents her as a medium of reception, through which culture is transmitted from one generation to the next. In this respect, the portrait mirrors the poet, who regarded his own mind as an "empty space" through which the "great minds" of history moved.

DuPlessis and Dilworth note an element of anxiety and self-criticism in "Portrait d'une femme."[70] DuPlessis argues that the poem reflects Pound's chagrin at being upstaged by Filippo Marinetti's explosive Futurist performances in London in March 1912.[71] This is impossible because the poem had already been submitted to and rejected by the *North American Review* by January 1912, and Pound had sent the entire typescript of *Ripostes* off to his publisher, Stephen Swift and Co., in February.[72] Rebecca Beasley has documented that Pound knew nothing about the revolution in the arts before mid-1912, when this poem was already in press.[73] Rather, the poem expresses an anxiety about originality already in evidence in his pre-1909 "Ode." In fact, the entire poem is predicated on Pound's uncertainty about how to become an American poet in a European tradition. This problem underlies Pound's choice of the "Sargasso Sea" as his metaphor for "your mind and you." Jean Rhys's later use of this title for her novel exploring the meaning of the European literary tradition in a postcolonial world retrospectively illuminates Pound's choice. The Sargasso Sea alludes to Swinburne's "tideless dolorous midland sea" but shifts the location of the body of water from the Mediterranean to the Atlantic, halfway between Europe and North America. The poet's mind is like a becalmed area between Europe and his native Pennsylvania, collecting whatever comes to it.

❧

Pound would soon develop the idea of a mid-Atlantic poetic in a positive program to encourage an "American Risorgimento." The undeveloped state of American letters was the theme of Pound's "Patria Mia" series, which ran in the *New Age* from September to November 1912. In "Patria Mia VII" Pound wrote, "How often do I hear it said of the American writers, by the Europeans, 'I can't see that they do anything but send us back copies of what we have already done.'"[74] "Portrait d'une femme" articulates the same accusation, but universalizes and transforms it into a virtue. Imitation has an important role to play in portraiture, whose worth depends partly on the portraitist's fidelity to his sitter. "Patria Mia VIII" presents two positive examples of expatriates whose work shows that "being born an American does not eternally damn a man or prevent him from the ultimate and highest achievement in the arts."[75] These men are Henry James and James McNeill Whistler. Pound specifically identifies portraits as their best work: James's *Portrait of a Lady* (1881) and Whistler's *Harmony in Grey and Green: Miss Cicely Alexander* (1872–73), *Grenat et Or: Le Petit Cardinal* (1900–1901); and *Brown and Gold: de Race* (1896–1900). Pound's choices may reflect an idea that portraiture was the most likely genre in which an American could achieve artistic success. His conception of the portrait as a "clear space" or medium in which figures of different times and nations encountered each other is also a potent metaphor for the internationalism that he sought to promote for the United States. In "Portrait d'une femme" and more explicitly in "Patria Mia," then, Pound was shifting his attention away from British Aestheticism and toward a contemporary, transatlantic world in which, he hoped, American artists such as himself would have more of a role to play.

In elevating James and Whistler as his heroes, Pound chose Americans of an earlier generation who were closely associated with Aestheticism. As the title "Portrait d'une femme" lets us know by alluding to Henry James's most famous novel, he is another of the "great minds" that intersect in the "Sargasso Sea" of the subject, the poem, and the poet's mind. James's "fine dissection of the dilettante" in this novel haunts Pound: "How well one knows this type! Have I not met 'Osmond' in Venice? He ornamented leather. What most distressed him in our national affairs was that Roosevelt had displayed the terrible vulgarity of appearing at King Edward's funeral in a soft felt hat."[76] A fear of descending into triviality by attention to objets d'art fuels both *Hugh Selwyn Mauberley* and "Portrait d'une femme." *Mauberley*'s eponymous subject shares a taste for medallions with James's Gilbert Osmond, while Pound's "femme" recalls Isabel, an unconventional woman whose role as society hostess threatens to imprison her. Isabel's fluid, sensitive consciousness seeks experience, knowledge, and connections with other people; Osmond, likened to a "fine gold coin," threatens to turn her into an object in his collection.[77] The struggle between Osmond and Isabel is particularly relevant to Pound's anxieties about his nationality, for both main characters are American, and their decline into mere connoisseurship warns of the dangers for expatriate Europhiles. Pound's portraiture after 1912 continues to debate the danger of reducing the human subject to a beautiful but exchangeable object, returning to the same cast of characters (Rossetti, Swinburne, Buchanan, James) and motifs (flowers, the sea, the gold medallion) in *Mauberley*. At the same time, James's novel provided Pound with an example of a successful portrait whose subject is less a single character than the way consciousness exists between characters. Increasingly important to Pound in the later nineteen-teens, *Portrait of a Lady* and other James novels showed him how to build on the concept of interspace without sacrificing the outlines of the individual figure. In "Moeurs Contemporaines," Pound expanded the aqueous, mediumistic selfhood proposed in "Portrait d'une femme" as a way of reintroducing interiority and mind itself into the human picture.

Pound's other American hero, James McNeill Whistler, also offered models of portraits built on the concept of interspace. Pound praised Whistler's *The Artist in His Studio* in "To Whistler, American: On the loan exhibit of his paintings at the Tate Gallery." He offered this poem to Harriet Monroe in September 1912 as an "informal salute" to "our only great artist."[78] The poem identifies "In the Studio" as one of the painter's most "perfect" works, along with "two portraits," the same ones noted in his "Patria Mia" essay.[79] Beasley suggests that Pound wanted "psychological insight" and "personality" from his paintings, rather than the abstraction that he would later endorse.[80] This is partly true; Pound continued to be interested in how to represent the qualities traditionally associated with portraiture—what I have called interiority rather than psychology. However, these portraits impressed him precisely by their lack of narrative content; as he wrote in "Patria Mia," Whistler's painting "has nothing in common with the picture which tells a story, against which sort he so valiantly inveighed."[81] For Pound—as for Whistler, Manet, and Rossetti—portraiture was the genre par excellence of "painting as painting," of the elevation of beauty apart from moral and religious content.[82] In 1912, "abstraction" per se was not part of Pound's equation; rather, like Rossetti, he continued to affirm nonnarrative "aesthetic" painting in contrast to those compositions that purported to tell a moral tale. While all three works that Pound hailed in his poem are portraits, *The Artist in His Studio* (fig. 6) places empty space at the center of the work in a way that has clear parallels in "Portrait d'une femme" as well as "To Whistler," written on the occasion of seeing the painting.

Painted in 1865–66 during Whistler's association with the Rossetti circle, this three-figure composition explores identity and "personality" as a hall of mirrors, experimenting with multiple reflections similar to those in *The Little White Girl* that inspired Swinburne's "Before the Mirror." The painting shows the artist at his easel on the right and two female figures to the left, one in a kimono standing with her back to him and to the beholder, the other in Western dress, reclining and looking up (this figure in white is probably Joanna Hiffernan). Whistler was right-handed, but the painter is shown with the brush in his left hand; a large mirror behind the artist's head at the center of the painting reminds us that the entire work was painted from a similar mirror standing where we are. A much smaller framed etching hangs to the right of this mirror echoing both its shape and its power to reverse images (an etching is a mirror image of the marked plate from which it was printed). The two women face each other, West and East, mistress and paid model. The woman in rose-colored Asian dress mirrors the artist in the sense that they stand back to back in similar positions, she with a touch of gray in her garment, and he with a touch of rose in the palette he holds. Finally, the painter's application of paint to his canvas echoes the painted blue and white china on the far left.[83] Each figure and object in this painting has its mirror image, even as the entire work presents itself as a reflection from the beholder's point of view.

As discussed in chapter 1, Whistler used reflection to recuperate a feeling of depth that could no longer be achieved by absorption; Fried calls

Whistler's painting "apparitional."[84] *The Artist in His Studio* particularly represents the painter himself as a reflection of the people and things around him; the perspectival focus of the work is not the features of his face, but the vanishing point in the mirror behind him. This mirror evokes absence by allusion to Diego Velazquez's *Las Meninas,* a painting greatly admired by both Whistler and Manet.[85] *The Artist in His Studio* is presumed to be a study for a monumental work that Whistler intended

FIG. 6. James McNeill Whistler (1834–1903), *The Artist in His Studio,* 1865–66. Oil on paper mounted on panel, 62.9 x 46.4 cm (24³/₄ x 18¹/₄ in.). (Friends of American Art Collection, 1912.141, The Art Institute of Chicago)

to paint of himself, Fantin-Latour, and Albert Moore in his studio, similar in scale and composition to *Las Meninas*.[86] Whistler's small painting
consciously replies to *Las Meninas* by reversing the right and left sides of
the composition (Velazquez has the artist on the left and courtiers on the
right). He also omits the central figures who dominate Velazquez's painting: the brightly lit figure of the Infanta in the foreground and the mirror
image of the King and Queen who preside over the entire scene from the
back of the room. The mirror on Whistler's wall instead reflects an empty
space. While the royal couple reside at the focal point of *Las Meninas* and
contribute the overriding raison d'être of the work, the guiding light of
Whistler's painting is absence and its reflection. His portrait of himself,
Joanna Hiffernan, and his model hover around this absence, not as fully
delineated individuals but as points of reference for each other.

Pound's "To Whistler, American" similarly evokes absence through
mirror images. The poem is a kind of double portrait in which Pound envisions himself as a reflection of Whistler, beginning "You also, our first
great."[87] For an act of hero-worship, the terms of Pound's praise are odd:
the chief characteristic that he attributes to Whistler is "uncertainty":
"Here is a part that's slight, and part gone wrong, / And much of little
moment"; "You had your searches, your uncertainties"; "You were not
always sure, not always set."[88] Whistler's repeated failures are the basis
for comparison with himself. Uncertainty is also a quality of Whistler's
painting—its indistinctness, the unfinished, sketched look of his figures.
As much as the poem builds Whistler up as an American hero on a par
with Lincoln, the portrait seems constructed over an abyss, "that mass of
dolts" below. While Pound seems to blame his own and Whistler's failures on the shortcomings of their audience, the emptiness at the heart of
the poem is not new; it is another version of the "nothing" that ends "Portrait d'une femme" or the "Nay" in "Portrait: from 'La Mère Inconnue.'"

Pound's response to the charge that "there is no man now living in
America whose work is of the slightest interest to any serious artist" was
similar to his own self-accusation that he lacked originality. Pound's earliest recorded poems practice imitation as a mode of hero-worship while
anxiously denying their derivative quality (as in "La Donzella Beata" and
"Ode: To La Mère Inconnue"). His solution to this poetic dilemma was
neither to break with the past nor to "find his voice," in the clichés of Modernist criticism, but to adopt imitation as a theme and principle of composition. "Portrait: from 'La Mère Inconnue,'" "Portrait d'une femme,"
and "To Whistler, American" recast reflection across an empty space as
the subject matter of portraiture. The 1909 "Portrait" and its companion

sonnet "Fair Helena" are primarily concerned with Pound's own lack of originality and the paradox that to become a poet he must echo the past. The two portraits of 1912, however, use the genre to address the general American problem of belatedness. Pound does not use portraiture to promote American individualism, as one might expect; rather, these poems explore the disintegration of the traditional qualities of the individual: agency, interiority, a sense of personal identity. This "negative" or "apparitional" idea of the self underwrites Pound's later expansion of the portrait poem into a canvas for avant-garde experimentation and social commentary. "Moeurs Contemporaines" and *Hugh Selwyn Mauberley* portray autobiographical protagonists whose failure and "nonidentity" dissolve the limits of individual consciousness and subjectivity.

Yet that story, like most told about Pound, leaves out an important strand of the plot. It would seem that with "Portrait d'une femme," he put Rossetti's poetics of presence behind him, finding his way toward Modernism by refiguring himself as a blank space. Yet in the spring of 1912 Pound conceived a completely different project: Imagism. The poems he wrote in the next five years embrace Rossetti's principles of condensation and visual orientation, elevate the concrete and the material, and place the poet's judging ego at the center of his utterances. The portraits in *Lustra*, a volume full of Pound's opinions and personality, experiment with all of Rossetti's tactics for creating presence. We turn to those in chapter 4. In the meantime, however, T. S. Eliot was also modernizing himself—like Pound—by practicing picture sonnets.

THREE

T. S. Eliot

GETTING OUT OF THE PICTURE

I N THE FALL OF 1908, the young T. S. Eliot composed two sonnets for publication in the *Harvard Advocate,* "Circe's Palace" and "On a Portrait." These poems are remarkable for their skilled integration of the Rossettian picture sonnet with the language of Swinburne. They are all the more remarkable for their very early dates of composition, before Eliot read Arthur Symons's *The Symbolist Movement in Literature,* discovered the poetry of Jules Laforgue, and sprang to life as a poet, as the story goes. In fact, these two sonnets suggest that Eliot's reading of Rossetti and Swinburne had brought him to the boiling point already and shaped some of his most fundamental concerns, for which Laforgue would provide the idiom and the irony. Eliot later acknowledged his early "rapture" for Rossetti, while summarily dismissing him from the scene of modern poetry. "Rossetti's *Blessed Damozel,* first by my rapture and next by my revolt, held up my appreciation of Beatrice by many years," he wrote in the 1929 essay on Dante, his only reference to Rossetti in the canon-forming *Selected Essays.*[1] Eliot does not say that it was Rossetti, the foremost English translator of the *Vita Nuova* and a leader in the modern revival of Dante, who introduced him to Dante in the first place. Nor does he allude to his family connection to the founder of the American Dante Society, Charles Eliot Norton, the most important supporter and collector of Pre-Raphaelite art in the United States.[2] Getting Rossetti out of the picture was important to Eliot's anti-Victorian project and self-presentation as the heir of European culture.[3] Yet his reading of Rossetti at the most formative stage of his life shaped Eliot's way of looking, his disposition to "portray." Rossetti's deployment of a double perspective—inner and outer "standing points"—entered Eliot's poetry through his early picture sonnets and became a central feature of his portraiture, culminating in "Portrait of a Lady" and revisited in *The Waste Land.*

Eliot's early picture sonnets indicate that his interest in perspective, which became a central feature of his poetry and the subject of his philosophical dissertation, initially arose in an engagement with painting. This is hardly surprising insofar as painters had been working to establish new relations between beholder and artwork since the 1860s, foregrounding the issue of perspective by flattening the appearance of the canvas and introducing multiple vanishing points. Eliot's two sonnets responded to paintings from two different movements: English Aestheticism and French Realism. Even as a college student, Eliot had a preternatural ability to combine divergent cultural threads in a way that brings out their common ground. His "On a Portrait" uses the language of Pater and Swinburne and the form favored by Rossetti to describe a painting by Édouard Manet, a surprising choice that shows many fundamental similarities between Aestheticism and Manet's protomodernism, including their shared technique of flattening and motif of mirrors. In running the ekphrastic sonnet through Manet, however, Eliot found an approach more consonant with his temperament and perception of modernity. While Rossetti's use of an "inner standing point" calls on the reader or beholder to feel desire or sympathy for the subject of the portrait, Eliot imagines ways of looking that do not entail entering either the painting or the mind of the figure portrayed. In "Mandarins," "La Figlia Che Piange" and "Portrait of a Lady," all composed from 1910 to 1911, Eliot experimented with a variety of approaches to portraiture, motivated by the project of releasing the viewer from the absorptive power of the image and—more important—from the idea of interiority per se. "Portrait of a Lady" recapitulates and revises the features of the Aesthetic portrait to represent the self as reflective, inherited, and without interiority. Finally, ten years later, Eliot returned to the scene of his original Aesthetic absorption in an ekphrasis of Rossetti's *Lady Lilith,* literally internalizing the genre of the portrait poem as an inset in *The Waste Land.*

"Circe's Palace" announces Eliot's entry into the poetic vocation under the sign of Aestheticism, rehearsing Rossetti and Swinburne's gestures and finding, within these, his own distinctive themes. "Circe's Palace" imitates Rossetti's picture sonnet "For 'The Wine of Circe' by Edward Burne-Jones" (1870), Rossetti's homage to the younger painter, his friend and protégé. In selecting this poem as his model, Eliot was hailing not only Rossetti, who continued to enchant and shock his audiences almost thirty years after his death, but also Burne-Jones, who had died at the height of his fame in 1898. The 1905 publication of the painter's biography had brought Burne-Jones much attention in the United States, and reproductions of his pictures, including *Circe Pouring Poison into a Vase and Awaiting the Arrival of Ulysses*, called *The Wine of Circe*, were available in an edition described by one reviewer as "one of the most artistic and most exquisite that has ever been published by an American publisher."[4] (Eliot must have been familiar with the picture from this or another book, because he correctly specifies the animals in the scene as "panthers," whereas Rossetti only calls them "beasts."[5]) Eliot's choice of Burne-Jones's picture was also routed through Swinburne, who had dedicated his first book of poems to the painter. In integrating Swinburnian language with Rossetti's form and subject matter to describe this painting by Burne-Jones, the young Eliot thus situated himself as the heir of these three great Victorian artists at a moment of their widespread fame in America.

Eliot's sonnet continues a conversation among Rossetti, Burne-Jones, and John Ruskin concerning the dual nature of Circe, and more broadly, of love. Originally commissioned by Ruskin, *Circe Pouring Poison into a Vase* (fig. 7) was Burne-Jones's response to the critic who had supported and encouraged him as a young artist and publicly defended the Pre-Raphaelite Brotherhood. Ruskin had described Circe as a figure of "frank, and full vital pleasure, which, if governed and watched, nourishes men; but, unwatched . . . turns men into beasts, but does not slay them,—leaves them, on the contrary, power of revival."[6] Both Burne-Jones and Rossetti followed Ruskin in bringing out Circe's complementary but opposed qualities. Rossetti conveys the brilliant contrasts of Burne-Jones's painting by pairing Circe's gold robe and her dark hair, the golden wine and the black drops of her potion, the sunflowers (with their yellow petals and dark centers) with the coming night.[7] These color pairs set in motion the echo effect of the poem, centered on Circe, votaress of both "Helios and Hecate," the sunlit and darkened realms of passion, who "proclaim[s] / . . . all rapture in Love's name / Till pitiless Night give Day the countersign." The beasts also combine these contrasts in a different key. At once men and animals, they "echo back the sea's dull roar / With a vain wail from passion's tide-strown shore / Where the dishevelled seaweed hates the sea."[8] The beasts' "vain wail" repeats the inhuman sounds of the sea, yet expresses the human emotion of self-hatred. This wail is the beasts' version of the "countersign" that Night gives Day to signal the transformation of men into animals. "Countersign" is a crypt word that captures

Fig. 7. Edward Burne-Jones (1833–1898), *Circe Pouring Poison into a Vase and Awaiting the Arrival of Ulysses*, 1863–69. Watercolor on paper, 70 x 101 cm. (The Bridgeman Art Library)

the mirror-imaging at work throughout the poem. Rossetti's Circe is not a figure of feminine trickery, but a symbol of the inexorable tie between love and despair—the heights and depths of passion—as reflections or echoes of each other.[9] Similarly, the "Lords of their hour" (Ulysses and his men, whose ships are pictured in the upper right-hand corner of the painting) mirror the beasts, their opposite, but soon to be their double. The poem is suffused with a painful mixture of pity for those brought low by passion, and the poet's recognition of himself in their state.

As readers and beholders, then, we are brought into the work by sympathy and desire, in an effect that Rossetti named the "inner standing point," in "The Stealthy School of Criticism," his reply to Robert Buchanan's attack on "Jenny" and other poems. Rossetti protests that to treat such a subject (in this case, prostitution) "the motive powers of art reverse the requirement of science, and demand first of all an *inner* standing point. The heart of such a mystery as this must be plucked from the very world in which it beats or bleeds." "To such a speaker," Rossetti continues, "many half-cynical revulsions of feeling and reverie, and a recurrent presence of the impressions of beauty (however artificial) which first brought him within such a circle of influence, would be inevitable features of the dramatic relation portrayed."[10] In other words, the inner standing point is not one, but several, consisting of the "self-questionings and all-questionings" of the ambivalent speaker/beholder, who keeps one foot outside the picture even as he ventures in with the other. Eliot's response to Burne-Jones's painting employs a partial inner standing point, yet resists being drawn into the "circle of influence."

In his "Circe's Palace," Eliot avoids looking directly at the figure of Circe and transfers her qualities onto her symbols, the sunflowers. He imagines these as man-eating blossoms "that no man knows":

> Their petals are fanged and red
> With hideous streak and stain;
> They sprang from the limbs of the dead.—
> We shall not come here again.[11]

Eliot elaborates Rossetti's contrasts with a touch of Swinburne's "Dolores," another figure who unites pleasure with pain. Dolores, "Our Lady of Pain," has a "cruel / Red mouth like a venomous flower." Eliot's mouthlike flowers mirror Dolores's flowerlike mouth. Swinburne asks, "From the lips and the foam and the fangs / Shall no new sin be born for men's trouble, / No dream of impossible pangs?"[12] Eliot answers this question literally by evoking blood-stained flowers that grow from the limbs of the dead. This is the first instance of plants growing from corpses in Eliot's oeuvre. In imagining the inhuman growing from the bodies of humans, the nonliving bringing forth the living, Eliot responds to the paired contrasts of Rossetti's sonnet, especially the idea—derived from Ruskin—of Circe's power of revival. Eliot's second seven-line stanza describes Circe's panthers, python, and peacocks that "look at us with the eyes / Of men whom we knew long ago." These final lines repeat Rossetti's gesture of identifying the beasts and the approaching men as two aspects of the same self. Eliot's recognition of the humanity in the panthers has a cooler tone than Rossetti, however, expressed in the language of knowledge rather than feeling. There is hardly any "inner standing point": the speaker sees himself briefly reflected in the beasts' eyes but he remains outside the palace, looking in.

Eliot's readjustment of the beholder's position reflects not only his characteristic preference for the observer's pose, but also Rossetti's own experiments with perspective. Many of Rossetti's poems and paintings offer not a single but multiple standing points. In "The Blessed Damozel," as Helsinger writes, the interspersed voices of the Damozel, her lover, and a narrator create "a *mise-en-abîme* of consciousness more than a true dramatic situation," in which a later, more skeptical mind tries to imagine an earlier, more naïve, or otherwise alien sensibility.[13] The outer or skeptical voice (of the lover) invites us to sympathize with the inner voice (the Damozel), while marking our distance from her place. This situation entails both a desire for union and a consciousness of difference and remoteness. Even without dramatic voices, "For 'The Wine of Circe' by Edward Burne-Jones" similarly combines two contrasting yet inextricable points of view, inviting us to see ourselves both as the men approaching in ships and as the beasts (the before and after, so to speak). Eliot retains the two perspectives, but rewrites Rossetti's invitation to sympathize as a mere flicker of similarity between the beasts and speaker, in a setting so strange and inhuman that it seems impossible to imagine ourselves there.

In his 1908 apprentice poem, then, Eliot followed Rossetti and Burne-Jones in complicating the relationship of the beholder or reader to the artwork, but he took their project a step further by turning off the flow of sympathy and identification. Indeed, without either the figure of Circe or the ships of the approaching men, his description lacks any human form toward which we could direct our feeling. Though he sees his reflection in the beasts' eyes, the speaker/beholder does not go inside the palace. The art historian Richard Wollheim describes a similar project in Manet's work from the same decade:

> Get the spectator to imagine someone in the represented space, someone who tries, tries hard, tries importunately, and fails, to gain the attention of the figure who is represented as there in the space; get the spectator moreover to imagine this person from the inside so that, this imaginative entry into the picture over, it will then be for him as if he had himself experienced some of the tedium, some of the frustration, some of the sense of rejection, that must attend any attempt to establish contact with the represented figure—and then the content of the picture will be brought home to him with clarity and cogency.[14]

Wollheim is describing the effect of Manet's *Jeune Dame en 1866*, or *Young Lady in 1866*, previously called *Woman with a Parrot*, the painting to which Eliot turned for his next picture sonnet, "On a Portrait." Responding to Manet, Eliot's ekphrasis explores the inaccessibility of the female figure, trying out various standing points in the painting. Given that we cannot enter the woman's mind, where should we imagine ourselves? The absence of interiority in the painting rebounds on the beholder so that he experiences not feeling, but a sense of flatness, of being a reflective surface. In this picture, Eliot found an occasion for developing a mode of looking that he had already begun to explore in his engagement with Burne-Jones's *The Wine of Circe.*

Eliot's "rapture" with Rossetti and Swinburne was an inescapable condition of being an aspiring poet in 1908, but he discovered Manet on his own, as if searching for a counterpoint to their influence. According to his college friend Tinckholm-Fernandez, he saw *Young Lady in 1866* in a book on French Impressionism.[15] Eliot's choice of this painting indicates many things about the direction of his tastes and his future poetry: his preference for French culture over English, for the cool and disengaged rather than the passionate attitude, and of course, for the modern over the Victorian. Manet, not Rossetti, is hailed as the "father of Modernism." Clement Greenberg claimed that Manet's Modernism lay in his rejection of the illusion of depth: "Manet's paintings became the first Modernist ones by virtue of the frankness with which they declared the surfaces on which they were painted . . . Flatness, two-dimensionality, was the only condition painting shared with no other art, and so Modernist painting oriented itself to flatness as it did to nothing else."[16] According to Greenberg's influential account of Modernist painting, Manet pioneered a set of techniques for producing this flattened look that the Impressionists would emulate and intensify, leading to the breakdown of representation and emergence of abstraction. Eliot's choice of *Young Lady in 1866* dovetails with this history; following Manet, Eliot remade his art by refusing to provide the coherence of narrative or a single speaking voice. His poems, too, frankly announce the materials out of which they are made, and withhold the pleasures of absorption and identification.

The Manet connection is consistent with the familiar story of Eliot's modernization through his exposure to Laforgue and French symbolism, which enabled him to triumph over the enervating influence of late Victorian verse. "On a Portrait" introduces complications to that narrative, however. In Eliot's poem, French and English influences do not so much strive against each other as work together toward a revised conception of the subject. The surprise element of the story is the consonance between Manet and Rossetti, two painters so rarely spoken of in the same breath, though they were born and died within four years of each other, lived a mere two hundred miles apart, and had significant acquaintances in common, especially Whistler, who associated with Manet and Courbet during his Realist years in Paris before he moved to London and joined the Rossetti circle. Both Manet and Rossetti cultivated two-dimensionality and drew attention to the use of paint on canvas, the trait that Greenberg picks out as the hallmark of Manet's Modernism. Moreover, both Rossetti and Manet preferred portraiture above other genres, where they could avoid the obligation to tell a narrative or moral. Working from paid models rather than paying clients gave both painters the freedom to experiment with the conventions of the genre, including the inside/outside model of subjectivity. Their portrait-like compositions are characterized by notably enigmatic or empty expressions on the sitters' faces.

Eliot chose Manet's *Young Lady in 1866* because his "rapture" for Rossetti had prepared him to see and understand the painting. While Manet's tone and technique accorded with Eliot's inclination to turn down Rossetti's emotional temperature, the basic composition of this painting would have corresponded to what Eliot already knew well from Rossetti's paintings and picture sonnets, particularly *Lady Lilith* and "Body's Beauty." As discussed in chapter 1, this double work had a significant impact on Modernist writing. In particular, Walter Pater interpreted Leonardo da Vinci's female portraits in the light of Rossetti's, famously drawing attention to *La Gioconda*'s "unfathomable smile, always with a touch of something sinister in it."[17] One of the central features of the Aesthetic portrait was this "unfathomable" self-absorption that drew the beholder's attention yet gave no answers. Pater's lyrical description of *La Gioconda* was responsible in particular for passing this image on into Modernism.

Manet's portrait-like representation of a woman in a peignoir with a parrot by her side features a similarly enigmatic look (fig. 8). Many aspects of this painting are similar to *Lady Lilith* and other Rossetti portraits: the sitter's suggestive half-dressed state, the ambiguity of her social status, large areas of white paint that push the image toward the viewer, lack of background depth, and most of all the sitter's vacant expression. The audience that encountered this painting when it was first exhibited in 1866 objected to Victorine Meurent's enigmatic, almost blank expression, which she also exhibits in the famous *Olympia* (1863) as well as *Victorine Meurent, Mlle V . . . in the Costume of an Espada* (both 1862), *The Street Singer* (1863), and *The Fifer* (1866).[18] One contemporary critic complained that "you will find yourself surrounded by personages endowed with all the appearance of reality, [but] at bottom devoid of precisely what constitutes it, I mean expression. Everything there is cold, without accent; nothing is stirred in you."[19] Contemporaries found the expressions of these figures "inexplicably blank, opaque, noncommunicating, without psychological interiority of any kind."[20] These viewers perceived a deficit in Manet's paintings: the lack of some special quality that turns a likeness of a body into the likeness of a person. For them, Manet's figures offered only the exterior appearance of life without the suggestion

FIG. 8. Édouard Manet (1832–1883), *Young Lady in 1866*, 1866. Oil on canvas, 185.1 x 128.6 cm. (The Metropolitan Museum of Art, Gift of Erwin Davis, 1889 [89.21.3]; Image © The Metropolitan Museum of Art)

of an interiority to animate that life. Unlike Swinburne, who saw a new and different kind of eroticism in Lilith's disengaged expression, Manet's viewers felt threatened by his revision of the conventions of portraiture. Even so, *Lady Lilith* must have seemed too bold either to the painter or its owner, for Rossetti took it back in 1872 and substituted the head of a different model, with a less unapproachable expression.

Rossetti's and Manet's contemporaries were accustomed to "absorptive" poses that gave clues about the sitter's inner life and created an imaginative space for the viewer inside the painting, as discussed in chapter 1. Wordsworth's "Lines Suggested by a Portrait" describes such a pose (the girl looks at a bouquet of flowers in her lap) and the feelings of sympathy that it evokes. Absorptive attitudes draw the beholder into the painting and, presumably, engage him or her in inward contemplation similar to the activity depicted. One of the signal differences between Manet and his fellow Realist Courbet was Manet's explicit challenge to the convention of absorption in paintings such as this one.[21] He favored frontal poses in which the figure looks out disconcertingly at the viewer, with the peculiar absent look that Manet's contemporaries always complained about on the faces of his models.[22] Neutral backgrounds, as in this painting, give no sense of three-dimensional space. The brushy, unfinished-looking execution also rejects the illusion of depth.

Young Lady in 1866 affronts a specific tradition of representing a female figure absorbed by her pet parrot. For example, Manet was familiar with two seventeenth-century paintings by Frans van Mieris and Gaspard Netchser, both entitled *Woman with a Parrot,* in which the woman concentrates on feeding her bird (both reproduced in Manet's copy of Charles Blanc's *Histoire des Peintres*).[23] Several English examples from the previous decade represent the woman communicating or sharing a moment of reverie with her bird. The Pre-Raphaelite painter Walter Deverell painted two portraits of Elizabeth Siddal in such a pose, *The Pet* and *The Grey Parrot* (both 1852). Manet would certainly have been familiar with works by Eugène Delacroix (1827), and Gustave Courbet (1866), in which an eroticized female figure plays with her parrot. In all these scenes, the parrot provides an opportunity to showcase either the woman's tenderness or her flirtatiousness; she appears engaged in an interpersonal exchange with a pet that stands in for a person (the beholder is invited to take her position or the bird's). In the nineteenth century, parrots were considered appropriate pets for women, especially lonely ones, as an outlet for their emotions.[24] As a kind of genre-painting (or treatment of daily life), the scene emphasized an interior capacity for emotion attributed specifically to women. Manet thus took a radical turn when he chose to depict the woman and the parrot standing apart from each other and showing no interest in one another.

By contrast to those of Courbet and Delacroix, Manet's figure is fully clothed, staring back at the viewer rather than dallying with her parrot. Every detail that Courbet used to whip up the viewer's interest is here deployed to push back at the viewer, to refuse entry into the painting. An erotic narrative is both suggested and withheld, for example by the bouquet of violets in her hand. Violets signified modesty in the nineteenth-century language of flowers, but her coquettish gesture with the bouquet suggests that it might be the gift of a male admirer. We can't see the outlines of her body under her massive loose-fitting pink gown, but her attire is informal, suggesting the possibility of undress. At the foot of the parrot's stand, a half-peeled orange reminds us that outer coverings can be removed to reveal what is underneath. Interiority is thus teasingly suggested by some details but canceled by others. "Identity," comments one critic about the ambiguity of the jeune dame's appearance, "resides nowhere but on the fluid surface of the canvas. And that flat surface is composed of false bottoms, inducing a certain vertigo."[25] The monocle that she wears on a string around her neck might be the symbol of this baffling strategy. The monocle is a man's accessory; women conventionally carried a lorgnette, as Manet's audience would have instantly recognized.[26] An eyeglass is intended to help us see better, but in this picture it serves only as decoration, and an ambiguous one at that. Similarly, Manet emphasizes the eyes of the woman and those of the parrot, but they see neither each other nor us, apparently. Seeing brings us not interior depth, but painted surface.[27]

The reflective—as opposed to representational—aspects of the painting are intensified in the figure of the parrot. By choosing the talkative African Grey rather than the brightly hued macaw depicted by Delacroix and Courbet, Manet draws our attention to the parrot's facility at copying language. Visually, the bird "parrots" the figure of the woman by repeating on a smaller scale the tints and strokes that make up her appearance.[28] The work copies Victorine Meurent without revealing anything about her besides surface; it also copies Courbet's *Woman with a Parrot* (and earlier precedents) while doing away with the illusion of access to a reality behind the surface of the canvas. More generally, the parrot draws our attention to the characteristic of Manet's work that contemporaries found the most outrageous: "the literalness and obviousness with which he often quoted earlier paintings."[29] His contemporaries interpreted this practice as either outright copying (lack of originality) or parody (lack of respect). There is evidence that Manet was quite self-consciously addressing the issue of copying in this painting. In Blanc's *Histoire des Peintres,* which Manet often consulted, the text directly below the engraving of Netscher's "Woman with a Parrot" disapprovingly indicts imitation: "An artist without personality would have done what they all do: he would have copied his master and retraced the same types in a weakened imitation."[30] *Young Lady in 1866* is obviously interested in substituting copying, reflection, and imitation for the traditional illusion of access to the real, to the origin or inside of the subject. In a sense, Manet merely makes explicit the mimetic condition of all painting.

The painting's critics have differed on its meaning and what it asks of its beholders. For Wollheim, the subject of this and Manet's other figure-paintings is being "locked up in . . . private thought."[31] Wollheim thus sees Meurent's expression as a kind of absorption that excludes the beholder. Fried, by contrast, has described Manet's refusal of absorption as a "facingness" or "strikingness" that he locates in the frontal poses of the figures, compositional depthlessness, and rough texture of the paint. All these qualities repel the beholder rather than drawing us into an imaginary three-dimensional space. "Facingness" is also thematized in this painting as the relationship between the parrot and the woman. The parrot's invisible eye on the other side of his head looks back at Victorine Meurent, but without implying any communication between them. Similarly, her blank stare meets that of the beholder without inviting identification or sympathy. The relationship between parrot and woman, and between painting and viewer, is that of reflection: two surfaces looking back at each other.

Manet's *Young Lady in 1866* offers no inner standing point in Rossetti's sense; rather, we experience two standing points, both "in" the painting, but neither promising access to a conscious mind. A painting such as Rossetti's *Ecce Ancilla Domini!,* organized around more than one vanishing point, suggests such a multiperspective strategy, but at the same time, the figure of the frightened girl invites our sympathy. Manet forces the figure's solitude back on us by ruling out this emotional identification; what his painting communicates is not only her isolation, but our own, symbolized by the impassive, gazing parrot.

The place where Eliot most likely first encountered the idea that aesthetic experience may isolate as well as please the beholder was not Manet's painting but Pater's "Conclusion" to *The Renaissance.* A philosophical way of looking at painting was Pater's specific contribution to

Aestheticism. From his study of German Idealism, Pater carried over into art criticism the idea that the mind has access only to sense perceptions, not to objects in the world—or, it would have to be said, to other people. The consequence of this view is a profound isolation that Pater expressed in a paragraph that reverberated through the literature of the later nineteenth century and into Modernism.[32] In the most famous passage of *The Renaissance* (originally published in a review in 1868), Pater remarks:

> Experience, already reduced to a group of impressions, is ringed round for each one of us by that thick wall of personality through which no real voice has ever pierced on its way to us, or from us to that which we can only conjecture to be without. Every one of those impressions is the impression of the individual in his isolation, each mind keeping as a solitary prisoner its own dream of a world.[33]

Pater's description of the individual's imprisonment in his own "dream" mirrors his account of *La Gioconda;* her enigmatic look rebounds upon the beholder to make him aware of his own isolation. Pater here elaborates and translates into philosophical discourse the implications of *Lady Lilith,* understanding that painting not only as the object of the beholder's fascination but a commentary on his or her own condition.

> Art and poetry, philosophy and the religious life, and that other life of refined pleasure and action in the conspicuous places of the world, are each of them confined to its own circle of ideas, and those who prosecute either of them are generally little curious of the thoughts of others.[34]

The situation Pater sketches out in both passages is one of mutual isolation, each individual locked, as Wollheim writes of Manet, in his or her own thoughts. Pater's use of the term "circle of ideas" helps to mark the descent of this concept from Rossetti (who described Lilith as being within her "own circle") to Eliot, who describes Manet's figure as standing "Beyond the circle of our thought."[35]

As is well known, Eliot would later explore the idea of confinement within one's own point of view in a philosophical register. His Harvard dissertation, *Knowledge and Experience in the Philosophy of F. H. Bradley,* uses nearly the same language of "circles," such as "How can we issue from the circle described about each point of view?"[36] Bradley's Absolute Idealism was a version of Hegel that attempted to solve the isolation inherent in the idea that knowledge is limited to sensation, and that the "real" is limited to ideas. Eliot's analysis of Bradley accepts the Idealism without the Absolute, ending in a Paterian isolation and subjectivism, essentially rejecting Bradley's solution without proposing another. What makes the problem insoluble for Eliot is precisely his multiplication of identical points of view, each inscribed in its own circle. The seeds of Eliot's philosophical relativism about perspective can be found in his application of Pater's thought to Manet's painting.

&

"On a Portrait" describes Manet's *Young Lady in 1866* as seen by a beholder who is drawn into the picture to imagine the woman portrayed:

> Among a crowd of tenuous dreams, unknown
> To us of restless brain and weary feet,
> Forever hurrying, up and down the street,
> She stands at evening in the room alone.

He finds himself first absorbed, and thereby relieved of his "weary" self-consciousness, but then baffled by her inscrutable look. She seems "evanescent" and "an immaterial fancy of one's own"—throwing the beholder back on himself. She is "unknown" both in the world of the painting and by the viewer himself, who cannot get access to her "dreams": "Her dark eyes keep their secrets hid from us, / Beyond the circle of our thought she stands." Her expression reveals nothing about her thoughts, only suggesting that she must have "secrets." The beholder ends by turning his gaze to the parrot, who stands in for the beholder and his relationship to the portrait: "The parrot on his bar, a silent spy, / Regards her with a patient curious eye."[37] Throughout the poem, the speaker/beholder moves back and forth between attributing isolation to the figure and to himself, making his condition a reflection of hers, or perhaps the other way around. The parrot described in the concluding couplet is the symbol of this mirror-imaging.

The poem opens by framing the woman in the painting, setting her at a distance from the speaker. This is a gesture made familiar by Rossetti's ekphrases, particularly "Soul's Beauty," the picture sonnet that accompanies *Sybilla Palmifera*. A cooler figure than Lilith, *Sybilla* has much in common with Manet's young lady with a parrot: "Under the arch of Life, where love and death, / Terror and mystery, guard her shrine, I saw / Beauty enthroned."[38] As in Eliot's opening, the grammatical core of the sentence ("I saw"; "she stands") is delayed by modifiers that locate the figure in space and distance her from the speaker. But Eliot distances the speaker from the figure emotionally, in contrast to Rossetti's highly charged "love and death," "terror and mystery." Eliot's tone has more in common with Swinburne's "The Garden of Proserpine":

> Pale, beyond porch and portal,
>   Crowned with calm leaves, she stands
> Who gathers all things mortal
>   With cold immortal hands.[39]

Here, too, the grammatical core of the sentence is delayed in order to place the figure visually, and Eliot in particular echoes the words "she stands" from this passage.[40] Numerous meanings revolve around the word "stand," which refers to Proserpine's pose in Swinburne's poem, the Lady's pose in Manet's painting, and her parrot's vertical perch, or "stand." The parrot's "bar" at the end of Eliot's poem thus reflects the lady's standing posture at the opening. There are literally two "stands" in the poem, as there are in Manet's painting, yet neither is clearly our own. Rather, the relationship between these two stands, or standing points, generates the meaning of the poem and the picture it describes. We find ourselves somewhere in the exchange between them.

This reflection between two "stands" is the poem's way of forestalling the impulse or obligation (who knows how Eliot experienced it?) to become absorbed in the painted figure by imagining her interiority. The poem seeks to experience her in a different way. Indeed, while using a Romantic vocabulary, Eliot rewrites the concept of interiority, shifting its function from originality to reflection. His use of the two words "fancy" and "lamia" in particular hail the Romantic investment in interiority as the source of emotion and ideas. The figure in Manet's painting is "evanescent, as if one should meet / A pensive lamia in some wood-retreat, / An immaterial fancy of one's own."[41] The word "lamia" is conspicuous in a poem laden with the language of Romantic poetry. In Keats's poem by that name, the lamia generates a self-sustaining world of aesthetic and erotic pleasure through her imagination. All the benefits of life are due to her power, even if they cannot stand up against the "percent eye" of the skeptic philosopher. Rossetti's *Lilith* and Pater's *La Gioconda*, whom he calls a "vampire," are versions of Keats's lamia, dangerous but compelling creatures of imagination. Yet Eliot emphasizes the immateriality of imagination, its evanescence, rather than its power. Coleridge distinguished between organic creativity and "fancy," which he defined as a mechanical process of recall and repetition, a "mirrorment . . . repeating simply, or by transposition, and again involuntary (as in dreams)."[42] Fancy may thus be "immaterial" in two senses: issuing from the disembodied inner world (literally *not made of matter*), but also *not important* because it is mechanical, lacking originality.[43] Significantly, it was not even Eliot's idea to use the word "lamia" in this poem: according to Powel, Eliot's friend Frederic Schenk suggested "pensive lamia" in place of "young chimera."[44] "Young chimera" actually better captures the now-you-see-her, now-you-don't quality of Manet's young woman, though "lamia" fits the meter better. Eliot no doubt recognized "lamia" as an appropriate choice for the way it chimes with his Romantic vocabulary and identifies the female figure with *Lilith* and *La Gioconda*. This substitution also draws attention to the self-conscious thematic of repetition and reflection in the poem.

Eliot's poem is a hall of mirrors, which was perhaps not what A. D. Moody meant when he dismissed it as "remote and artificial, its images not original but reproductions."[45] As a picture that Eliot saw in a book, the woman with the parrot is hardly "a fancy of one's own." The painting's portrait-like qualities place it in a genre often denigrated in the nineteenth century because the painter's contribution was thought to be imitative and unoriginal. As an ekphrasis of a portrait, Eliot's poem is a copy of a copy. Finally, "On a Portrait" not only works in a well-worn mode popularized by Rossetti, it is also saturated with references to Swinburne, Tennyson, James Thompson, Lionel Johnson, Ernest Dowson, and other fin de siècle poets. At every level, the poem emphasizes not only its own unoriginality, but also the emptiness of the very idea of originality.

Just as in Manet's painting, the appearance of the parrot in Eliot's closing couplet signifies flatness and copying as against depth and originality. The parrot is a "spy" on a private scene, but what can it tell us? If it could speak, it would only repeat things that other people have said. Indeed, the poem itself is a kind of "parrot's eye": the poet/viewer stands before a painting and repeats what he sees. The parrot's "eye" with which Eliot ends the poem is a classic pun on the pronoun "I." What would a parrot's "I" be? The Romantic lyric "I"—expressing the unique inwardness of the poet—implies a conception of self that "parroting" would seem to cancel. The pronoun "I" never appears in Eliot's poem except by implication in this pun, indicating a disappearance of the speaker that matches the woman's evanescence. If the Romantic self is predicated on expression of original thoughts and feeling, what kind of self can a poet have if he only repeats and imitates?

The eye/I pun concludes "On a Portrait" with an echo and reversal of the last line of Rossetti's "The Portrait": "They that would look on her must come to me." Both endings allude to the ekphrastic mode of the poem by referring to acts of looking ("regards" / "look on her") and to the authorizing poet. However, whereas Rossetti takes credit for both the image and the poem, affirming his role as creator and originator, Eliot suggests reflection or imitation as the basis of his poem and the painting. The figure of the parrot returns us to the surface of the painting and to consciousness of the imitative rather than expressive quality of thoughts or interior speech. This move, on the one hand, cancels out the most deeply cherished concept of English lyric poetry—the feeling, thinking self—yet, on the other, wipes away the poetic and philosophical problems that come with such an investment in individuality and originality. The isolation that the speaker seems to experience is merely a reflection of the picture, which itself is a "copy" of the sitter: he is wrapped in dreams, but they are not his own dreams. The lack of depth—the lack of an inner standing point, of a creative and emotional source from which the poem issues and to which it draws us—becomes not a problem in this poem, but a solution. With no substantial self to express, there is also no confining "circle" to escape from.

⚜

Eliot elaborated and experimented with this realization in his next portraits, trying out different configurations of sitter and beholder, and varying length and point of view. Eliot began "Portrait of a Lady" in February 1910 and composed "Mandarins" in August of the same year. He completed "Portrait of a Lady" in November 1911, when he also wrote "La Figlia Che Piange."[46] These three works reflect Eliot's intense interest at this time in the portrait poem. Though strikingly different from one another, all three portraits experiment with ways of detaching the speaker from the figure portrayed. Rather than seeking to become absorbed in the figure and interpret the meaning of her look, these speakers "observe," "remain self-possessed," and "leave." While "On a Portrait" asks questions about the subject that can't be answered, these poems don't seek answers about the subject's interiority. They represent meaning as outside of and between figure and speaker, rather than inside the portrait subjects. This exteriorization of meaning and "soul" also goes hand in hand with a loosening of the ekphrastic dependence of the poem on a painting. While "Mandarins" and "La Figlia" appear to be at least notionally ekphrastic (the specific visual sources are not yet known, if they exist), the poems resist absorption by distancing the viewer/poet from the image in various ways. The most experimental of these three poems, "Portrait of a Lady," carries out the implications of "On a Portrait" by imagining a relationship between sitter and beholder—or beloved and lover—in which the two parties merely "parrot" each other.

"Mandarins"

Since its publication in *Inventions of the March Hare* in 1996, "Mandarins" has received less attention than other poems in this collection, but as one of Eliot's most explicitly ekphrastic works, it reveals a good deal about his changing approach to the visual image and to portraiture. With the mandarin's "sword and fan," his "screen and cranes," the "gold-wire dragons," and the ladies' porcelain cups, "Mandarins" toys with the late-nineteenth-century craze for all things Japanese, with perhaps a touch of the interest in Chinese art that began to take hold around the turn of the century. Its japonisme taps into the same aesthetic of flatness found in Manet's painting and Eliot's ekphrastic response. Indeed, Japanese art influenced Manet and Whistler in the 1860s and 1870s as they developed techniques for reducing the depth of the canvas and emphasizing its decorative and "painted" qualities. The flattening effect of *Young Lady in 1866* was itself probably influenced by Manet's study of Japanese prints.[47] Eliot's "Oriental" theme and his anti-absorptive treatment of his portrait subjects connect closely with developments in late nineteenth-century art.

Eliot also surely saw Asian artifacts in Boston homes, where they were popular as decoration at the turn of the century, and probably visited the Museum of Fine Arts in Boston, which had (and has) one of the largest collections of Japanese art outside of Japan. The MFA moved and reopened at its new Huntington Avenue building in the fall of 1909, featuring Japanese galleries designed to present artifacts, such as the priceless collection of Buddhas, in more spacious and sympathetic surroundings. In the spring of 1910, Eliot took Fine Arts 20B (Florentine painting) with Professor Edward Forbes, a trustee of the MFA and director of Harvard's Fogg Art Museum, who regularly led his students to view original artworks. (The final examination for this course included a query about the "four galleries" they had visited during the semester.) Eliot also was acquainted with the curator of Asian art at the MFA, Okakura Kakuzo, whom he may have met at the house of Isabella Stewart Gardner, herself a collector of Asian art.[48] At the MFA, Eliot would have seen examples of the kinds of artifacts and images mentioned in "Mandarins," as well as crowds of museum-goers who flocked to the new galleries.

Section 3 of "Mandarins" refers to "cranes that fly across a screen," suggesting that the entire scene, including "the eldest of the mandarins" and the cranes, is painted on a screen. On display at the MFA in spring 1910 was an exhibit of screens by the sixteenth-century Japanese artist

Kano Eitoku, who introduced the practice of using gold leaf, as in the "Gift Bearers at the Chinese Court," a pair of six-paneled screens prized by the museum at this time.[49] The formality of the figures in Eitoku's screen, the theme of paying homage, and most important, the stiff and apparently impassive attitude of the figures correspond with that described in "Mandarins 1." Other screens and hanging scrolls in the MFA collection from this era represent cranes and egrets as well as mandarin-like figures. Asian screens also appeared in European paintings beginning in the 1860s. Manet's *Portrait of Emile Zola* (1868) shows Zola flanked on the left by a screen depicting a bird on a branch, and on the right by a woodcut by Utamaro depicting a large man in Japanese dress. At least two paintings by Whistler, *The Golden Screen* (1864) and *La Princesse du pays de la porcelaine* (1864), feature a painted screen that fills the background while pushing into the foreground and effectively blending with the Japanese dress of the sitter.

La Princesse brings together three elements of "japonisme" in one composition: the screen, the figure's elaborately decorated robe, and a porcelain pot. "Mandarins" also links these elements; the robes and the porcelain appear in "Mandarins II." Other paintings by Whistler feature porcelain objects both large and small (such as *Purple and Rose: The Lange Leizen of the Six Marks,* also 1864). Whistler also introduced the porcelain craze to Rossetti, as reflected in the blue-and-white tiles of the latter's *Blue Bower,* 1865. The last line of "Mandarins 4," "How life goes well in pink and green!" evokes Whistler's characteristic color titles, such as *Variations in Flesh Colour and Green: The Balcony* (1864–65), a painting that includes a tea service, a "distant prospect of the sea," and perhaps the "abstract sunset (rich, not crude)" referred to in "Mandarins 2." None of these paintings by Whistler show male figures, and so cannot be thought of as the single source of "Mandarins." Yet Eliot's poem is definitely visual, and the description of "crowds that ran, / Pushed, stared, and huddled, at his feet" in "Mandarins 1" suggest that the setting is a museum or gallery.[50] It is very likely that Eliot was responding to a number of different images; his ekphrasis picks out easily recognized, somewhat stereotypical features of Asian art. What is most significant is Eliot's astute perception of this artistic style as the source of the flattening effect in European painting from the 1860s onward.

Eliot links the visual aesthetic of the painted screen with a psychologically flat representation of the figures in each portrait. The figure in "Mandarins 1" is "indifferent"; he "merely stands and waits . . . With fixed regardless eyes—/ Looking neither out, nor in." The "eldest of the mandarins" in 3 is described as an "indifferent idealist, / World in fist," and the poem concludes, "how life goes on different planes!"[51] These expressions could just as well describe the woman in Manet's painting, and indeed Eliot echoes much of his language from this earlier poem, including the watchword of "On a Portrait," "stands," which leads off the sequence. "Mandarins" and "On a Portrait" each contrast the self-contained standing of the main figure to the restless hurrying of those around him or her, sharing the key terms "crowds," "feet," and "eye." However, the speaker of "Mandarins" is not engaged with the image as he is in "On a Portrait"—now he too is "indifferent," dissociating himself from the "crowds that ran, / Pushed, stared, and huddled," in contrast to the speaker of "On a Portrait," who refers to himself as "us of restless brain and weary feet." The speaker of "Mandarins 1" does not even try to enter into the figure's thoughts; rather, he imagines that the Mandarin, who "merely stands and waits," has no thoughts at all. With "fixed," meaningless gaze, the mandarin *is* the parrot of Manet's painting (this identification is hardly accidental, as we will see again in "Portrait of a Lady": both are non-Western "others"). "Mandarins" fully inhabits the flattened world of Manet's painting in a way that "On a Portrait" only approaches in its closing couplet. The references to "screens" and "planes" suggest a two-dimensionality that is both visual and psychological: "The cranes that fly across a screen . . . Observe him with a frivolous mien . . . how life goes on different planes!" and "How very few there are, I think / Who see their outlines on the screen."[52]

"Mandarins" departs from the nineteenth-century portrait poem by focusing chiefly on appearances, and only commenting on the figures' states of mind to emphasize their "indifference" and "tranquility," their adherence to "formalities" that seem to take the place of feeling and thought. Rather than the attempted journey into the sitter's mind that we find in "On a Portrait," these poems investigate the relative positions and "attitudes" of the figures vis-à-vis each other: the mandarin and the "crowds" in 1, the two ladies drinking tea in 2, the "eldest of the mandarins" and the painted cranes in 3, and the dignified conversation of the "demoiselles and gentlemen" in 4. Yet while they are "indifferent" to each other, nonetheless the figures are all engaged in a complex exchange of gazes, thematized by the many instances of looking ("stared" and "fixed regardless eyes" in 1; "Regard" in 2; "observe" in 3; "see" in 4). This exchange of gazes picks up and develops the detail of the parrot's "patient curious eye" from 1909. Seeing is not treated as an occasion for an imaginative reverie about the figure's inner life. Rather, we see a sequence of "shifting scenes," of interactions that bring figures into relation with each other (such as the two ladies who "Regard / A distant prospect of the sea" while drinking tea together) without going beneath their surfaces.

"Mandarins" intensifies the flatness of "On a Portrait" while also contracting and hardening its aesthetic. The description of the ladies in "Mandarins 2" captures the quality of the sequence: "outlines delicate and hard." Formally, each section is an emaciated sonnet. Discounting one- and two-syllable lines, three of the four poems are fourteen lines long, and all conclude with two- to three-line stanzas that deliver a "point" similar to the epigrammatic couplet that closes the Shakespearean sonnet. The use of tetrameter lines interspersed with dimeter half-lines gives the poems a diminished feel, however. This formal reduction reflects the two-dimensional representation of the portrait subjects, a pair of features that often go together in portraits of 1912–1915 (including Eliot's "Cousin Nancy" and "Aunt Helen"), as discussed in chapter 4. Like the portraits described in the next chapter, "Mandarins" focuses on the material accessories that symbolize the portrait subject, reduces people to objects, and treats visual images as objects rather than windows. The hallmark of such portraits is contraction and condensation, and in this process the Rossetti picture sonnet remains the formal model even as the language and images change. "Mandarins" can thus be understood to spell out the implications of aestheticized portraits by Whistler, Manet, and Rossetti, exploring what it would mean to truly dwell on the surface—in a poem, rather than in a painting. The portraits that result are intentionally superficial, or to use Eliot's word, "frivolous."

"La Figlia Che Piange"

Written within a year of "Mandarins," "Portrait of a Lady" and "La Figlia Che Piange" explore superficiality as an alternative to emotional engagement and absorption. The slighting, even cruel treatment of the female figures in these two poems is intentionally shocking, and changes in attitudes toward women have made these poems even more discomforting to read in the twenty-first century than at their first appearance in print. The project in these poems is similar to that of "Mandarins": to disengage the viewer/speaker from the absorptive power of the image, and in particular, from the image of the Beloved. While his personal discomfort with women may be a proximate cause for the unsympathetic treatment of the girl and the lady in these poems, Eliot also responds here to the overblown discourse of the soul that pervades Victorian poetry. "La Figlia" stages a self-conscious rupture with the idea that female beauty embodies or represents the meaning of the soul. In this poem, Eliot remains within the parameters and language of the Rossettian ekphrastic portrait while violently refusing its implications. "Portrait of a Lady" aims at an easier target, mercilessly parodying Matthew Arnold's "The Buried Life" for its sentimental conception of the soul and the capacity of love to awaken interiority. Eliot's strategic targeting of Arnold enables him to distance this aspect of Victorian poetry while less obviously following Rossetti's and Swinburne's own deflation of interiority through the motifs of reflection, surface, and flatness.

"La Figlia Che Piange" describes an image of a woman clasping flowers, with sunlight in her hair, and a look of "pained surprise" and "fugitive resentment in her eyes."[53] These details correspond to many portraits of women from the Rossetti circle, especially the flowing hair, which is a consistent feature of major Pre-Raphaelite and Aesthetic paintings, from *Lady Lilith* and *Fazio's Mistress* to Whistler's *White Girl* and *Little White Girl* and John Everett Millais's *Ophelia*. Like many of Eliot's epigraphs, the line from Virgil that introduces the poem—"O quam te memorem virgo"—leads away from the proximate Victorian source of the poem's ideas by introducing a historically remote and more erudite context.[54] Eliot also commented that the title of the poem (meaning "The Weeping Girl") referred to a statue in an Italian museum that he had not seen; but, as Derek Roper observes, a statue he never saw cannot have had much impact on the content of the poem.[55] Roper instead places Eliot's poem in the context of Victorian picture-poems, particularly Rossetti's, noting that the imperative voice found in the first stanza of "La Figlia" can be found in Rossetti's "Cassandra," "For 'Ruggerio and Angelica' by Ingres," and "For a Venetian Pastoral by Giorgione," among others.[56] These poems interpret the intriguing expressions on the figures' faces by putting the painting into time and imagining what might have happened before or could come after the moment depicted. Similarly, in "La Figlia," the speaker begins by telling the figure in the image to do exactly what she is already doing: "Stand on the highest pavement of the stair— / Lean on a garden urn." The next stanza puts this moment in perspective by dramatizing the picture involving a man who has just left or is about to leave the woman pictured: "So I would have had him leave."[57] Finally, according to Roper, the third stanza "closes the episode by moving the woman's imagined movement into the past," where it becomes "a memory of memories."[58] This tripartite structure—description of the image, dramatization of its events, and meditation on memory—follows the pattern of Swinburne's "Before the Mirror." Eliot's ending, "[she] Compelled my imagination many days, / Many days and many hours" echoes Rossetti's "Soul's Beauty," "How passionately and irretrievably, / In what fond flight, how many ways and days!"[59] Eliot's choice of image, method of development, tripartite form, and verbal echoes follow the Aesthetic portrait poem that, as we have already seen, he knew well.

Eliot pays homage to Rossetti in "La Figlia" but also defines his difference from the elder poet. Rossetti's speaker swears to follow his lady "passionately and irretrievably," but Eliot's speaker imagines a brutal separation from the girl: "So he would have left / As the soul leaves the body torn and bruised, / As the mind deserts the body it has used."[60] The violence of the poet's departure from the Rossettian Beloved measures his "rapture" and the difficulty of breaking free of it. Whatever personal feelings these lines express, they also stage the poet's attempt to disengage from ekphrasis—from the power of images and the conventions for interpreting such images. Indeed, the speaker does not break entirely free from the image, for he continues to meditate on and be compelled by it. Unlike his models, Roper notes, Eliot does not open out to a broader conclusion at the end of his poem.[61] That is because, I would suggest, the poem itself attempts to "turn away" from the ekphrastic convention of finding the meaning of the woman's soul in her facial expression. The speaker isolates the image of "her hair over her arms and her arms full of flowers" as "a gesture and a pose"—as a theatrical "stand" that does not reveal a deeper meaning but rather follows a generic convention. He "wonder[s] how they should have been together" (the union that is the goal of Rossetti's poetics), but prefers a repetition of the image *without* further interpretation. This ending is, finally, not entirely different from Swinburne's; both poems conclude with reflection and repetition, with "formless gleams" that reveal nothing about the interior state of the figure, or for that matter, the speaker. In a few lines, this conclusion recapitulates the essence of "Portrait of a Lady," which Eliot had just finished when he wrote "La Figlia": the speaker's soul and mind—in this case called his "imagination"—is not the site of original feelings and thoughts, but rather reflects the world in a nearly automatic way.

"Portrait of a Lady"

Of Eliot's portraits, "Portrait of a Lady" goes the farthest in revising the Victorian portrait poem, probably doing more to change the genre than any other single work. Eliot's adoption of free verse, his mixture of interior monologue and quoted speech, and the striking, even shocking refusal to idealize the female subject made the poem a benchmark for

Pound and Williams, who both struggled to match Eliot's inventiveness in their own portraiture. An important sign of Eliot's departure from convention is the absence of ekphrasis, notional or actual. Moving away from the visual image and its implied conception of identity, the poem is less a portrait of an individual than of a relationship between the lady and her male companion, who narrates their interactions to himself. Like Pound's "Portrait d'une femme," Eliot's "Portrait of a Lady" rejects the traditional Cartesian conception of the subject as consisting of an interior and exterior, exploring the way that ideas, including our very sense of interiority, migrate back and forth in an infinite exchange of reflections. Rather than remaining in the ekphrastic sonnet mold, "Portrait of a Lady" allows the implications of "On a Portrait" to unfold at the level of form. Under this changed idea of self, the "portrait" must be a different kind of poem.

Eliot's most inventive portrait is, nevertheless, composed of features and traits from existing Victorian conventions and sources. The poem openly parodies Matthew Arnold's "The Buried Life" (1852), while continuing to draw on Rossetti and Swinburne at a subterranean level. From Arnold, Eliot adopts many turns of phrase (including the title of Arnold's poem, which appears in the poem's second section) and the narrative framework of a man seeking affirmation of his "soul" in the eyes of his beloved, all of which Eliot treats ironically. From Arnold he also takes up music as a metaphor for interiority, but sets Arnold's music in counterpoint with Swinburne's, exploring the way that this motif captures the intersubjective and reflective aspects of self. Again, Eliot retains the tripartite structure of "Before the Mirror," translated from a spatial to a temporal dimension. Eliot's mixture of dramatic voices follows the hybrid form that appears in both "Before the Mirror" and Rossetti's "The Blessed Damozel," framing the female figure's speech with the internal monologue by a male speaker. Finally, "Portrait of a Lady" picks up and develops the compositional strategy of *mirroring* from both Rossetti and Swinburne—though to a different effect—imagining the male speaker as the lady's reflection.

Eliot evokes music beginning with the opening scene of "Portrait of a Lady," in which the two characters return from hearing a concert of Chopin Preludes, and continuing to the closing lines, where the male speaker thinks, "This music is successful with a 'dying fall.'" Eliot's choice to make music the figurative medium of his "Portrait" follows the pervasive analogy between art and music in painting of the Rossetti and Watts circles, as discussed in chapter 1. The appeal of music as a model of art for its own sake was articulated most famously in Pater's dictum that "all arts should aspire to the condition of music." John Xiros Cooper claims that Eliot used music in this and other early poems to "cast a sardonic light on the late nineteenth-century aestheticist obsession with music," a "sound world" that he experienced "as a regressive state of conventionalized sensations and a parallel sclerosis of musical thought."[62] This interpretation places Eliot, as usual, in the role of scourge to the "exhausted," "corrupt" culture of the nineteenth century. But Eliot's deployment of music and his response to Aestheticism in this poem are more complex than that.

In Swinburne's "Before the Mirror," music absorbs individual human griefs and renders them insignificant in the larger flow of time. In "Portrait of a Lady," we hear not one music but several; the tonal disparities among musical instruments "play out" the competition between the lady and her male companion. Eliot thus keeps the analogy with music but observes that music is not always harmonious. The "lady" is characterized by late-Romantic expressive music: Chopin and the "attenuated tones of violins / Mingled with remote cornets." She wishes to engage the male speaker in a "friendship" of "understanding" that reflects her conception of the self as having "feelings" (her words). She echoes the language of Matthew Arnold's "The Buried Life," as if she were the addressee of that poem, having outlived Arnold to see a younger generation less receptive to "friendship." The male speaker, on the other hand, asserts his distance from her by imagining himself as a "dull tom-tom" and a "capricious monotone," and their conversation as "a broken violin." This dissonance creates an opportunity for Eliot to differentiate his poetry from Victorian lyricism, although ultimately the disparity is not as great as the male speaker would like to think.

In "The Buried Life," Arnold reincarnates the Romantic expressive lyric as a dramatic monologue, in which the speaker tries to reach his own "hidden self" by making contact with his beloved. She has been conducting a merry "war of mocking words" with him. He enjoins her, "Yes, yes, we know that we can jest, / We know, we know that we can smile!" But, he pleads with her, "hush awhile / And turn those limpid eyes on mine, / And let me read there, love! thy inmost soul."[63] Arnold opposes superficial smiling, an expression of the mouth, to sincere tears that come from inside the eyes (tears being an important feature of Victorian sentimentality). On this basis the speaker attempts to break through the triviality of life—"the thousand nothings of the hour"—to access the "buried life" in himself and his beloved. This buried life is variously described as "the inmost soul," "the buried stream," "his genuine self," "our true, original course," "the soul's subterranean depths," and "a lost pulse of feeling." All these terms are familiar grist for the portrait poem, which similarly attempts to find its subject's inner life.

Most important, Arnold describes the interior life as musical "airs":

> Yet still, from time to time, vague and forlorn,
> From the soul's subterranean depth upborne
> As from an infinitely distant land,
> Come airs, and floating echoes, and convey
> A melancholy into all our day.[64]

Echoing the "thoughts that do often lie too deep for tears" of Wordsworth's "Immortality Ode," the trope of music as the expression of interior "depth" flows from Arnold to Swinburne to Eliot. But when it surfaces in "Portrait of a Lady," the "airs" have been transformed to "ariettes / Of cracked cornets." The lady continues to insist on a model of selfhood that seems coercive and outdated to the male speaker; when she remarks that "youth . . . smiles at situations which it cannot see," he comments "I smile, of course, / And go on drinking tea." Despite his smile, she continues to reassure herself by ever more explicit reliance on Arnold:

> Yet with these April sunsets, that somehow recall
> My buried life, and Paris in the Spring,
> I feel immeasurably at peace, and find the world
> To be wonderful and youthful, after all.[65]

The lady's references to Arnold give her a paradoxical relationship to interiority. She asserts her belief in an interior space of sincere feeling, which can be accessed through the privileged relationship of two lovers or "friends." Yet, she can only express her own feelings through the quotation of Victorian clichés. Whereas the lady's "music" once seemed spontaneous and expressive, now it is sickening to a modern hearer, as Eliot's allusion to a "dying fall" indicates ("That strain again! It had a dying fall; / . . . Enough; no more: / 'Tis not so sweet now as it was before").[66]

In contrast, the male speaker goes to great lengths not to be sincere and blocks the lady's attempts to draw him into friendship. Inside the privacy of his "brain" he develops another self that is out of key with the "ariettes" of her performance.[67]

> Inside my brain a dull tom-tom begins
> Absurdly hammering a prelude of its own,
> Capricious monotone
> That is at least one definite "false note."[68]

This important passage has been much noted for Eliot's use of "primitive" subject matter.[69] The "tom-tom" is at once the poet's name ("Tom"), the sound of his thudding heart, the discordant Modernist music of his rebellion against Victorian convention, and the signature of the "other," an echo of a primordial ritual whose meaning is inaccessible to the speaker or anyone in his culture. Rawson links the "dull tom-tom" to sounds Marlow recalls in *The Heart of Darkness:* "The monotonous beating of a big drum filled the air with muffled shocks and a lingering vibration," and "the beat of the drum, regular and muffled like the beating of a heart."[70] The note of pure "savagery" is supposed to be the note of pure authenticity: Kurtz's behavior shows the "horror" latent in every civilized heart, a horror that is as intrinsic as the actual heartbeat of life. The value of the savage drumbeat, to the speaker, is twofold. It appears to be a true expression of self, rather than the ultracivilized "attenuated tones of violins" in which the lady wishes to snare him. As long as he maintains this secret "monotone," it proves that there is more to him than his half-hearted role-playing.[71]

Eliot relies on the contrast between Arnold's "lost pulse of feeling" and the male speaker's own "dull tom-tom" for ironic effect. But irony only partially conceals the structural similarity of the two sounds, which both define the interior by an analogy between heartbeat and musical or metrical rhythm. The very terms that denote the place of private expression inside his brain echo the cliché he is trying to avoid: his "capricious monotone" picks up Arnold's "capricious play." Indeed, like the lady, the male speaker turns out to be "parroting," as he discovers at length in section III:

> And I must borrow every changing shape
> To find expression . . . dance, dance
> Like a dancing bear,
> Cry like a parrot, chatter like an ape.
> Let us take the air, in a tobacco trance.[72]

The appearance of the parrot in section III directly parallels the "dull tom-tom" passage by virtue of their shared refrain, "Let us take the air, in a tobacco trance." The parrot's imitative, automatic speech would seem to oppose the authentic note of the "dull tom-tom." Yet the "borrowed" cry of the parrot and the speaker's "capricious monotone" have a lot in common. As Eliot represents them, the figure of the savage is like the figure of the parrot: both are non-European others, and both make sounds that can't be interpreted. We can't understand the tom-tom any more than we can understand the cry of the parrot (whether linguistic or nonlinguistic). The parrot presents a blank to our understanding because there's nothing there to understand; he is just imitating sounds without intending meaning. The tom-tom can't be understood because it precedes language, issuing from a place deeper within the self. It would seem that the parrot and the primitive drum would stand at opposite ends of the spectrum as models of self, and yet there is little effective difference between them.

Like the dancing bear and chattering ape, the parrot imitates or "borrows" human behavior, and the speaker's recourse to copying reflects the pressure the lady has placed on him to conform to the role of "friend" that she has in mind for him. She has tried to set the stage for his performance as parrot. This passage caps the development of a theme of imitation or performance (in the sense of following a script dictated by someone else) that pervades the poem. This theme is present from the opening lines: "You have the scene arrange itself—as it will seem to do / . . . An atmosphere of Juliet's tomb."[73] The idea of performance as automatic imitation also appears in "Convictions," a poem Eliot was working on at the same time as his first drafts of "Portrait of a Lady." It begins, "Among my marionettes I find / The enthusiasm is intense!"[74] In *The Symbolist Movement,* the book that introduced Eliot to modern poetry, Arthur Symons comments:

> Are we not all puppets, in a theatre of marionettes, in which the parts we play, the dresses we wear, the very emotion whose dominance gives its express form to our faces, have all been chosen for us? . . . so the words we seem to speak are but spoken through us, and we do but utter fragments of some elaborate invention.[75]

Like the parrot, the marionette expresses itself in words that are not its own (though it may not realize its lack of agency).[76] In "Portrait," automatic speech is particularly exemplified by the street piano that, "mechanical and tired, / Reiterates some worn-out common song." The street piano opposes the Romantic conception of lyric as the expression of individual feeling; this "song" just "Recall[s] things that other people have desired." The expression is mechanical both in the way it is reproduced on the street piano and in the way it reproduces (or "recalls") feeling in the speaker. The hackneyed tune of the street piano thus integrates the other two musical lines of the poem, the "violins" and the "tom-tom," for a conception of music (as well as speech) as inexpressive and automatic.

While this conception of music obviously runs against Arnold's, it is consistent with Swinburne's. The strangeness of Swinburne's turn to music in "Before the Mirror" is that the music seems essentially exterior to the figure—she hears the "stream" of "dead mouths," and the stream itself "hears / The flowing of all men's tears beneath the sky."[77] The song is not her own, nor does it capture her feelings, for she seems not to have any (neither "gladness" nor "sadness"). Both Swinburne and Eliot draw an analogy between this external quality of music and the experience of seeing yourself in a mirror:

> I feel like one who smiles, and turning shall remark
> Suddenly, his expression in a glass.
> My self-possession gutters; we are really in the dark.[78]

Rather than coming face to face with the beloved and thereby the subterranean true self (as in Arnold) or even with the abominable primitive self (as Conrad's Kurtz does), Eliot's speaker encounters himself simply as a reflection. He sees himself, suddenly, as if from the outside, and rather than emphasizing the difference between inside and outside, this experience reveals him as nothing but a surface onto which are copied (or mirrored) the appropriate facial expressions. He describes his feelings (supposedly the source of his inwardness) as a smile seen in the mirror—an expression faked and then reflected. The speaker of the portrait poem has moved from beholding the parrot to being the parrot, a migration already predicted at the end of "On a Portrait" by the pun on "parrot's eye" and "parrot's I."

The form of "Portrait of a Lady" reflects this conception of self as parrot-like. In quoting the female speaker to us, or to himself, the male speaker includes her words in his own silent monologue. Even as he attempts to distance himself from her ideas, his thoughts are also hers: not only through the complex reversals observed above but also in the simple fact that his voice includes hers. Framing quoted speech with silent commentary, Eliot follows both Rossetti and Swinburne in adjusting the Browningesque dramatic monologue to a less individualistic conception of selfhood. In particular, Swinburne's distinctions between narrator and quoted woman merely serve to emphasize that he is imagining her thoughts as he looks at the painting. Neither speaker has priority, for the painting precedes them both. Like Swinburne, Eliot uses this form to set up a cascading chain of echoes whose source cannot be located inside either speaker.

Understanding the male speaker as a mirror image of the lady complicates the gender relations ostensibly governing his portrayal of her. Gilbert and Gubar interpret Pound and Eliot's hostility to female literary figures as a defensive reaction to a feminized literary culture, and Carol Christ builds on their account to argue that in this poem Eliot "imagines the literary past as a woman, whom he deserts, dishonors, even murders while he appropriates her voice."[79] While Cooper applauds Eliot's censure of a "regressive" nineteenth-century culture, Christ reverses the values of this narrative to view the poet as a kind of domestic abuser of the "feminized idiom" of Victorian poetry. Both narratives, as I have been suggesting, overdo the contrast between Eliot and nineteenth-century culture. "Portrait of a Lady" certainly disparages a poetry devoted to the expression of love, associated with Arnold, but keeps many of the existing structures of the Aesthetic portrait poem in place. Like "The Blessed Damozel" and "Before the Mirror," Eliot's poem has two "standing points"; the only difference is that the male speaker who frames and interprets the female figure does not invite our sympathy with her. He also does not invite our sympathy with himself, however. Rather than moving into her view through his, we move back and forth between two characters who come to seem similar in fundamental ways. This movement is not so different from what we experience in a poem like "For 'The Wine of Circe' by Edward Burne-Jones," where Rossetti leads us through the opposing forces (day and night, love and shame) that Circe embodies. Though union is the aim of Rossetti's poetics, he cannot speak of the states he seeks to unify without separating them into sides. These two sides are bound together in an embrace he calls "love"; Eliot's two standing points are bound together as reflections of each other—both equally unoriginal—in a relationship that he calls a "parrot's cry." Though the feelings toward this relationship have changed, structurally it remains much the same. At some level, Eliot's discontented representation of both the male and female speakers in "Portrait of a Lady" is indebted to Aestheticism's willingness to explore ambiguities of gender and sexuality, to interrogate and destabilize the gender stereotypes and roles of Victorian culture. His mirror-image speakers owe something to Swinburne's "Hermaphroditus" and to the very masculine faces that look out from Rossetti's later portraits of women, making us wonder whether we are seeing Rossetti's beloved or himself—a merging of identities his poetry explores. It's important to remember, I think, that Eliot is neither abusing a specific woman nor affronting all of femininity, but rather detaching the portrait poem (and the practice of poetry in general) from the discourse of love that so dominates Victorian verse.

"A Game of Chess"

After "Portrait of a Lady," Eliot returned to female portraiture for the short satirical sketches "Aunt Helen" and "Cousin Nancy," discussed in the following chapter. While the freestanding portrait as such seems to disappear from his work at this point, it returns in *The Waste Land*, in what Fowler terms an "inset," where an abbreviated or miniature instance of one genre appears as part of a larger work.[80] While the genre of Eliot's long poem is indeterminate, individual passages indicate generic affinity, such as the double sonnet in "The Fire Sermon." "A Game of Chess" alludes to two of the most famous portraitists of the turn of the century, Rossetti and Henry James. Eliot used "In the Cage," the name of an 1898 novella by Henry James, as the working title of "A Game of Chess." This section recapitulates and updates Eliot's portrait practice from 1908 to 1922 with two short portraits in different modes. The first is a notional ekphrasis of a carefully framed and accessorized image of a woman combing her hair before a mirror, evoking Rossetti's *Lady Lilith*. The second is a conversation between a husband and wife in the same mixture of internal monologue and recorded speech as his 1911 "Portrait of a Lady." While "On a Portrait" followed Rossetti and Swinburne in gazing at the inaccessible and mysterious Beloved, "Portrait of a Lady" imagined the same figure as an older woman who has lost her power to charm the poet. "A Game of Chess," by contrast, restores the Lady's power and brings her into the modern era as a tormented and tormenting wife. In this picture of modern marriage, Eliot appropriately frames his pastiche of Rossetti, the Victorian poet of erotic love, under the sign of James, the novelist of disappointment.

The first sixteen lines of "A Game of Chess" describe a woman sitting at her dressing table. There are many precedents for this conventional scene, such as Pope's "Rape of the Lock," which was a model for parts of the *Waste Land* manuscript. Like Pope, Eliot satirizes the woman's vanity before her mirror. This opening section, like much of the whole work, operates by drawing an ironic or satirical contrast between the present scene and a similar one recorded in the literature of an earlier time, as in the opening lines: "The Chair she sat in, like a burnished throne, / Glowed on the marble."[81] These lines echo and parody Enobarbus's description of Cleopatra in Shakespeare's play by substituting "Chair" for "barge" and "marble" for "water." Shakespeare's Cleopatra provides Eliot with his foil but is not the object of his satire. The scene of a beautiful, seductive woman at her dressing table or before the mirror was a favorite one for

Aesthetic painters as an occasion for exploring the topic of self-sufficient and self-absorbed beauty. Rossetti, Whistler, and Courbet exchanged variations on this theme, including four by Rossetti: *Fazio's Mistress* (1863), the watercolor *Woman Combing her Hair* (1864), *Morning Music* (1864), and the most elaborate and erotically charged of these, *Lady Lilith* of 1868 (fig. 3). In this painting, the seated figure of Lilith combs her "fiery" red hair out straight while gazing at her reflection in a hand mirror. Beside her, on a chest or dresser with elaborate gold locks, a silver stand supports a mirror and two candles that are reflected in its surface. Before the mirror is a "vial of ivory" and gold, which, along with the locked jewel case, is a symbol of Lilith's sex, her self-contained erotic power, and her role as a vessel for the fantasies of men. All these elements appear in Eliot's description: the chair, the candelabra, the mirror, the vials, the jewel case, the fiery hair and comb. Eliot has added details but not subtracted any, and his additions only heighten the overdecorated, cluttered, even claustrophobic atmosphere that his description shares with Rossetti's picture.

"A Game of Chess" also connects with Rossetti's *Lady Lilith* by alluding to a violated Eden. Eliot refers to a "sylvan scene" pictured over the fireplace in the woman's dressing room:

> Above the antique mantel was displayed
> As though a window gave upon the sylvan scene
> The change of Philomel, by the barbarous king
> So rudely forced.[82]

In *Paradise Lost*, Eden is described as a "silvan scene" from Satan's perspective as he travels toward it to tempt Eve.[83] In *Lady Lilith*, a scene of trees pictured in the mirror on the bureau suggests Eden, Lilith's home before she fled from Adam, and it indeed appears framed "as through a window." Both Rossetti's and Eliot's dressing-room scenes include a picture of Eden, which in both cases has been violated. Lilith's story of violence involves her initial refusal to serve Adam and her subsequent role as the "witch" who lures, ensnares, and strangles unwitting young men, told in "Body's Beauty": "Lo! As that youth's eyes burned at thine, so went / Thy spell through him, and left his straight neck bent / And round his heart one strangling golden hair."[84] Rossetti's sonnet thus warns the viewer against the same seductive beauty that his painting represents and seeks to embody. Eliot's "sylvan scene" concerns the rape of Philomel by Tereus, a story that inaugurates a theme of sexual violence and loss of innocence developed across the entire poem. Eliot has reversed the genders of Rossetti's story of sexual violation by introducing Philomel into the picture, but the figure of Lilith is still present, indeed still dominates the scene, for it is her hair that "Spread into fiery points / Glowed into words, then would be savagely still."

In Eliot's image of modern married life, his reference to the "sylvan scene" does more than allude to Eden and Lilith, for the lines leading up to this moment in *Paradise Lost* concern regret, specifically Satan's regret of his rebellion against God:

> Be then his Love accurst, since love or hate,
> To me alike, it deals eternal woe.
> Nay curs'd be thou; since against his thy will
> Chose freely what it now so justly rues.[85]

The violated Eden in "A Game of Chess" is sexual innocence, but also the hopes and expectations brought to marriage, a state the poet now finds reduced (in Milton's words) to "infinite wrath, and infinite despair." Eliot's ekphrasis of a modern Lilith registers the erotic desires that Rossetti's painting knowingly stokes, as well as the strangulation of the young man's life that follows. Yet within this inset lies another ekphrasis, the description of Philomel, whose innocence and desires have also been violated; these two images reflect each other as the two sides of modern marriage.

These two sides are represented in the second portrait inset of "A Game of Chess," a conversation between husband and wife that inspired Pound to write "Photography" in the margin of Eliot's draft. The form of this episode is the same asymmetrical combination of interior monologue and speech that Eliot used in "Portrait of a Lady," and corresponds with similar narratives in both works. The male speaker tries to retain his sense of identity by not entering into scripted conversation with the woman, but finds himself simply repeating her words back to her, or remembering lines from Shakespeare ("Those are pearls that were his eyes"; "This music is successful with a dying fall").[86] The male speaker is an empty echo chamber, just as he was in "Portrait of a Lady." The situation has changed, however; now the speaker is married without the option of going away on a journey. "Portrait of a Lady" tentatively explores, and "Aunt Helen" gleefully announces, the male speaker's freedom from restrictive Victorian social conventions, but the euphoria doesn't last. As an early adopter of the modern theme of lives stifled by unhappy marriage, Henry James presides over this part of the section in particular. James's novella "In the Cage" concerns a young woman who works in a post office and tries to piece together the lives of her customers from their telegram messages. As her illusions about their lives are dispelled, the limits on her knowledge are gradually replaced by a different kind of cage: her recognition of the actual limits on the possibilities of her own life.

The two insets of "A Game of Chess" tell a history of the portrait genre after 1860 by condensing it into two moments: the ekphrastic portrait of an impassive woman looking in the mirror, and a dramatic dialogue between disappointed interlocutors, who have "nothing" in their heads. These two moments recapitulate Eliot's own practice of the genre in "On a Portrait" and "Portrait of a Lady." From the beginning, Eliot's portraiture explored the idea that interiority is a kind of "nothing," an idea that varies from mysterious to edgy to nihilistic. His continual undoing of interiority is one of Eliot's lasting contributions as a poet. Over the course of his portraits, the nothingness creeps closer. It begins as a quality the viewer sees in Manet's *Young Lady in 1866,* developing into an experience that the male speaker of "Portrait of a Lady" can end or evade by leaving the presence of the lady who makes him feel this way. In "A Game of Chess," it becomes the condition of his very being, a condition that seems to be the result not only of his marriage but also the war, the decay of European civilization, and other ills diagnosed in this poem.

Eliot's working title "In the Cage" captures the process of internalization and self-recognition that this section records: the vertiginous realization that he—the poet, probably, as well as the male speaker—is now *in* the portrait whose blankness so forcefully struck him fourteen years before. The episode is structured as a series of inclusions: the story of Philomel is framed as a picture on the wall in the wife's dressing room; the wife is framed by her accessories as a modern Lilith waiting to strangle the youth; and this picture of the wife is framed and updated by her unrelenting conversation with her husband. To go backward in time (toward Eden, or toward the first betrayal that led to this series of sufferings) is to move successively inward through the frames of memory. This series of frames reintroduces depth to the portrait as the interiorization of past events: "And other withered stumps of time / Were told upon the walls; staring forms / Leaned out, leaning, hushing the room enclosed."[87] The sense of interiority—of enclosing something—is achieved at a cost, for the specific memory recalled is of sin and violation; or as Satan says, "myself am hell." Yet in this mysterious passage the poem also registers its own origins in a "room" of "staring forms"—poetic forms that it now seeks to enclose in a larger work with little formal or generic definition. The speaker wishes to escape the room, dreading his encounter with the waiting lady, her glowing hair, her savage stillness. Yet in representing Lady Lilith's perfect self-absorption, the poem also seeks to take on her power. Finally, Eliot does not free himself from the appeal of the Aesthetic image so much as transform the ekphrastic portrait by drawing it into a new place.

PART TWO

Modulations 1912 to 1922

FOUR

Contraction

FROM PICTURE SONNET TO EPIGRAM

THE YEARS 1912 AND 1913 marked a sea change in many areas of literature and in modern life generally.[1] In poetry, a thorough rethinking
of form, style, and content were underway. From 1912 to 1922, poets who
had learned their craft under the influence of Aestheticism experimented
with changing the features of the portrait poem. While the genres of
many twentieth-century poems are hard to identify, relative consistency
in the titling and subject matter of portrait poems enables us to trace what
happened to this genre during the decade when Modernism went, so to
speak, from zero to sixty. The following chapters examine three modulations of the portrait poem. *Modulation* is Fowler's term for the mixing
and altering of traits in a generic repertoire without creating an entirely
new generic code, although it is difficult to determine in any given case
whether a work has transformed or merely modulated the existing genre.[2]
The three kinds of change explored here are contraction, expansion, and
pastoral modulation. Size is one of the most important, yet least noted,
aspects of genre.[3] Some genres are defined by their size, such as the sonnet, aphorism, or short story, but even genres whose identity is more tied
to other traits (like the portrait) can have their focus, effect, and subject
matter significantly altered by contraction or expansion. Rossetti's sonnet
"The Portrait" and his dramatic monologue by the same name marked
the approximate lower and upper length limits on a poem of this kind
in the nineteenth century. In contrast, poets after 1912 both shrank and
enlarged the portrait beyond these limits, contracting it to two or three
lines—in some cases just a few words—and expanding it to hundreds of
lines, even to the size of a book. Such variations in size had a profound
impact on how the portrait subject was represented and what kinds of
messages the work conveyed.

Contraction took place across the field of modern poetry, and was particularly a feature of Imagism. In the H.D.-Pound circle, portraits became shorter in length around 1912, corresponding with a reduced concept of the subject. Not interiority, but an almost thing-like quality in the subject characterizes these portraits, many of which are shaped by the modulating influence of epigram and epitaph. Schneidau wrote in 1968, "The epigram is more important in the ancestry of Imagism than the oft-noted haiku."[4] Yet because the art of epigram and epitaph are thought to have declined after the eighteenth century, little has been written about them as models for the Modernist short poem.[5]

Histories of ekphrasis identify the ancient epigram as one site where picture-description first emerged, and it is on the ground of its ekphrastic qualities that traits of epigram entered the portrait. Epigram means "written upon," and the form originated in inscriptions on monuments. These inscriptions typically dedicated a monument in the name of the giver or commemorated a dead person, as in the conventional epitaphic phrase "Beneath this stone." According to Jean Hagstrum, the Greek epigrams carved on monuments "spoke back" to the beholder, by which device "the mute statue was given a voice and the silent form was endowed with the power of speech."[6] As I will argue, Modernist poets moved from the Aesthetic picture sonnet to the epigrammatic portrait almost without missing a beat, and the explanation for this transition can be found in the shared ekphrastic basis for both kinds. Yet the epigrammatic inscription could also complicate the visual representation it accompanied, as Murray Krieger points out: it could "introduce an awareness of passing time . . . point to the illusionary effects of artifice in the plastic construct; and . . . allegorize the impact of the eternalizing shrine," thus separating the image from its referent.[7] Further, the epigram's independent existence since ancient times as a short poem displaying wit and "point"— not necessarily associated with a monument—also facilitated the movement away from ekphrasis in the Modernist portrait poem.[8] Instead of referring to an artwork, the epigrammatic portrait often turns that ekphrastic gesture toward itself, revolving around the description of some material object or visual image (not an artwork) that it analogizes to the portrait subject.

The most common type of ancient epigram, the epitaph, was particularly suitable as a model for portraiture, insofar as it refers to a single individual whose qualities it proposes to capture. E. A. Robinson, one of the most prolific portraitists of the time, experimented with epitaph-like portraits as early as 1902—anticipating, as he did in many ways, the experiments of H.D., Amy Lowell and Ezra Pound ten years later. The epitaph became particularly relevant as a poetic form during and after the Great War, ranging across movements to include Rudyard Kipling's *Epitaphs of War*, Edgar Lee Masters's *Spoon River Anthology*, and Pound's *Hugh Selwyn Mauberley*. Contraction also lent itself to the humorous and ridiculous, as may be seen in the satirical portraits by Pound and Eliot, and in the "Spectra" hoax, a spoof of Imagism perpetrated by Witter Bynner and Arthur Davison Ficke. Yet whether serious or comical, the reduced portrait communicated a diminished concept of personhood. Equating persons with things became a method of composition for Pound in the portraits of *Lustra*, which Bynner would later parody in *Pins for Wings* (1921). The more the poem was condensed, the less capacious its idea of the person, and the simpler the equation between person and thing. This feedback loop toward reduction and simplification had a natural limit (of about 3–4 words) that *Pins for Wings* consciously pushed for comic effect. By the time this collection was published, however, the transformation of the portrait had long since reversed direction and moved toward longer, more complex works.

The sonnet played a central role in the shortening and condensation of the portrait poem, and Rossetti presided over this process, even as it resulted in his being unseated as "king." His *House of Life* renovated the sonnet sequence for late Victorian poets, paring down the narrative element and extending the thematic breadth of the form.[9] In the context of the long Victorian narrative poem, a sonnet is short; and it was on the back of the sonnet that the spirit of brevity rode into the twentieth century. Robinson, Masters, Lowell, Pound, Eliot, Williams, and Cummings all mastered the sonnet early in their careers, learning from its discipline how to condense and contract. The sonnet and the epigram have a historically close relationship; they are "twinned and yet opposite," with the closing couplet of the Shakespearean sonnet the particular location of convergence between these two genres.[10] While the sonnet shares the qualities of point and brevity with the epigram, the popularity of the genres has often been inversely proportional. As the ranks of epigram swelled in the eighteenth century, the sonnet declined; but in the more elegiac and expressive poetry of the nineteenth century, the sonnet flourished and the epigram became the province mainly of classicists.[11] At least among the experimental Modernists of the early twentieth century, a similar reversal of fortunes occurred, in which the sonnet lost favor, while the epigram emerged as an appropriate vehicle for the sharper, more acerbic, less overtly expressive content of the modern poem. The epigram appeared from its place of hiding at the end of the sonnet in the years before the Great War, to carry the principle of condensation and reduction forward into the twentieth century.

The revival of the epigram was based on two different strains of the ancient form, the Greek and the Roman. The standard text and translation of Greek epigrams at the turn of the twentieth century was J. W. Mackail's *Select Epigrams from the Greek Anthology* (1890, revised in 1906). This is the source that Robinson, Masters, H.D., and Pound most likely used for their translations and imitations. Mackail defines the epigram as

> a very short poem summing up as though in a memorial inscription what it is desired to make permanently memorable in any action or situation. It must have the compression and conciseness of a real inscription, and in proportion to the smallness of its bulk must be highly finished, evenly balanced, simple, and lucid. In literature it holds something of the same place as is held in art by an engraved gem.[12]

The appeal of the epigram circa 1912 is immediately apparent from this definition, emphasizing concision, simplicity, and lucidity. Mackail's comparison of an epigram to an engraved gem dovetails with the values of both the 1890s—Pater's ideal of life "burning with a hard, gem-like flame"—and of the 1912–13 Imagist movement: directness, concreteness, and hardness.

The Scottish poet and scholar John Mackail (1859–1945) was the friend and biographer of William Morris and married the daughter of Edward Burne-Jones, so it is hardly surprising that his lengthy introduction to *Select Epigrams* is written in the language of Aestheticism. In particular, Mackail draws an explicit connection between the Greek epigram and the Rossettian picture sonnet. His discussion of Rossetti indicates how this form became a generic bridge from the Aesthetic to the Imagistic versions of portraiture. Mackail praises an ekphrastic epigram by Theocritus as "worthy to take rank with the finest 'sonnets on pictures' of modern poets." He particularly has Rossetti's "For a Venetian Pastoral by Giorgione" in mind when he writes that Theocritus

> seems to place the whole world of ancient pastoral before our eyes. The grouping of the figures is like that in the famous Venetian Pastoral of Giorgione; in both alike are the shadowed grass, the slim pipes,

the hand trailing upon the viol-string. But with an almost Venetian glow of colour, the verses are still Greek in their simplicity, their matchless purity of line.[13]

Mackail's reference indicates how impossible it was in 1890 to speak of the poetry of images without recourse to Rossetti, whose own condensation of language sets Mackail's terms of praise for a kind of poetry that he claims is "purer" and simpler.

❦

The epigram's condensation, ekphrastic origins, and compositional focus on the individual made it a likely successor to the portrait sonnet. Even before the epigram became a popular vessel for the Imagists, the process of reduction and diminution was at work in the portraits of Edwin Arlington Robinson at the level of both theme and form. A prolific poet, Robinson published many long narrative poems, especially later in his career, after *The Man Against the Sky* (1916) established him as an important poet. Yet his early volumes contain a predominance of sonnets and short poems in other exacting forms, which are often considered his best work. Many of these short poems are character sketches, leading Robinson's midcentury critics to refer to them as portraits.[14] The theme of Robinson's portraits is failure: failure to achieve worldly success, to enjoy it if achieved, and to find love or appreciate another's love, as well as the failure of modern society to provide opportunities for self-realization. In pairing reduction with a belittling attitude toward the individual, Robinson was alert to the history of the epitaph, which in the sixteenth and seventeenth centuries served twin purposes of Protestant self-abasement and a dismissive treatment of the "low."[15] Robinson's combination of approachable language, mastery of traditional forms, and attitude of disillusion made him a prominent modern poet during the years when Eliot and Pound were struggling to establish themselves. His work was well known by them (Pound and Frost discussed "Miniver Cheevey" when they first met in London).[16] Robinson's sonnet portraits offered a striking change of tone from the Rossettian praise-poem, a change of tone that is similar to and may have influenced the turn in Pound's portraiture around 1912 toward a more belittling, satirical view of human nature.

Robinson remarked to a reviewer in 1897, "The world is not a prison house, but a sort of spiritual kindergarten, where millions of bewildered infants are trying to spell God with the wrong blocks."[17] The portraits in *Children of the Night,* published the same year, emphasize the childish, foolish, or feeble characteristics that lead to failure. "Aaron Stark" begins,

"Withal a meager man was Aaron Stark, / Cursed and unkempt, shrewd, shriveled, and morose."[18] Stark's eyes are compared to "little dollars in the dark," his words to "sullen blows." Such belittling analogies between the subject and contemptible things play an important role in Pound's *Lustra* and in the contracted portrait generally. The description of Stark as "shriveled" and "meager" do not entirely eliminate the possibility of an inner life, but work to diminish the scope of that interiority. The very littleness of his spirit is captured in the smallest space of the sonnet, its closing lines:

> And oftentimes there crept into his ears
> A sound of alien pity, touched with tears,—
> And then (and only then) did Aaron laugh.

In Robinson's Petrarchan sonnets, the epigrammatic point or twist usually occurs in the last three, rather than the last two lines. Another portrait, "Charles Carville's Eyes" similarly closes by pulling away the veil to reveal the blankness of the soul within. Beginning "A melancholy face Charles Carville had," it ends,

> we were out of touch
> With all his whims and all his theories
> Till he was dead, so those blank eyes of his
> Might speak them. Then we heard them, every word.[19]

Carville's eyes are no different, in a sense, from those of the "pensive lamia" in Eliot's "On a Portrait"—blankness has nothing to tell—but Robinson determinedly deflates the Romantic associations between melancholy and hidden feeling to emphasize the lifelessness of the subject's interior ("His insufficient eyes, forever sad: / In them there was no life-glimpse, good or bad / Nor joy nor passion in them ever gleamed"). These portraits grant interiority to the subject, but it is negligible, even contemptible.

Robinson constructs an alternative genealogy for the portrait poem that does not go through Cowper and Wordsworth. As discussed in chapter 1, the foundational Romantic portrait poems seek to reveal the richness of the subject's soul, affirming her personal and religious fidelity and ultimately strengthening the viewer's own faith. Instead, Robinson praises writers who have revealed the very littleness of the human soul: Emile Zola, Thomas Hood, George Crabbe, and Paul Verlaine. These writers appear in *Children of the Night* as the subjects of portrait sonnets entitled with their names. "George Crabbe," for example, shows us

> the shame
> And emptiness of what our souls reveal
> In books that are as altars where we kneel
> To consecrate the flicker, not the flame.[20]

In contrast to the Cowperian virtuous circle where clarity of representation leads to stronger faith, in Robinson's downward cycle, the best portrayals reveal our emptiness most starkly. Yet Robinson still essentially shares the Romantic values that privilege "soul" as a good in life as well as in poetry. He indicts contemporary poets who write "songs without souls," implying that the theme of modern poetry must still be the soul. In his "Sonnet," Robinson identifies the villains of contemporary poetry as the "little sonnet men,"

> Who fashion, in a shrewd mechanic way,
> Songs without souls, that flicker for a day,
> To vanish in irrevocable night.[21]

and he asks for "a poet . . . To spirit back the Muses, long astray." "Sonnet" suggests that the "flicker, not the flame" of the human soul is manifest in ephemeral, mechanical poems. Although "George Crabbe" indicts human nature across a broad sweep of time, "Sonnet" targets contemporary poetry for failing to "shine," and in particular he appears to target *sonnetry* as the site or even the cause of this failure. Indeed, in 1897 the sonnet was hardly the place for exploring the modern condition of soullessness; it had served as a vehicle for representing the soul through four centuries of English poetry.

Much of Robinson's work is concerned with or ends in death, both in longer narrative poems such as "Annandale" and in his shorter character sketches. Death is a common theme in portraiture, as nearly all of the major examples discussed in this book suggest: Cowper's "On the Receipt of My Mother's Picture out of Norfolk," Wordsworth's "Lines Suggested by a Portrait," Tennyson's "The Gardener's Daughter," Browning's "My Last Duchess," and Rossetti's dramatic monologue "The Portrait." It might almost be said that the portrait poem is made possible by death, which brings the subject's life to a close and ushers him or her into history. Yet death may be treated in many ways, and the Victorian portrait poem typically makes the subject's death the occasion for an elegiac description of her life and soul, and for expression of the poet's emotions in response to her death. This treatment is in keeping with the predominantly elegiac character of nineteenth-century poetry.[22] Robinson's portraits, however, are more likely to treat death as a sign of the brevity and fundamental emptiness of life, rather than an occasion to explore the character, soul, and faith of the subject. While death may reveal a hidden truth about the portrait subject, for Robinson it is a truth that never expands, but instead diminishes the picture. "Richard Cory" is the most famous poem in *Children of the Night*, perhaps in all of Robinson's oeuvre, and demonstrates his skill in deploying death in this way. In this poem, suicide cuts short a life that seems charmed to outsiders, revealing Cory's judgment on his own life as not worth living. The four-quatrain poem is not a sonnet, but its closing lines execute a twist or turn similar to the endings of many of Robinson's sonnets: "And Richard Cory, one calm summer night, / Went home and put a bullet through his head."[23] This summary of Cory's fate is not unlike those given in epitaphs, and it was to this form that Robinson tentatively turned in his next volume, *Captain Craig* (1902).

As the summation of an individual's life on the occasion of his or her death, the epitaph is perfectly suited for portraiture driven toward reduction and diminution. Although the classical epitaph may be considered the origin of elegy, in modern times the elegy and the epitaph represent divergent approaches to death and commemoration. As Peter Sacks has admirably shown, the traditional English elegy guides the poet and audience through a process of mourning and is oriented toward bringing the living to recognize and accept the subject's death.[24] The epitaph, by contrast, summarizes the deceased person's life and death with the greatest economy possible and frequently purports to be spoken by the dead person him- or herself. It often conveys a message about the brevity of life and finality of death. Epitaph is perhaps the most condensed poetic form, and certainly the most condensed of the genres that treat death. Scodel claims that the few examples of poetic epitaph composed in the twentieth century, such as Yeats's at the end of "Under Ben Bulben" prove its "overall obsolescence" in this period.[25] It appears as an influence on portraiture from Robinson through Pound, however, as an alternative to the more expressive elegy that, as Ramazani has shown, also had to be transformed during this period to meet changing attitudes toward death.[26]

Published in *Captain Craig*, Robinson's "Variations of Greek Themes" consists of eleven translations from the *Greek Anthology*, eight of which are epitaphs. Rarely anthologized or discussed since then, these short translations are formally and thematically close to the experimental Modernism that would emerge within the decade. The resemblance to poems by Richard Aldington and H.D. may simply reflect a shared model. Yet this resemblance also indicates the appeal of the epitaph as a generic vessel or model for reduction. Ranging in length from sixteen lines to four, the "Variations" explore what is the least that can be meaningfully said of a person's life. The endings aim for epigrammatic condensation: "For what I was I cannot be, / And what I am I will not see," concludes "Lais to Aphrodite" (X); "Leave me to my quiet rest / In the region of the blest," ends the "Happy Man" (I); "And with Eutychides in Hell, / Where's a poor tortured soul to dwell?" asks the joking minstrel Eutychides (IV); "'One stays with him,' you said, / 'And this one I bring with me to the dead,'" says the epigrammatist to Aretemias (VII).[27] The collection includes two complaints about old age that similarly close with epigrammatic thrust: "Must you find only at the end / That who has nothing has no friend?" and "You will see me in the evening?—And what evening has there been / Since time began with women, but old age and wrinkled skin?" (VIII and IX).[28] Although these are translations, it is clear that Robinson chose carefully from the thousands of epigrams in the *Greek Anthology* for originals that matched his existing preoccupations with portraiture, death, and a minimalism about life's possibilities.

Robinson's choice of epitaphs also reveals an interest in the way that inscriptions combine the portrait subject with the material object on which the text is written. That is, the epitaph refers both to an individual (the person memorialized) and to an object, the marker on his or her grave:

> When these graven lines you see,
> Traveler, do not pity me
>
> This dust was Timas
>
> No dust have I to cover me,
> My grave no man may show;
> My tomb is this unending sea,
> And I lie far below.[29]

When the epitaph is spoken in the first person, as in the opening and closing pieces of the sequence, the assimilation of subject and object is more intense. The device strangely both reduces the subject to mere "dust," while also perpetuating his or her voice beyond death, if only as a reminder of life's brevity and insignificance. Yet this effect is in keeping with Robinson's picture of the modern soul as a mere shadow of its former self—an insubstantial, but persistent shadow.

Robinson's early portraiture exemplifies the formal and aesthetic shift away from sonnet and toward epigram as the model of portraiture. Robinson's minimal expectations for humanity found an appropriate vessel in the epigram, even as his sonnets explored a conflict about what the proper subject of poetry should be: the soul, or soullessness. This conflict was as much about *how* to represent as what to represent, for the sonnet, much deployed in the nineteenth century for themes of love, faith, and praise, made an uncomfortable or even ironic fit with Robinson's dark view of human life as short and empty. He was not the only writer to struggle with and modify the sonnet as a vehicle for portraiture: Lowell, Pound, Eliot, Masters, and Arthur Ficke rang changes on the sonnet as they sought the appropriate form for deprecating their subjects.

In *Modern Poetry in Miniature,* a 1963 study of Imagism, William Pratt likened the Imagist poem to the Elizabethan sonnet as the most important form of its age. He drew this analogy in order to contrast the formal restrictions of the sonnet with Imagism's free verse, which he saw "as a measure of the greater uncertainty, the deeper spiritual unrest of our time in comparison with that of the Elizabethans."[30] Yet the affinity between the sonnet and the Imagist "miniature" goes beyond their respective importance at different eras in history, as I have suggested. The sonnet had long served as the site for condensation and nonnarrative poetics, and the resurgence of the epigram around the turn of the century meant not the invention of a new sensibility but a transfer and adjustment of the sonnet-sensibility to a new form. The Imagist poem did inherit the role of the sonnet, but not only in the simple sense that it became more popular than its precursor. They are in contact with each other at the point of the couplet of the Shakespearean sonnet, where the epigram passed into English poetry. Although many Imagist poems are not epigrams at all, most of the poets associated with the movement wrote portraits in epigram form. In passing through the narrow neck of the epigram, the portrait was transformed to a spare, rather unforgiving instrument for reducing and satirizing modern man and woman. Yet this change in form and tone also preserved elements of Aesthetic portraiture: Rossetti's condensation and privileging of surface were intensified in the epigrammatic portrait, rather than left behind. Epigrammatic portraits by Pound, H.D., and Amy Lowell, as well as Eliot's thirteen-line satiric portraits that straddle the two forms, demonstrate the simultaneous continuity and modernization of the portrait as it contracted and "hardened."

According to Pound and to H.D., Imagism was founded when they sent a group of poems to Harriet Monroe for inclusion in the first volume of *Poetry* magazine (1912–13). H.D.'s "Epigram (After the Greek)" was the final poem in the group printed in *Poetry*, and it is a work that, according to David Ayers, exemplifies the aesthetic of Imagism.[31] Ayers identifies H.D's use of classical models to develop a more direct mode of writing as the means by which she and Aldington "helped provide the basis for a key element in English modernism—neo-classicism."[32] But, as Laity argues, it was Swinburne's "Anactoria" and "Sapphics" that had made Sappho available to H.D. as a stylistic model as well as "the example of an open sexual narrative."[33] H.D. remained fascinated with Swinburne throughout her career; the title of her autobiographical novel *White Rose and the Red* alludes to "Before the Mirror," and is nominally set in the circle of Swinburne and Rossetti. In *Asphodel*, a fictional autobiography composed in 1921–22, the poet heroine claims, "We are children of the Rossettis, of Burne Jones, of Swinburne."[34] H.D.'s many poems about sea plants—reflected in the title of her first collection, *Sea Garden*—combine Swinburne's signature motif (the sea) with Rossetti's (flowers).

"Epigram" both builds on Aesthetic portraiture and transforms it stylistically. The poem is adapted from an epitaph that H.D. most likely found in J. W. Mackail's *Select Epigrams*, Epitaph XLVI, there given in a more discursive prose.[35] H.D. changed the perspective from first to third person, detaching the speaker's voice from the poem's subject and reorienting the work toward description rather than utterance, while cutting back the length and substituting epithets ("the golden one") for Mackail's clauses ("I who was more golden"):

Epigram
(After the Greek)

> The golden one is gone from the banquets;
> She, beloved of Atimetus,
> The swallow, the bright Homonoea:
> Gone the dear chatterer;
> Death succeeds Atimetus.[36]

In its simplification, scale, and "laconic detachment," according to Ayers, H.D.'s version achieves the ideals of Imagist verse.[37] Yet in its condensation, visuality, and objectification of the subject, "Epigram" is also employing and intensifying Rossettian effects. H.D. chose to translate a work that recalled motifs familiar from Aesthetic poetry: a once "golden" woman, now dead (as in the "Blessed Damozel") who is a "swallow" (Swinburne's famous "Itylus" begins, "Swallow, my sister, O sister swallow").[38] Unlike Robinson and Pound, who point to the "meager" and diminished quality of the modern person, H.D. cherishes the subject even as she embalms "the golden one" in a polished aesthetic artifact. Her "Epigram" is like Rossetti's "shrine" in "The Portrait" that both honors and substitutes itself for the portrait subject's living presence.

❧

In Amy Lowell's short but prolific career, she wrote many portraits and portrait-like poems, moving from sonnets to concise, pictorial poems. Her first volume, *A Dome of Many-Coloured Glass* (1912), included a group of sonnets exhibiting different methods of portraiture, such as "On Carpaccio's Picture: The Dream of St. Ursula," "Epitaph in a Church-Yard in Charleston, South Carolina," and "Francis II, King of Naples." This group is particularly notable for Lowell's echoes of Rossetti. "On Carpaccio's Picture" recalls Rossetti's picture sonnet "The Holy Family, by Michelangelo." Both sonnets describe religious paintings, contrasting the innocence of the figure in the picture with our knowledge of the violent death yet to come. Rossetti exhorts the figure of Jesus in Michelangelo's painting,

> Turn not the prophet's page, O Son! He knew
> All that thou hast to suffer, and hath writ.
> Not yet thine hour of knowledge.

Lowell tenderly explains of St. Ursula,

> And she lies sleeping, ignorant of Fate,
> Enmeshed in listless dreams, her soul not yet
> Ripened to bear the purport of this day.[39]

Lowell follows Rossetti in capturing the calm, not-yet-tragic moment in the life of a martyr (which is, in a sense, a metaphor for the still moment of the visual image withdrawn from temporality), while translating the gender of the figure from male to female. The theme of Lowell's portraiture in subsequent volumes is precisely this suspension, the cherishing of a fragile yet significant image, while she increasingly seeks to detach the image from works of visual art and give it concrete substance on its own.

The very title *Pictures of the Floating World* (1919), as well as one of its subheadings, "Lacquer Prints," suggests the visual orientation of the poems contained in this volume, yet few if any are ekphrastic. Instead, the poems describe material objects and identify these things metaphori-

cally with aspects of a person. "A Lady to Her Lover" reflects on the gap
between person and aesthetic object:

> The white snows of Winter
> Follow the falling of leaves;
> Therefore
> I have had your portrait cut
> In snow-white jade.[40]

This is a double portrait representing the lady by her speech, and her
lover by a notional ekphrasis of the jade portrait. The lover's likeness "cut"
in jade is compared to the concise utterance of the lady (which is both
"cut" short and curtailed in its unexpressed emotion). At the same time,
his aging and fading is contrasted to the permanence of his portrait. Not
the jade carving, but the "white snows of Winter" convey the fragility and
ephemerality of the lover and his relationship with the lady. Or rather,
Lowell makes his portrait out of the contrast between these two things. "A
Lady to Her Lover" also develops the theme of flat, hard surfaces found
throughout "Lacquer Prints." Lowell's three-line "Middle Age" compares
"the dulled surface of my heart" to "black ice / Scrolled over with unintelligible patterns by an ignorant skater."[41] The polished surfaces of Rossetti's canvases thus enter Lowell's poems in the form of material objects
that she identifies with her portrait subjects.

Lowell's practice remained closely allied with the picture sonnet, while
she worked to condense her images and detach them from dependence on
visual artworks. Her "Venus Transiens" refers to Botticelli's *The Birth of
Venus* and echoes Rossetti's sonnet to the same artist ("For Spring, By Sandro Botticelli")—as well as, perhaps, his sonnet and painting "Venus Verticordia." Like Rossetti, Lowell proceeds by a series of rhetorical questions
that pay homage to beauty—"What masque of what old wind-withered
New-Year / Honors this Lady?" asks Rossetti; "Tell me, / Was Venus more
beautiful / Than you are?" asks Lowell—and observes the suspension of
Botticelli's figures in the air, "hovering" (Rossetti) or "poised" (Lowell).[42]
Yet rather than paying homage to Botticelli's painting, "Venus Transiens"
proposes that the beauty of the poet's "vision" is "fairer" than his. Indeed,
Lowell offers no description of the lady in question, whose "too great loveliness" she seeks to "cover" with words, rather than (like Botticelli and
Rossetti in *Venus Verticordia*) leaving her naked for everyone to see. At
sixteen lines, the poem is vertically longer than a sonnet, but each line
consists of only a few syllables, thus contracting horizontally. The slim

poem clearly embraces an aesthetic of "less is more," both where words and nudity are concerned.

While *Pictures of the Floating World* is still in conversation with ekphrasis, Lowell's posthumous *Ballads for Sale* (1925) makes the move away from visual artworks to assert the independence of the portrait poem. Works such as "Silhouette with Sepia Background," "Aquatint Framed in Gold," "Miniature," "Easel Picture," as well as several "Portraits" capture the essence of their subjects without making reference to existing (or notional) artworks. "I thought of him in an oval gilt frame / Against sprigged wallpaper," Lowell writes in "Miniature," offering her description of the "little gentleman" as the equivalent of a painted miniature.[43] The epigrammatic "Portrait of an Orchestra Leader" insists that the "young man on a platform" is really "a white flame upreared in a silver dish." Lowell bridges the sensory gap between sound and sight, describing the orchestra music as "wind" and "waves" that cause the "flame" to bend and sway.[44] Such a synthesis, the poem suggests with its defiant insistence on the flame as a "portrait," can only be achieved in poetry, whose metaphorical structure allows the interpenetration of identities and of sight and sound.

A similar metaphoric substitution takes place in Lowell's unrhymed sonnet "Portrait (E.R.B.)," which compares "this lady" to "a grass-blade sheathed in ice," "hoar-frost running along the borders of a formal garden," and "violets under the misted glass of a cold frame / On an Autumn morning with the sun scarcely above the trees."[45] Working from the conventional comparison of a woman to an enclosed garden, Lowell suggests that her subject combines both the garden (the grass and violets) and its enclosure (the frost edging the garden and the glass in the cold frames), as a fragile being encased in a hard protective layer. This metaphor gestures also to the Victorian portrait's conventional body-soul dualism, except that here, both "inside" (garden, grass, violets) and "outside" (frost, cold frame) seem equally visible to the eye. At the same time, Lowell's portrait does not depict any aspect of the lady's physical appearance, but rather evokes her whole character. The "frame" and the subject are made out of the same material. Lowell's sonnet again echoes Rossetti's "For Spring, by Sandro Botticelli," with similar rhetorical questions ("But what can equal the glitter of the frost grass-blades?") and an emphasis on the figure's suspension—the "rigid radiance, / Bent and motionless"—in a cold atmosphere. The frame, the frozen moment, the questioning of the image: all these elements carry over from Rossetti, yet Lowell's portrait creates its own image that bears no relation either to a visual artwork or to the body of the subject. Like Rossetti's sonnet "The Portrait," Lowell's sonnet aspires to self-sufficiency, yet in a different way: not by substituting itself for the living subject, but by freeing poetic description from dependence on visual artworks.

H.D. and Lowell treat their subjects tenderly, as if breakable. Indeed, fragility or evanescence is a theme of many Imagist portraits. Lowell's "A Lady" of 1914 compares the subject to "an old opera tune / Played upon a harpsichord"; Richard Aldington's "R. V. and Another," which appeared in his 1915 *Images,* compares "delicate strangers / In a gloomy town" to "crocus blossoms in a drab lane."[46] The fragile quality of the subject suggests that he or she is in some danger of disappearing or being lost. In contrast, Pound endows his subjects with substance, and treats them more coarsely. Both approaches, however, draw our attention to the portrait subjects as things in the material world.

Like Robinson, Eliot, and Lowell, Pound began his portraits in sonnet form before experimenting with both shorter and longer variations. Already an accomplished sonneteer in 1910, Pound undertook the translation of Guido Cavalcanti's *Sonnets and Ballate,* a work to which Rossetti's translation (in *Dante and His Circle*) had introduced him. *Canzoni* (1911) was written very much under the influence of this massive translation project and his renewed contact with Rossetti's work during 1910–11. *Sonnets and Ballate* appeared in May 1912, a few months before he published *Ripostes,* the volume regarded as Pound's watershed "Modernist break." *Ripostes* bears the mark of the discipline imposed by his translation project, though in a different way. Opening with a sonnet, this volume documents the reduction of the portrait from the sonnet to a shorter, epigrammatic form.

While Pound would compose many epigrammatic poems between 1911 and 1915, he gave the generic term "Epigrams" to only two, which appeared together under this title in *Canzoni* (1911), composed while he was completing the Cavalcanti translations. Like *Hilda's Book, Canzoni* is steeped in late-Victorian poetics, especially the sequence "Und Drang," which quotes explicitly from Swinburne, Rossetti, Morris, and Arthur Symons. "Epigrams" combine a Rossettian visual sensibility with epigrammatic condensation more characteristic of *Ripostes* and *Lustra* than the volume in which they appear. These two poems point to the reduction of the portrait, but at the same time they demonstrate the very continuity between the picture sonnet and the epigram. The first of these, with its "ivory" and "rose" color scheme, is quoted and discussed in chapter 2. The second epigram also seems to connect with Rossetti, in particular the background of the *Blessed Damozel,* where pairs of lovers float above the Damozel's head on a flat backdrop of gold:

II

(THE SEA OF GLASS)

I looked and saw a sea
  roofed over with rainbows,
In the midst of each
    two lovers met and departed;
Then the sky was full of faces
    with gold glories behind them.[47]

The addition of the "sea" is a nod to Swinburne that neatly combines the styles of the two writers—glassy in Rossetti's case, oceanic in Swinburne's. Unlike the poems in *Hilda's Book,* these epigrams make no reference to "soul," but rather focus on the material aspects of the subjects and the aesthetic effect of spatial arrangements and color combinations. "Epigram I" specifically identifies the subject as a thing: ivory, then rose. The epigrams lack the "point" that those in *Ripostes* and *Lustra* cultivate; rather, they reveal Pound's basic conception of the epigram as a short object-centered poem.

The epigrammatic portraits of *Ripostes* and *Lustra* drop the ekphrastic orientation of "Epigrams," while adopting objecthood as the central trait of the portrait subject. The primary model for these works is the epigrams of Catullus, a poet Pound had studied in graduate school and continued to admire throughout his career ("If you want to go to the gist of the matter go to Sappho, Catullus, Villon," he wrote in "A Retrospect," 1918).[48] Catullus and Martial, the best-known epigrammatists in English, set the prevailing tone of wit and satire in the genre. Martial in particular provided the primary model for the English epigram in the sixteenth and seventeenth centuries, securing the genre's lasting reputation as a two-line witty remark with a twist or point.[49] A pointed, judgmental conclusion is the essence of Pound's epigrammatic portraits in *Ripostes.* "Portrait d'une femme" illustrates this conclusion at the end of a longer poem: "No! there is nothing! In the whole and all, / Nothing that's quite your own. / Yet this is you."[50] The spirit of this ending is distilled in the four-line portraits "An Object" and "Quies." Along with "A Girl" and "Phasellus Ille," Pound designated these poems as "sketches" in his list of "Portraits and Personae" at the back of *Umbra* in 1920. All exhibit the same condensed, epigrammatic close.

"An Object" is perhaps most representative of the group:

> This thing, that hath a code and not a core,
> Hath set acquaintance where might be affections,
> And nothing now
> Disturbeth his reflections.[51]

This fascinating poem modulates the Rossettian sonnet through epigram to produce a completely different kind of portrait. Pound's pre-*Ripostes* method of portraiture was to praise the subject by comparing her to aesthetic objects such as roses, golden tapestries, and ivory. In *Ripostes*, "Apparuit" still follows this method. Echoing the *Vita Nuova* and Rossetti, "Apparuit" envisions the subject framed and sheathed in gold: "Golden rose the house, in the portal I saw / thee, a marvel, carven in subtle stuff . . . frail alabaster, ah me!"[52] "An Object" similarly compares the subject to a "thing," thereby emphasizing flatness and lack of interiority. The male subject of this portrait has no "core," but rather lives by convention ("code") and in the eyes of others ("acquaintance"). Mao writes that this poem expresses "the danger of succumbing to an absolute privileging of the thing for its own sake."[53] Like the subject of "Apparuit," he is "superficial" in the sense that there is nothing beyond his reflecting surface, which is alluring in her case and objectionable in his. The change of mode from elegiac to epigrammatic makes possible the change of tone from expressive longing to sharp criticism.

At the same time, Pound's new topic—a man—also facilitates this abrupt change, for the same qualities that might seem praiseworthy in a woman can be criticized in a man. The expansive subjectivity and agency that "The Seafarer" idealizes (for example) are rarely represented in nineteenth-century female portraiture. When Pound applies the more limited horizon of female existence to a male subject, the resulting portrait has the tone of disapproval or disappointment: the person is *less* than expected. In other words, the epigrammatic mode enables Pound to make the switch from female to male subjects, and from praise to criticism. Before *Ripostes*, Pound's portraiture is strictly reserved for female subjects; his male figures are the speakers of dramatic monologues. Yet in *Ripostes* and beyond—especially in "Moeurs Contemporaines" and *Mauberley*—Pound's portraits describe and judge male figures rather than making them the narrators of their own stories. Indeed, Pound himself becomes the chief object of epitaph and satiric portraiture in "Moeurs" and *Mau-*

berley. While the sonnet was associated in Pound's mind with female portraiture and the relation of love, the epigram permitted a shift to masculine portraiture, with completely different results.

"Phasellus Ille" exhibits Pound's portraiture in transition from sonnet to epigram, both echoing and repudiating his earlier female portraits
in a satirical sketch of a conservative editor. It recapitulates the ideas of
"An Object" in fourteen lines rather than four. "Phasellus Ille" is only
sonnet-like in length, however; it has no rhyme scheme.[54] The poem is
a parody—Peter Davidson calls it a "grotesque echo"—of Catullus's Carmen IV.[55] Writing near the end of the Roman Republic, Catullus drew
on Greek models of epigram and renewed the form for personal, expressive, and erotic themes. Nearly half of Catullus's poems are composed
in elegiac couplets. Pound's affinity for Catullus at this time is further
evidence of the importance of the epigram during his process of scalar
reduction. Although the length and iambic trimeter of Carmen IV puts
it outside the epigram proper, it was intended as an inscription, probably for a votive model of Catullus's favorite ship.[56] As an inscription,
the poem thus has a family association with epigram. Pound has condensed the original twenty-seven lines to fourteen, shortening it by half
and marking its affinity with the sonnet. However, the last three lines are
separated from the rest of the poem by a space and display the point and
brevity of epigram.

Pound's shaping of his material thus combines Latin and nineteenth-
century English influences in a telling, if "grotesque" hybrid. In the original dedicatory inscription, Catullus praises the yacht ("phasellus") that
brought him home to Sirmio from his travels. Though his boat "was a
lively vessel that could make / The quickest voyages," she has come to rest
in "this fair inland lake . . . [to] pass the remnant of her days" (according to an 1874 translation Pound might have consulted).[57] Pound's version describes not a boat but a conservative editor, whom he refers to
as "papier-mâché," "it," a "thing." While Catullus reflects nostalgically
on his boat, Pound attacks the editor for his failure to change: "Its mind
was made up in 'the seventies,' . . . Nor will the horrid threats of Bernard Shaw / Shake up the stagnant pool of its convictions."[58] The "stagnant pool" refers to Catullus's "inland lake," but also recalls the persistent
theme of reflecting surfaces in Rossetti and Swinburne, and in Pound's
own work, including the "reflections" in "An Object." The pool even
strangely echoes Buchanan's critique of Rossetti's mind as "a surface so
thickly sown with water-lilies that it retains its glassy smoothness even in
the strongest wind."[59] As usual, Pound's relationship to Rossetti is ambiv-

alent: while the form of his poem hearkens to the "king" of the sonnet, its tone of biting criticism recalls Rossetti's nemesis Buchanan.

The detached closing tercet of "Phasellus Ille" has the condensation and economy of the Shakespearean couplet or the Latin epigram. In combining sonnet and epigram, "Phasellus Ille" becomes the staging ground of Pound's own poetic dilemma as he repurposes the Rossettian portrait from praise to criticism:

> Come Beauty barefoot from the Cyclades,
> She'd find a model for St. Anthony
> In this thing's sure *decorum* and behavior.[60]

Pound proposes a conflict between "Beauty" and "decorum," with the papier-mâché editor representing the side of decorum against the nakedness of beauty. Yet previously Pound had found beauty in decorum, as his many stylized, conventional descriptions of women as gold and ivory suggest. While "Epigrams" epitomizes Pound's conception of beauty as stilled, smooth, and unchanging, "Phasellus Ille" attempts to separate the quality of stillness from Beauty. Although the poem essentially promises to defend Beauty against the stagnating effect of decorum, its real work is to subtract Beauty from the portrait, which shows her absence by its diminished scope and reduced picture of humanity.

The portraits of *Ripostes*, like those of Robinson ten years before, show Pound pushing the genre into a shorter, more condensed form, while changing the tone from idealization to criticism, and the subject matter from female beauty to male character. Pound's portraits from 1913 to 1916 combine miniaturization with deliberate deflation. Reviewers noted his newly critical attitude disapprovingly when he collected these poems in *Lustra* (1916–17): "This almost excessive air of detachment about Ezra Pound's work gives an impression of coldness, of almost bitter aloofness from the common run. His rebelliousness is purely aesthetic and intellectual. . . . without emotion, he does not move one. The natural métier of such an attitude is the epigram."[61] In this volume, formal reduction goes hand in hand with the cold, detached representation of other people. The group of portraits includes some of Pound's shortest poems, such as the three "Epitaphs," "Phyllidula," "The Patterns," "Albâtre," and three groups of short portraits: "Ladies," "Amities," and "The Social Order." While some, such as "Epitaphs," allude to Chinese influence, most take the Latin epigram as their model, indicated by the choice of names such as "Agathas," Phyllidula," and "Erinna." "Lesbia Illa" in "Amitiés" is a translation of Catullus's "Carmen LVIII." Pound's

Roman orientation contrasts with Allen Upward's imitation of Asian models in "Scented Leaves from a Chinese Jar," a series of short poems that identify stock figures as their subjects, such as "The Coral Fisher" or "The Commentator."[62] In contrast, Pound tends to specify a name for the subject even when it is clearly a pseudonym. The influence of Catullus in particular is felt in the epigrammatic portraits: their brevity, satirical wit, use of epithets ("The bashful Arides"), and the device of switching from formal to casual diction in the last line to give a deflating feeling to the ending.[63]

Pound's "Epitaph" of December 1913 concisely articulates the idea of deflation:

Epitaph

Leucis, who intended a Grand Passion,
Ends with a willingness-to-oblige.[64]

"Leucis" has been reduced in a number of ways. The idea of a "Grand Passion" confers nobility on his romantic intentions, implies agency and will, and signifies an interior origin of feeling. In contrast, "willingness-to-oblige" shifts desire away from him to another person, renders him passive, and makes his role ridiculous rather than heroic. Leucis is Prufrock, the romantic lover who discovers that he's merely playing a role rather than acting on feeling. In "Amitiés" and "Ladies"—four-part sequences of short portraits—each individual portrait also follows this pattern of deflation:

Agathas

Four and forty lovers had Agathas in the old days,
All of whom she refused;
And now she turns to me seeking love,
And her hair also is turning.[65]

As in "Epitaph," which pivots on the word "ends," "Agathas" pivots on the word "turns": the woman's turn from the role of inaccessible object of desire to humble seeker of love is compared to the unerotic graying of her hair. This process is imagined as a historic change in the representation of love, from elevated emotions and unconsummated relationships to sexual self-gratification. The "turn" is also a structure in the epigram form itself, as a point delivered in the second line or second couplet of the work. This turn is brought over from Catullus and Martial, in whose epigrams "the technique of presenting a situation and then crowning it with a dismissive final line thus reveal[s] a system of false logic in the preceding lines."[66] In both "Epitaph" and "Agathas," Pound specifically identifies the movement from false to true as a chronological or historical change, rather than a sudden realization. Thus, these epigrams internalize their own status as commentary on the Victorian sonnet and love elegy, coming after and passing judgment on the form in which they originated.

While Robinson's theme is failure of self-realization, Pound is more interested in the downgrading of love to sex. In "Agathas," this reduction is represented as a shift in the power dynamic between men and women, in which women give up the cachet of inaccessibility in exchange for sexual satisfaction. "Phyllidula," "Arides," and "The Patterns" develop this theme. Other portraits focus on the system of economic exchange that reduces girls to items for sale in the marriage market, such as "Society" and "Lesbia Illa," a translation of Catullus's "Carmen LVIII" (in the original, "Lesbia" is described as a prostitute, whereas in Pound's version she is "now wedded / To a British householder").[67] "Mr. Styrax" of "Moeurs Contemporaines" (1918) also picks up this theme. Criticizing the economic system in which girls and women are traded on the marriage or sex market is an interesting variation on Pound's familiar motif of women metaphorized as gold. In a sense, this variation only makes explicit what is already implied in *Bocca Baciata*, where the sitter wears earrings of gold coins. Portraits such as "Albâtre" and "Society" make some attempt to analyze this system, while also participating in it by relentlessly identifying women with things. This variation draws attention to the way that people—women in particular—are made analogous to material things in the "real world," not only in poetry.

Like many of Pound's earlier portraits, "Albâtre" (1914) frames and objectifies the female subject by comparing her to her accessories. Yet in reducing the scale of this familiar style of portrait, Pound has reversed his tone so that the poem criticizes the process rather than appearing to enjoy it. The text and title of "Albâtre" refer to Théophile Gautier's "Symphonie en blanc mineur," from *Émaux et Camées* of 1852. This famous poem may well have suggested the title *Symphony in White* to Whistler when he renamed the three portraits in his "White Girl" series. Given Pound's long admiration for Whistler (his homage "To Whistler" was published only two years before), it is not surprising that he was particularly drawn to Gautier's poem. Pound was reading Gautier and other French symbolist poets in or before 1912, and their influence on his modernization is profound and carefully documented. Yet the differences between Gautier's

"Symphonie" and Pound's "Albâtre" are as striking as the shared frame of reference; Gautier's seventy-two-line description of a beautiful woman playing the piano "discovers an absolute beauty within the quotidian world," according to one critic, "fashion[ing] a poésie pure to rival the purity of music."[68] At seven lines, Pound's "Albâtre" reduces not only the scale of Gautier's work but the social class of the female subject (from performing artist in an aristocratic salon to "mistress of my friend"), the formality of attire (white camellias on a white satin gown to "the white bath-robe which she calls a peignoir"), and the nobility of the objects she is likened to (a swan, the moon, snow, glaciers, marble, ivory, and so on, to "the delicate white feet of her little white dog" and "two indolent candles"). Even though Pound often praised the "hardness" of Gautier, taking his spare quatrain form as a model when he became disillusioned with free verse, "Albâtre" essentially deflates Gautier's lyrical and expansive portrait of a lady in white. The poem does to Gautier's vision of female beauty what "An Object" does to Rossetti's vision—recycles it in an epigrammatic mode with the poles of feeling reversed.[69]

☙

The previous examples from H.D., Lowell, and Pound show a process of contraction at work in a variety of tones ranging from nostalgic to satirical and biting. In all these tones, the shift from sonnet to epigram as the model for portraiture seems linked with a sense that the human subject itself has shrunk. This reduction of scale and content extended beyond the Imagist movement. In 1915, Harriet Monroe accepted two short portrait poems from Eliot that share a number of traits with those already discussed in this chapter: "Aunt Helen" and "Cousin Nancy." The slightly longer "Mr. Apollinax" was also written at this time. In length, "Aunt Helen" and "Cousin Nancy" are each 13 lines, falling symbolically short of the sonnet by one line; "Cousin Nancy" alludes to George Meredith's sonnet "Lucifer in Starlight" to emphasize this formal frame of reference. Both works subversively mock the conventions and proprieties of the older generation, represented by Miss Helen Slingsby in "Aunt Helen" and the aunts in "Cousin Nancy." Whereas in "Portrait of a Lady," the figure of the older woman threatens the young male speaker's sense of himself, here she poses no threat and is only the object of humor. Indeed, the two poems effectively announce the changing of the guard from the Victorian era, overseen by "Matthew and Waldo / The army of unalterable law," to the modern era, characterized by smoking, dancing women, and the footman holding the housemaid on his knees. The shortness of the two portraits signals the fate of the older generation—and the Victorian muse figure first evoked in "On a Portrait"—reduced and brought to an end.

"Aunt Helen" is a true miniature in that it retains in shrunken form many of the traits of the nineteenth-century portrait poem, including Eliot's own "On a Portrait." The poem is epitaphic in the sense that it is occasioned by death. In keeping with the conventions for such portraits from Cowper to Rossetti, "Aunt Helen" assesses the subject's soul, but unlike these earlier models, finds only "silence in heaven / And silence at her end of the street."[70] The previously immortal soul is now imagined simply as a silence, an "end." This discovery corresponds with Robinson's and Pound's findings of human diminishment in their own reduced portraits. In place of the soul, the poem enumerates the material accessories of life: her "small house near a fashionable square," her cul-de-sac, her servants, her pets, and the Dresden clock on the mantelpiece. The Dresden clock is a nice touch that contrasts the durability of Aunt Helen's possessions with her own transience. The statues of Waldo and Matthew serve a similar function in "Cousin Nancy," standing as relics of a past era. The one possession that expires with Aunt Helen is her parrot, which "died too." The appearance and death of the parrot mark the final migration of this potent symbol from Manet's *Young Lady in 1866* to Eliot's "On a Portrait" to the crying parrot of "Portrait of a Lady." In these earlier portraits, the parrot stands in for the uncomfortable "I" who sees himself as an imitation of the lady. In "Aunt Helen," this anxiety about originality seems temporarily put to rest along with the now defunct generation that made the poet feel secondary. It is hard not to see the death of the parrot as Eliot's personal account-settling with his previous self and with the portrait-of-a-lady genre. Both the genre and the anxiety about parroting return, however, for a significant cameo appearance in *The Waste Land*, as discussed in chapter 3.

❧

The formal modulation of the portrait from Rossettian sonnet to the Modernist epigram was not a phenomenon limited to the Pound-Eliot circle. It may also be seen in the work of three other American poets of the era: Arthur Davison Ficke and Witter Bynner, authors of the Spectra Hoax, and Edgar Lee Masters, whose *Spoon River Anthology* is the most ambitious and certainly the largest collection of epitaphic portraits in Modernist poetry. Ficke and Bynner rendered the Imagist portrait ridiculous by contracting it to its smallest possible dimensions. Masters's representation of the individual is similar to Pound's and Robinson's in that his portraits emphasize the element of failure, but the scale of *Spoon*

River aspires to tragic or perhaps epic dimensions. Despite their very different versions of the Modernist portrait, Ficke, Bynner, and Masters began their careers in a familiar place, in imitations of Swinburne and the *House of Life*.

Under the pseudonyms "Emmanuel Morgan" and "Anne Knish," Bynner and Ficke spoofed Imagism and Vorticism in *Spectra*, the 1916 collection of extravagant parodies that were received in all seriousness as the latest poetic movement. For Ficke and Bynner, the two-year-long hoax proved the emptiness of the new avant-garde poetry, but their own careers also demonstrate the closeness in form and spirit between the Rossettian picture sonnet and the satirical modern portrait. Ficke and Bynner became lifelong friends at Harvard, where they graduated several classes ahead of T. S. Eliot. Ficke was a friend of Harriet Monroe and kept one foot in Chicago's literary circles while pursuing a career as a lawyer in Davenport, Iowa. The first volume of *Poetry* magazine includes more works from him and Bynner than from any other contributors. The February 1913 issue gives a taste of their Aesthetic sympathies, beginning with Ficke's eighteen-part "Swinburne: An Elegy," which frankly acknowledges the elder poet's influence (it opens, "The autumn dusk, not yearly but eternal / Is haunted by thy voice . . .").[71] Bynner's "Grieve Not for Beauty" evokes Yeats, particularly "Fallen Majesty," printed in a previous number of *Poetry*. In the same year, Ficke published a short volume of ekphrastic verse, *Twelve Japanese Painters*, mostly consisting of portrait poems that follow the standard formula of seeking the subject's "soul" or "secret" from the image. For example, "Dramatic Portrait by Sharaku" begins, "Whence art thou come, / Tall figure clasping to thy tragic breast / Thy orange robe . . . ?" and concludes, "How shall I wrest / From thee the secret of thy lofty doom . . . ?"[72] This volume shows Ficke's mastery of the nineteenth-century ekphrastic portrait and makes an interesting comparison with Eliot's "Mandarins," a sequence displaying many of the same visual details but emphasizing the flatness of the images and emptiness of the subjects' gazes.

Even as he rehearsed the Victorian portrait poem, Ficke was also experimenting with a dark inversion of its conventions. Published in the same issue of *Poetry* as his "Swinburne: An Elegy," Ficke's "Portrait of an Old Woman" repudiates beauty and the idea that the face reflects the subject's soul:

> She limps with halting painful pace,
> Stops, wavers, and creeps on again;

Peers up with dim and questioning face
Void of desire or doubt or pain.[73]

While it is a cliché of the Victorian portrait poem to call a woman the temple of the Lord, here she is described as an "empty temple of the Lord/ From which the jocund Lord has passed." Rather than revealing interiority with a blush, her face shows no emotion: "Her cheeks hang gray in waxen folds / Wherein there stirs no blood at all."[74] The "tight line" of her lips conveys her "writhing gasps" in contrast to Rossetti's "sea-line of her soul." Her body is compared to various objects, but not gold and roses: "bundled cornstalks," "a knot," "a ropy throat." The woman in the portrait is both an individual who has been "abandoned to the final night" in her old age, and also a muse figure transformed from the Rossettian Beloved to a "limping," "bleak," "unhuman" character appropriate to the modern urban condition that inspires this poem (her plight is contrasted to the "city's pomp"). Like Robinson, Ficke ties modernity to interior emptiness; like Eliot, he ages the female figure so that she can no longer be an object of desire; like Pound, he compares the subject with concrete, mundane objects. The contrast between this poem and other works Ficke published in the same year suggests an ambivalence or uncertainty about how to adjust poetic language and generic features to modern subject matter.

Ficke's most ambitious work, "Sonnets of a Portrait Painter," weighs the realism of "Portrait of an Old Woman" against an aesthetic Ficke calls "enameled softness." Published in *Forum* magazine in August 1914, this fifty-seven-part sonnet sequence draws heavily on Rossetti's *House of Life* for its form, title, and many allusions. The speaker imagines himself as an updated Rossetti, a modern portrait painter who also writes sonnets for his Beloved, chronicling the vicissitudes of their relationship. Ficke adopts such Rossettian elements as the color combination of gold and rose (Sonnets XII and XV), comparison of his beloved to Dante's Beatrice (XLI), and a celebration of postcoital rest (XVI), from Rossetti's famous "Nuptial Sleep." He often depends on the trope of interiority as revealed by the face of the beloved, as in Sonnet XIII: "I am in love with all unveiled faces, / I seek the wonder at the heart of man . . . turn toward me for a space / The marvel of your rapture-lighted face." Yet the sequence also is concerned with ugliness in a way that Rossetti is not: "Fate, with devoted and incessant care, / Has showered grotesqueness round us day by day" (V). In Sonnet XXX, the speaker represents himself as a painter of reality rather than idealized beauty:

> You mean, my friend, you do not greatly care
> For these harsh portraits I have lately done?
> You like my old style better,—like the rare
> Enamelled softness of that princess-one?
> True, this old woman, with the sunken throat
> Painted like cordage, is not sweet to view.
>
> .   .   .   .
>
> So these disturb? I fear this is the end
> Of days when I shall please your taste, my friend.[75]

These lines clearly refer to Ficke's "Portrait of an Old Lady" of 1913, pos-
ing a conflict between the stark realism of that poem and the "enamelled
softness" of Rossetti's idealized, soft-focus portraits. "Sonnets of a Portrait Painter" heralds a change in portraiture from the beautiful to the
ugly, while preserving the framework of the Rossettian sonnet sequence.
What is striking about the work is how well the "new style" integrates
with the old form, indeed suggesting that many "new" elements (such
as disillusion and stark realism) are present in the work that Ficke imitates. Rossetti, after all, shocked and disturbed his audience; perhaps it
is precisely the response of Buchanan-like reviewers that Ficke hoped to
defuse in this sonnet. Yet as Ficke was soon to learn, a "new style" did not
necessarily mean alienating his audience.

In February 1916, on the way to visit Ficke in Davenport, Witter Bynner stopped in Chicago to see a performance of *Le Spectre de la Rose*,
danced by Sergei Diaghilev's Ballets Russes.[76] He came up with the idea
for an avant-garde poetry "school" during the performance, based on associations between the ballet title "spectre" and the Imagist and Vorticist
movements. Bynner wrote several experimental poems on the train to
Davenport the next day and quickly drafted his friend into the project
when he arrived at Ficke's house. Written in a hotel room over the next
ten days, the poems by "Knish" and "Morgan" were published by Mitchell Kennerley in the fall of the same year with a preface and illustrations
by Ficke. The preface announced, "It is the aim of the Spectric group to
push the possibilities of poetic expression into a new region,—to attain a
fresh brilliance of impression by a method not so wholly different from
the methods of Futurist Painting."[77] The preface mixes references to the
avant-garde with the language of Aestheticism, such as "These specters
are the manifold spell and true essence of objects,—like the magic that
would inevitably encircle a mirror from the hand of Helen of Troy."[78] This

language reflects both Ficke's own investment in Rossetti and Pater, and perhaps his perception that these influences also had shaped Imagism and Vorticism.

The poems of *Spectra* vary in topic, but tend to make use of visual description in a way that is more similar to the poems in *Some Imagist Poets* than *BLAST*. The poems especially rely on the description of material objects to create their visual images and their humorous effects. For example, Knish's "Opus 131" catalogs objects that the speaker (striking a fin de siècle note) claims she is "weary of":

> Ivory on a fan of Venice,
> Black-pearl of a bowl of Japan,
> Prismatic lustres of Phoenician glass
> Fawn-tinged embroideries from looms of Bagdad.

Portrait poems by both Knish and Morgan employ the familiar device of comparing the subject to a thing, usually with humorous contrast, such as Knish's "Upstairs there lies a sodden thing / Sleeping" ("Op. 122"), or "Her fair and featurous face / Writhed like / An albino boa-constrictor" ("Op. 195"). Morgan's blazon-like "Op. 40" pivots on a "turn" that renders the list of things ridiculous by comparing them to parts of the subject, such as:

> Two cocktails round a smile,
>   A grapefruit after grace,
> Flowers in an aisle
>   . . . Were your face.[79]

The comparisons go only one step beyond Lowell's appreciative "She is like violets under the misted glass of a cold frame" or Pound's disapproving, but still serious, comparison of a woman to her white lapdog in "Albâtre." In keeping with the conventions of traditional portraiture, Bynner ends the poem with the subject's soul, while making sure to deflate this concept as well:

> Sun on the Hellespont,
>   White swimmers in the bowl
> Of the baptismal font
>   Are your soul.

In brevity, point, and use of person-thing comparisons, these satirical portraits perfectly capture the style and form of the Imagist portrait. Reduction is, in a sense, the formal solution that Ficke was seeking in "Sonnets of a Portrait Painter," where his message about the diminished scope of modern love seems unsuited to the courtly form of the sonnet and the elaborate narrative of the sequence.

Portraiture remained a favored genre in the Spectric movement beyond the initial volume by Ficke and Bynner. Many of the poems withheld from the original volume or published later in periodicals announced their generic affiliation plainly in their titles, as in Bynner's "Self-Portrait" and "Portrait of a Poet" and Ficke's "Portrait of a Poetess" (representing his friend Edna St. Vincent Millay). The poet Marjorie Sieffert joined the group as "Elijah Hay" after the publication of *Spectra,* and contributed a new subgenre of portrait that she called a "Spectrum." Alfred Kreymborg's *Others* ran a "Spectric Issue" in January 1917, and a group of Sieffert's contributions are entitled "Spectrum of Mrs. X," "Of Mrs. Y," "Of Mrs. Z," and "Of Mrs. & So Forth," playing on the name of the movement to suggest that each poem yields a picture of its subject. In "Of Mrs. & So Forth," Sieffert compares "old ladies" to "house-flies" and the subject, "you," to "a fly drowning in a cocktail!"[80] These short poems, none longer than six lines, incorporate the point of epigram to achieve their humorous effect. Sieffert's contributions suggest that she understood portraiture to be at the heart of the movement: Spectrism itself was a parody of Lowell, Pound, and other members of the Anglo-American avant-garde, as Morgan's contribution entitled "The Little Review" makes explicit: "A candle with no holder, lighting / A Victory with no head."[81]

Bynner found the epigrammatic portrait such a suitable vessel for his sense of humor that he continued to compose in this form after the hoax was discovered in 1918. In 1920, "Emmanuel Morgan" published a volume consisting entirely of two-line epigrammatic portraits of contemporary literary figures. Bynner's *Pins for Wings* beautifully demonstrates the tendency of reduction in the modern portrait poem. Each poem consists of a title that names the subject—"Richard Aldington"—and an object that stands for the individual: "an Attic vase / full of tea." Typically, the object has elevated connotations that are negated in the second line for humorous effect. Thus each portrait diminishes its subject by raising expectations for poetic loftiness and then dashing them:

> T. S. ELIOT
> the wedding cake
> of two tired cultures

H.D.
Winged Victory
hopping

WALLACE STEVENS
the shine of a match
in an empty pipe[82]

In these poems, Bynner has reduced the Imagist portrait to its fundamental formula: person = thing. Even as he parodies this formula, Bynner's capacity to spin out endless variations reflects its vitality. His noun-
phrase epigrams mark the point of greatest condensation of the short
portrait, and indeed the lower limit of brevity consistent with describing
a subject. *Pins for Wings* also reflects the tendency toward aggregation
that accompanies the contraction of the portrait. Whereas longer portraits
such as Eliot's "Portrait of a Lady" have the mass to stand alone in the
pages of a literary magazine or in a collection of varied genres, the contracted portrait is too insubstantial to stand alone, and seeks others of its
own kind.

Perhaps the best example of short portraits gathered in a sequence is
Masters's *Spoon River Anthology,* a work that also demonstrates the continuity between the Rossettian sonnet sequence and the modern epitaphic portrait. *Spoon River* is at once an exemplary instance of Modernist
portraiture and also not a perfect fit with the genre, for the more than
240 character sketches in this collection combine first person dramatic
speech with the objectivity and concision of epitaph. Like Pound and
Eliot, Masters's work might be seen as the hybrid product of Rossetti and
Browning. Masters acknowledged his debt to Browning in the penultimate portrait, "Elijah Browning." His apprenticeship to Rossetti is less
obvious. In 1910, Masters published *Songs and Sonnets,* a collection ending with a twenty-eight-sonnet sequence concerning an unhappy love affair, complete with many of the narrative highlights of the *House of Life,*
such as the moment of meeting outdoors (IV) and the consummation of
the relationship (VI). Like Ficke's "Sonnets of a Portrait Painter," Masters's "Sonnet-Sequence" reflects on his Beloved's decline from the Pre-
Raphaelite ideal, which makes the sonnet itself a less fitting vehicle for
describing her:

> Sometimes, meseems, your heart has turned a rose. . . .
> And yet, betimes, the old unwelcome tone

> Turns the soft poem of your voice to prose,
> And your heart hardens to a scentless bud.
> Something within your life has made you rock,
> O'er which thin earth defeats deep husbandry.[83]

Masters contrasts her current hardness with the poetic "rose" that she was or should be; yet, as Ficke's expression "enamelled softness" suggests, this hardness was always a quality of Rossetti's beloved, whose lacquered surface is aesthetically appealing but not, finally, an opening to interior recesses. The change from Rossetti to Masters or Ficke is a slight adjustment of attitude, a chilling acknowledgment of the loss of interiority that Rossetti's visual and verbal gorgeousness literally glosses over. And, like Ficke, Masters found that the sonnet sequence was not quite the right form for exploring this diminished subject.

Masters was a literary naturalist, an approach that has surprising connections to Aestheticism. The naturalist, like the aesthete, has an essentially materialist view of human beings as constituted by their bodies; for both, sensory experience and particularly sexual experience are paramount. Rossetti and Swinburne's willingness to treat sexuality with unprecedented frankness no doubt made it possible for naturalists such as Masters and his friend Theodore Dreiser to push the boundaries even further.[84] While Rossetti finds transcendence of the self in sexual union, however, *Spoon River* represents sexuality as a misunderstood force that drives lives to ruin: "Hear me, ambitious souls, / Sex is the curse of life!"[85] Masters's representation of life as a "rat trap" reflects his religious skepticism and his reading of other naturalists including Dreiser and Stephen Crane.[86]

Masters's naturalist pessimism and unvarnished treatment of modern life also had a poetic source, however: the *Greek Anthology*. "It would have been fitting had I dedicated Spoon River Anthology to you," Masters wrote to Marion Reedy in the dedication of his 1918 *Toward the Gulf*. "You know that it was you who pressed upon my attention in June, 1909, the Greek Anthology. It was from contemplation of its epitaphs that my hand unconsciously strayed to the . . . first written and first printed sketches of The Spoon River Anthology," which *Reedy's Mirror* had introduced to the world in 1915.[87] In the epigrams of the *Greek Anthology*, Masters found a poetic form that was "something less than verse, yet more than prose," a variety of tones, "ironical and tender, satirical and sympathetic," that suited his needs, and most of all, the idea of shaping his material in the form of epitaphs.[88] A frank acceptance of the finality of death and the futility of human aspirations also carries over from the Greek epitaphs to those of Masters. Masters often expressed such views in a concluding turn at the end of the poem: "These are driving him to the place where I lie. / In death, therefore, I am avenged" ("Ollie McGee"); "But I proclaim from the dust / That he slew me from his hatred" ("Amanda Barker").[89] This device reflected both the influence of the Greek epigram and his proficiency as a sonneteer. Indeed, Masters's free verse poems average only a few lines over fourteen. Thus he was able to translate his Aesthetic disposition and skill as a sonneteer into the naturalist epitaph expressing the downward trajectory of human life into the grave. From ekphrasis it is a short step to the pointing gesture of epitaph: "this granite pedestal / Bearing the words, 'Pro Patria.' / What do they mean, anyway?"[90]

"In the *Spoon River Anthology,* Mr. Webster Ford unites something of the feeling and method of the Greek Anthology with a trace of the spirit of Villon," wrote Ezra Pound approvingly in *Poetry,* soon after the first installment of *Spoon River* appeared in *Reedy's Mirror,* under the alias of Ford.[91] Pound was quick to recognize a project similar to his own (already explored in poems such as "Epitaph" of 1913), and he likely also took inspiration from Masters's more ambitious use of the epitaphic portrait to represent a social system through its effect on individual lives. Indeed, Pound soon echoed the rhythms and structures of *Spoon River* in *Hugh Selwyn Mauberley,* a similar collection of epitaphs commenting on modern existence.[92] *Spoon River* and *Mauberley* thus exemplify not only the epigrammatic modulation of the portrait, but also its tendency to aggregate, to gather together. The loose structure of *Spoon River* again derives from the model of the *Greek Anthology:* not a sequence per se but a "gathering of flowers."[93] While Masters's *Songs and Sonnets* preserves some elements of the Rossettian autobiographical sequence (itself not strictly chronological, but shaped by an emotional arc of fading love), *Spoon River* instead relates a wide variety of characters through a neutral medium, the ground that they share. Pound surely observed Masters's simplifying solution to the problem of organization in *Spoon River.* The problem, in short, is how to enlarge the canvas of the portrait to include multiple figures and yet keep it coherent as a single work. This is the challenge of expansion, to which we now turn.

FIVE

Expansion

EZRA POUND AND AVANT-GARDE PORTRAITURE

IN THE YEARS FOLLOWING its Imagist contraction, the portrait poem breathed out, multiplying into collections and expanding into longer and more complex forms. From Masters's book-length *Spoon River Anthology* in 1915 to the twenty-nine portraits in E. E. Cummings's *Tulips and Chimneys* (1922) and Melvin Tolson's 1935 *Gallery of Harlem Portraits,* the Modernist portrait collection became a site for exploring social relationships through a multiplicity of characters, rather than (as in earlier stand-alone portraits) the nature of consciousness and identity. Placed in this context, Ezra Pound's sequences written between 1913 and 1920 are evidence of a change in the shape and aims of portraiture. From the early group portrait "Les Millwins" of 1913 to the sequences "Moeurs Contemporaines" (1918) and *Hugh Selwyn Mauberley* (1920), Pound gradually expanded the scale of his canvas by adding figures, concluding with *Mauberley,* his longest and final work of lyric poetry. Unlike *Spoon River* or *Harlem Portraits,* which are organized geographically to tell the story of the inhabitants of a place, Pound superimposed the multiple figures of each group portrait on the shadowy outline of a single quasi-autobiographical protagonist, thereby retaining traits of the single-figure portrait. By setting multiple short portraits inside the frame of a single-figure composition, "Moeurs" and *Mauberley* test the capacity of the genre for expansion. How big can a portrait poem get before it becomes a catalogue of names, before it loses its distinctive concern with interiority, consciousness, and face-to-face engagement?

Epigrammatic modulation had diminished the significance of the individual subject while shrinking the scale of the portrait, but kept the single figure as its focus. Pound's many devices for expanding the scale of his portraits subjected the genre to a more thoroughgoing revision, perhaps to the point of transforming it into something else—though in 1921 he was still content to collect "Moeurs" and *Mauberley* under the title *Three Portraits and Four Cantos*. In this chapter I examine what happened to the portrait poem as Pound added figures and tested out a variety of avant-garde techniques drawn from the visual and performance arts. The test, as I see it, was to see how far the core concerns of single-figure portraiture could go when mapped onto the larger canvas of multifigure compositions. In particular, "Moeurs" extends the work of "Portrait d'une femme" in detaching interiority from the individual subject and reconfiguring it as a fluid medium. This sequence draws from a variety of avant-garde arts to develop a multimedia approach to the group portrait. The exchange among arts comes to serve as a model of intersubjective exchange. In *Mauberley*, by contrast, the project of reanimating interiority falters, and the sequence becomes more concerned with the object-like impermeability of individual figures.

Pound's movement toward multifigure portraiture owed much to his involvement in the avant-garde revolution in London from 1913 to 1919. The density and disjunctiveness of "Moeurs" and *Mauberley* reflect Pound's avant-garde commitment and also the difficulty of revising a nineteenth-century genre for Modernist purposes. Avant-garde art posed a special challenge to the portrait poem. As early as 1906, painters in France and Italy challenged the composition of the portrait and its very identity as a genre of painting. In the history of early twentieth-century painting, Marcia Pointon writes, "modernism and the portrait might be said to be impacted, welded together," but this is true more for Cubism than Futurism, which attacked the single-figure portrait.[1]

These two artistic movements operated as catalyzing influences on modern poetry, in ways that have been much examined by critics.[2] Early Modernism could be dated from the masklike face of Picasso's *Portrait of Gertrude Stein* (1906), through the apex of Analytic Cubism in his portraits of Kahnweiler and Vollard (1910), to the synthetic portraits of Eva Gouel (such as *Woman in an Armchair*, 1913, and *Portrait of a Girl*, 1914), ending with his return to representation in the neoclassical studies of the spring of 1914. During this period Picasso painted and drew many portraits of himself, his lovers, and his acquaintances, progressively "analyzing" the features of the face, first into blank masklike elements (as in the portrait of Stein), then gradually "slicing" the face and figure into more and more geometric shapes and planes with an emphasis still placed compositionally on the face (as in the *Portrait of Ambroise Vollard*), and finally, returning to portraiture through the lens of collage, reassembling the figure of the body in a referential but nonillusionistic way.[3] While this artistic adventure questioned the most fundamental principles of portraiture, especially that the painting should represent a recognizable, unique individual, still Picasso continued to work with reference to the portrait genre.[4] Picasso's return to representational portraiture in 1914, and the continued centrality of the genre throughout his career, suggests that his experimentation never significantly undermined the validity of portraiture for him, and he continued to work within the framework of single-figure composition.

The compatibility of Cubism and portraiture is exemplified by Picasso's fruitful friendship and artistic collaboration with Gertrude Stein, the subject of his first proto-Cubist portrait. Stein's interest in issues of mimesis and her close relationships with avant-garde painters in Paris make her experimentation with portraiture seem inevitable in hindsight. As early as 1908, Stein began composing prose portraits of individuals in a "Cubist" style. The earliest of these, such as "Picasso" and "Matisse," experiment with linguistic representation by multiplying the portraitist's point of view into many similar but slightly varied descriptive statements that correspond to the multiplication of angles of vision in the Analytic Cubist portrait. Stein composed over 130 literary portraits of individuals in a variety of styles between 1908 and her death in 1946. Wendy Steiner argues that her work in this genre was driven by a paradox at the heart of literary portraiture: how language can imitate an individual. Steiner finds that, finally, the outcome of her experimentation was "tragic" in the sense that she found the aims of portraiture could not be carried out in writing: "The desire to tell the strict 'truth,' to put upon the canvas or page an exact copy of what is in the mind, by-passes reality and leads quite predictably . . . to nonrepresentational work."[5] Stein's experimentation tends in much the same direction as abstraction in painting—toward pure form. She continued to compose short prose pieces titled with their subjects' names throughout her career, however, a testament to her commitment to the single-figure composition even as she emptied the genre of its representational content.

The challenges for writing under the influence of Futurism were quite different from the issues that Cubism raised for Stein. While Cubism undermined the mimetic function that had motivated and justified visual art for millennia, Futurism instead attacked the tradition of an art that privileged the single human figure. Futurism elevated the machine over the human body, dynamism and speed over the stasis of portraiture, and groups over single figures. The 1910 *Manifesto of Futurist Painters* exhorts its readers to "throw out" and "finish off . . . the Portraitists."[6] The *Technical Manifesto of Futurist Painting* established the values of the movement against single-figure compositions (the nude in particular). Instead, the manifesto promoted movement and interpenetration as compositional principles. In contrast to the Cubist technique of analyzing the many geometric units by which a single figure is composed, the Futurists would demonstrate the fundamental interpenetration of figures previously seen to be separate:

> Who can still believe in the opacity of bodies, since our sharpened and multiplied sensitiveness has already penetrated the obscure manifestations of the medium? Why should we forget in our creations the doubled power of our sight, capable of giving results analogous to those of the X-rays? . . .
>
> The sixteen people around you in a rolling motor bus are in turn and at the same time one, ten, four, three; they are motionless and they change places; they come and go, bound into the street, are suddenly swallowed up by the sunshine, then come back and sit before you, like persistent symbols of universal vibration.[7]

The concept of interpenetration was a major component in the program of dynamism by which the Futurists distinguished themselves from past painters, and more important, from Cubism. Titles such as Giacomo Balla's *Iridescent Compenetration* indicate this orientation.

It is well known that Vorticism, officially represented in the spring of 1914 by Wyndham Lewis's Rebel Art Center and in June of that year by the first issue of *BLAST,* had close ties with Futurism. Until shortly before the publication of *BLAST,* the periodical was conceived of as a review of new art movements, including Futurism, rather than a defensively hostile attack on Futurism's founder, Marinetti. In its attitude to portraiture, Vorticism was far more like Futurism than Cubism. The titles of illustrations in the first issue of *BLAST* suggest the painters' disposition toward groups of figures: Lewis's *Slow Attack* and *Plan of War* (as well as his famous oil painting of 1914, *The Crowd*), Edward Wadsworth's *March,* W. Roberts's *Dancers,* Cuthbert Hamilton's *The Group,* and so on. In Vorticist painting, according to Dasenbrock, "Portraiture as such is almost unknown."[8] There are exceptions to this rule, including Lewis's *Portrait of an Englishwoman,* reproduced in *BLAST* 1. Without its title, however, the painting would be unrecognizable as a portrait (unlike, for example, Picasso's portrait of Ambroise Vollard, which is clearly oriented around a face, however distorted). Walter Michel, Lewis's cataloguer, writes that the painting "could be viewed as a plan for an apartment house," and for Richard Cork, it "transforms the theme of femininity into a series of frankly mechanistic shapes."[9] Even in a representational interpretation, such as that offered by Paul Edwards, the thickest of the diagonal black bars might be understood either as a goose-stepping, dark-trousered leg, or as a phallic protrusion, but in either case this suggestion runs absolutely counter to the idea of "Englishwoman" indicated by the title. Lewis's "Portrait" in a sense confirms his programmatic objection to single-figure composition, declared in *BLAST* 1:

> We all today (possibly with a coldness reminiscent of the insect= world) are in each other's vitals—overlap, intersect, and are Siamese to any extent. . . .
>
> The human form still runs, like a wave, through the texture or body of existence, and therefore of art.
>
> But just as the old form of egotism is no longer fit for such conditions as now prevail, so the isolated human figure of most ancient Art is an anachronism.
>
> THE ACTUAL HUMAN BODY BECOMES OF LESS IMPORTANCE EVERY DAY.
>
> It now, literally, EXISTS much less.[10]

Lewis's statement that "the actual human body becomes of less importance every day" would soon be proved true by the grisly realities of the war. But that is not the context in which it was written. Lewis's artistic manifesto illuminates the already reduced size of the poetic portrait *before* the impact of Futurism, let alone war. Robinson, Pound, H.D., Lowell, Eliot, Ficke, Bynner, and Masters had each in their own way diminished or bade farewell to the individual portrait subject. Furthermore, Pound had been experimenting since 1913 with portrait sequences and group portraits that emphasize a combination of figures over the free-standing individual. "Amitiés," "Ladies," "The Social Order," "Epitaphs," and "Impressions" of *Lustra* are short sequences of individual portraits, while "Les Millwins" and "Bellaires" each assemble multiple figures in a single composition. "Dompna Pois" combines these approaches by representing a single "lady" composed of traits drawn from other women. As he developed more complex ways of assembling figures that went beyond a simple numbered list, Pound was working toward an expanded form of portraiture. In this form he sought to accommodate the Futurist-Vorticist aesthetic of multiplicity. Yet, unlike Marinetti or Lewis, Pound continued to be committed to portraiture as a genre, retaining its traditional

traits even as he dispersed them among overlapping or intersecting figures. Pound had a longstanding interest in the way that interiority can
be shared between two people, and he now sought ways of spreading out
that interspace among larger groups of figures.

I examine three different strategies that Pound employed to expand
his portraits: the concept of intersection in a "futurist X," the narrative of
failed development adopted from the modern Bildungsroman, and the
metaphor of the gallery or museum. To preview these three strategies, I
turn first to a prose work that has been described both as a portrait and
as his most avant-garde composition: *Gaudier-Brzeska: A Memoir* (1916).
As well as a monument to Pound's friend Henri Gaudier-Brzeska and the
short-lived Vorticist movement, Pound's memoir uses the more flexible
and adaptable medium of prose to try out a number of devices used in his
portrait sequences of 1917 and 1919. Combining narration of Gaudier's
life, quotation from his letters and remarks, the testimony of people who
knew him, Pound's own articles on Vorticism from *The New Age,* and an
illustrated catalog of Gaudier's work accompanied by Pound's commentary, this highly experimental work has often been offered as "exhibit
A" in the case for Pound's radical break with the past and embrace of
avant-garde techniques. Marjorie Perloff calls it a "portrait of the artist as
collage-text" and compares it to Gino Severini's 1913 *Portrait of Marinetti,*
which combines collage (the printed titles of Marinetti's major works
pasted on to the canvas over his head) with a Cubist-inspired rendering in
paint of Marinetti's face from several angles.[11] Her reading of the memoir emphasizes its narrative discontinuity and similarities to avant-garde
visual art. The use of surprising intersections that echo Futurist visual art
is the first of the three strategies that Pound developed in response to the
avant-garde challenge in portraiture, as early as "Les Millwins" of 1913.
This poem about a performance of the Ballets Russes explores the theme
of intersection among art forms and between individuals, offering what
it calls a "futurist X" as a pattern for the shocking encounter of audiences
with modernity.

As Perloff's allusion to James Joyce's *A Portrait of the Artist as a Young
Man* suggests, however, *Gaudier-Brzeska* also follows a novelistic model.
In telling the story of Gaudier's development into an artist, discovery of
a personal style, and entry into a group of like-minded artists, Pound
adopts the novelistic narrative of development. The basic narrative of education and socialization underlies many if not most nineteenth-century
novels, including some of Pound's favorites: Flaubert's *Sentimental Education,* Henry James's *The Portrait of a Lady,* and Joyce's *Portrait.* Indeed, as

these titles suggest, the term "Portrait" may be a generic flag for the novel of development.[12] While the term "portrait" in painting indicates treatment of a single figure to the exclusion of other topics, within the capacious form of the novel the single figure is seen against the background of a social network, with the protagonist as narrative focal point. The novel of development typically traces the protagonist's coming to terms with this social network. Franco Moretti calls the Bildungsroman "the symbolic form that more than any other has portrayed and promoted modern socialization."[13] The "portraits" of James and Joyce—as well as novels of development by Stendhal and Flaubert—provided Pound with models for portraiture within a social context, where a primary character develops in relation to other figures.

Pound's *Memoir* of Gaudier brings together the formal structure of rupture—cutting and pasting elements in order to emphasize their disconnectedness—with a narrative of development that attempts to suture together the broken elements.[14] The memoir begins with Gaudier's death notice, commenting, "It is part of the war waste."[15] Pound's choice of pronoun, "it," emphasizes the shocking reduction of his living friend to a thing, recapitulating the familiar process of Imagist portraiture (where a person is analogized to an object) in a new, ghastly light. The work that follows attempts to recast that shocking information in such a way that it can be understood within an intelligible narrative of artistic progress and achievement. Pound offers conventional details of the artist's life, such as the hardworking father, his talent as a youth, and success in school. Despite Gaudier's "revolt" against academic art at the age of twenty and his resulting loss of public support, the story of the young man's life ultimately follows the traditional pattern of the novel of development, in which the isolated youth is educated and establishes himself in a social context. Gaudier's appearance in an art gallery next to Pound—"like a Greek god in a vision"—marks the beginning of his relationship with the poet and the Vorticist movement. The avant-garde art gallery is, in effect, the institution where he finds his social place. The illustrated catalog of Gaudier's work at the end of the memoir is this place, a virtual community of art-lovers into which Gaudier must now be dispersed because he is dead.

The portrait sequence "Moeurs Contemporaines" roughly follows the same pattern of development, except here Pound emphasizes an element of failure that is latent in *Gaudier-Brzeska* (but which Pound avoids because he is paying homage to his friend). As in *Gaudier-Brzeska*, the protagonist of "Moeurs" seeks to integrate himself in conventional institutions (school, work, and marriage), finds his avenues for self-development blocked, and turns to a virtual community symbolized in Pound's memoir by the catalogue of Gaudier's works and in "Moeurs" by the memory and echoes of conversation. *Hugh Selwyn Mauberley* similarly contains many of the elements of the modern Bildungsroman, emphasizing development less and failure more, but still seeking to place the central protagonist in a context of other figures as a compositional strategy. *Gaudier-Brzeska,* "Moeurs," and *Mauberley* are all punctuated with moments of death, actual and metaphorical, moments that make the necessity of finding an adequate form of portraiture all the more pressing.

Gaudier-Brzeska thus experiments with different strategies for assembling the portrait of one man out of many pieces of his life and social milieu. The collage is one such strategy; a second is narrative, telling the story of Gaudier's development and his relationships with other people; and a third is the gallery, an institution that selects and arranges works of visual art for viewing. They differ, of course, in how we experience each one: collage aims for sudden impact, for instantaneousness, while narrative is chronologically organized and experienced over time. The art gallery as a model has both spatial and temporal aspects. In a gallery, all the works may be seen at once, or one by one; the works may all date from the same time, or they may document the past and trace the changes in art over periods of history. The scene in the gallery where Pound meets Gaudier for the first time brings together the temporal dimension of the memoir—the narrative of Gaudier's search for a like-minded community—with its spatial dimension as the place where Gaudier's works are gathered for sale and for posterity. The gallery suggests a different model for the memoir as a whole: not the flat collage but a three-dimensional location where figures intersect in space and even across time. Likewise, "Moeurs" is set in several interior spaces where figures from different times encounter each other: the house of the novelist, the opera, and the bedroom of the "very old lady." As in *Gaudier,* Pound invests an almost mystical significance to such places, as though they hold out the possibility for remaining "in" a living tradition with deep roots in the past. *Mauberley,* however, likens the portrait sequence to a museum (or bottle of pickled bones) where figures of the past are preserved for our viewing. Revisiting major figures and monuments of Aestheticism, the work is both a museum of individuals and of portrait types, reviewing a dazzling array of subgenres (ekphrastic, epigrammatic, epitaphic, dramatic, etc.). The sequence expands the portrait to an unprecedented length and complexity, then bids farewell to the genre along with London and

Pound's career as a lyric poet. The journey toward avant-garde portraiture that began at the Russian Ballet in 1913 ends in *Mauberley*, paradoxically returning to the Rossetti circle where the modern portrait poem began.

"Les Millwins" and the "Futurist X"

"Les Millwins" of 1913 specifically identifies the group portrait with avant-garde art, associating its own style with both the Ballets Russes and Futurism.[16] Dorothy Shakespear mentioned "Les Millwins" in a letter of March 14, two weeks after she and Pound had made plans to attend a performance of the Ballets Russes.[17] The poem portrays a group of Edwardian ballet-goers, comparing their "mauve and greenish souls" to "unused boas" "lying along the upper seats," in an analogy typical of Pound's Imagist thing-portraits.[18] The Millwins are not the whole subject of the poem, however. Their attention is focused on the excited Slade students who are also attending the performance. The focal point of the poem is the image of the art students' arms "Crossed in great futuristic X's," a shape that reflects stylistic motifs of both Nijinsky's choreography and Futurist artwork.

Pound's "futuristic X" identifies a motif characterizing the avant-garde movements in painting and dance, importing it into his poem as a sign of intersection and combination. Daniel Albright's concept of an "aesthetic pre-entity" can help explain Pound's "futuristic X." Albright explains how some Modernist works combine multiple artistic media by "understand[ing] music and poetry and painting as interchangeable, a set of easy, fluid transforms," originating in some "thing" that lies beneath the medium. "At the origin of the . . . work of art lies some aesthetic pre-entity that dwells in a kind of limbo, not yet literary or musical or pictorial—though it may extend itself into any of these domains."[19] An aesthetic pre-entity provides the basis for intermedial connections, which flourished in early Modernism, especially in the multimedia productions of theater, opera, and dance. Pound's "Les Millwins" registers such an entity, an "X" found in both Nijinsky's choreography and Futurist art. Although the poem refers to *Cleopatra* as the ballet on stage, Pound had tickets for the March 1 performance of Nijinsky in *L'Après-midi d'un faune*, which expressed a raw, primitive, and hard-edged aesthetic, in contrast to the popular orientalism of *Cleopatra*, a revival from 1910. While *Cleopatra* would have been more to the taste of the Millwins (whose "mauve and greenish" souls reflect the purple and green color scheme of that ballet), the Slade students would have been unlikely to get so excited about it. The responses of the Slade students suggest that *they* are seen viewing the much more experimental *Faune,* featuring "rigid poses and angular movements."[20] Contemporary comments on Diaghilev's ballet emphasize its two-dimensionality: "The bodies of the dancers were invariably facing the audience while their heads and limbs were rigidly in profile. There were few contiguous movements; they passed by rapid change from one static pose to another."[21] Nijinsky made only one leap (his stock in trade) in the entire ballet. Writing in 1921, W. A. Propert described the ballet as the "most irritating performance imaginable," in which the humanity of the dancers was "ruthlessly suppressed."[22]

Perhaps the most notoriously confrontational aspect of the ballet was its raw sexuality, expressed in the concluding scene by Nijinsky dancing the part of the Faun. Having stolen a scarf from a fleeing nymph, the besotted Faun fondled the scarf and then, lying face down on it with his hands under his body, simulated masturbation with a sudden jerk of his body. This ending had caused a public disturbance at the Paris premier the year before, leading to American headlines such as "WICKED PARIS SHOCKED AT LAST."[23] In both *Cleopatra* and *Faune,* a fabric prop provided the occasion for an erotic climax, but in contrast to Cleopatra's strip-tease, the Faun's unlicensed display of his aggressive sexuality on top of the nymph's scarf was calculated to affront and shock, not to entice, the audience. This moment introduced a new era in the relationship of the artist to his audience, which was fully announced by *Le Sacre du printemps* and the ensuing riot.[24] With reference to the Ballets Russes, then, Pound's "X" evokes both the angular, jerky style of dancing it featured, and also its confrontational relationship to the audience. This confrontation is mirrored in "Les Millwins" by the relationship between the shocked but fascinated Millwins and the "rigorous," "exalted," and "exult[ing]" Slade students. In "Les Millwins," the two eras and aesthetic styles represented by these two groups of figures meet, intersect, and clash, in an event that is very well captured by the sign "X."

By identifying the appreciative art students with Futurism, Pound explicitly links dance with painting. In the avant-garde milieu that Pound entered in 1913, dance was the metaphor par excellence of interpenetration and intersection. While this metaphor had a basis in nineteenth-century English and French poetry, beginning in 1909, Diaghilev's Ballets Russes had shifted its meaning away from harmony and transcendence and toward dissonance, primitivism, and angularity. A number of important Futurist paintings from 1912–1913 reflect the integration of Futurist themes with those of Diaghilev's dancers, including Gino Severini's *The Blue Dancer* and *Dynamism of a Dancer* (1912), and Francis Picabia's *Star*

FIG. 9. Wyndham Lewis (1882–1957), *The Dancers*, 1912. Ink and watercolor on paper, 30.2 x 29.2 cm. (Manchester City Art Galleries; © By kind permission of the Wyndham Lewis Memorial Trust [a registered charity])

Dancer and Her School of Dance (1913). In England, as Cork notes, the theme of dance more than any other "fired rebel artists in their search for the perfect equation between form and content."[25]

Wyndham Lewis, himself a former Slade student, explored the subject of dancing figures in many prewar works. When Pound became friendly with Lewis at the beginning of 1913, he may well have seen two of these in particular: *The Dancers* (a watercolor study for the lost oil painting *Kermesse*), and a larger oil painting *Danse* (now lost). In *The Dancers* (fig. 9), three figures with impassive, masklike expressions form the shape of a "dynamic 'X' composition, with many subsidiary rhythms among the variously dislocated members of the figures."[26] Lewis's watercolor is composed out of numerous X and V shapes made by the crossed bodies of the dancers, as well as single arms bent in V shapes, bent legs, parted legs, crotches, the shapes of the three dancers' faces, and the angles of their eyes. In the context of the overall X structure of the painting, the V shapes have the appearance of dislocated halves of Xs. It is perhaps this X configuration that appears in "Les Millwins" as a "futuristic X" of arms. In early 1913, Pound would have associated Lewis with Futurism, a movement that Lewis at that time saw as a healthy alternative to the Bloomsbury-Paris axis of art.[27]

"X" was to become an important sign in 1913–14. In the summer of 1913, Nijinsky's choreography for Debussy's *Jeux* would place dancers in the shape of an X, in a "rigid and geometrical" formation noted by reviewers and compared to Cubism in painting.[28] The X shape also appears in a number of Futurist works from these years, including Giacomo Balla's *Compenetration* series of 1913, experiments with colored diamond and triangular shapes in an uncharacteristically orderly pattern of repeated Xs. Severini, the Futurist painter for whom Pound expressed the most admiration, painted a self-portrait in 1912–13 with lines intersecting in the face in the shape of Xs.[29] Carlo Carrà's "words in freedom" compositions, which profoundly affected Vorticism and Pound's writing specifically, favor a radial pattern that suggests the intersection of a spiral with an X. This pattern bears a strong resemblance to the vortex shape adopted by Lewis late in 1913 as a symbol for their nascent group.[30] The mere choice of the name "Vortex" foregrounds not only the shape of the X, but also the letters X and V, a fortuitous conjunction that may have reinforced Pound's sense of the symbolic significance of this shape or letter.[31]

In "Les Millwins" as well as Lewis's *The Dancers,* the X shape captures the intersection of *media* as well as of bodies. "Exalted" by the spectacle, the Slade students raise their arms to reflect the movements they see on stage, thus suggesting an intersection of painting and dance. Lewis's painting, too, is intermedial in this sense, with the X background drawing attention to the flat, still picture plane, while the figures represent the movement and three-dimensional space of dance. The X also marks the intersection of painting and dance with language. Although Pound is unlikely to have seen any of the new collage art at the time he wrote this poem, his X functions to blur the lines between visual and linguistic representation much the way Futurist word pictures and Cubist collages of newspaper clippings do. Pound further draws attention to the intermediality of X by repeating it in "exalted" and "exulted," where it functions phonetically rather than referring visually to a shape. This intersection of media seems to point to a shared idea expressed by avant-garde artists and dancers in 1913. Though he would quickly distance himself from the powerful influence of Futurism by collaborating with Lewis on building Vorticism, the idea of spatial and intermedial intersection remained a structuring principle of his multifigure portraits.

The idea of intersection is also represented in the embedded structure of three different views in the poem: the Millwins' view of the Slade students; the speaker's view of the Millwins and the Slade students, and everyone's view of the dancers on stage, at the invisible center of the poem.

> And the little Millwins beheld these things;
> With their large and anaemic eyes they looked out upon this
>   configuration.
>
> Let us therefore mention the fact,
> For it seems to us worthy of record.[32]

The speaker/portraitist watches the Millwins watching the Slade students, who themselves watch and are engrossed in the Ballets Russes performance. With their boa-like souls and "anaemic eyes," the Millwins cannot internalize what they see, because the world of Slade, Futurism, and Nijinsky is beyond their comprehension. The speaker's deadpan "recording" of the scene is little different from their numbed shock. The intersection of the various observers follows the pattern of the "futurist X," suggesting the depthless surface of collage or words-in-freedom.

Yet the site of the encounter in "Les Millwins" suggests another sign or symbol as well: the Royal Opera House, the public space where these disparate figures come into contact with each other. Launching the Russian Ballet at the Royal Opera in Covent Garden ensured a degree of social prestige to the event, despite the potentially scandalous content of the performances.[33] In selecting this venue, the Russian Ballet drew both a fashionable audience and theater-goers interested in the avant-garde, a mixture registered in "Les Millwins." The three-dimensional opera house provides what none of the individual audience members can: an interior that in some sense "comprehends" the meeting of unrelated individuals and the encounter between past and futurity. In the Opera, Pound finds a metaphor for the "empty space" of self that he had articulated as early as "Histrion" and developed in "Portrait d'une femme" as the medium of the sea. Instead of an abstraction, here, the space of intersection is a real place in which people meet and exchange ideas. This setting offers to recover some of the interiority lost by the shocking encounter with modernity, not within the individual figures but between them.

"Moeurs Contemporaines"

Writing *Gaudier-Brzeska: A Memoir* in 1915 prepared Pound for expanding the framework of the poetic portrait. Like his memoir, "Moeurs Contemporaines" combines the narrative of individual development with sketches of other figures whose lives are in contact with the central subject. Working with the portrait's traditional focus on the character of a single figure, Pound broadened the scope of the genre to take into consideration the many relations of intersection, connection, and conflict in which an individual life takes shape. In what follows, I read "Moeurs" as Pound's take on the Modernist novel of development (with a downward trajectory toward failure or nonidentity), featuring a thinly disguised autobiographical protagonist. Indirect references to Pound's marriage to Dorothy Shakespear in 1914, the Vorticist movement and his friendship with Henri Gaudier-Brzeska from 1914 to 1915, and the 1916 death of Henry James place the poet at the center of the sequence. The first half of the sequence consists of a series of portraits of individuals who fail to mature or realize their ambitions, ending with a satiric self-epitaph, "Stele." As the protagonist of these sections gradually acknowledges his condition of "nonidentity," a different model of interiority emerges, not predicated on the individual. If the first half deconstructs the idea of individual development, the second half builds the theory that interiority is like a room in which two or more people are conversing. Unlike a physical space, however, this "embedded" interiority admits the presence of figures from across time, as in the bedroom of the "very old lady" in the closing "Ritratto" (portrait) of the sequence. This room incorporates the idea of intersection from the "futurist X" while recuperating an older conception of three-dimensional interiority, now spread out over multiple figures in space and time. Like Swinburne's "Before the Mirror," "Moeurs" expands out beyond visual art to draw on dance, instrumental music, opera, and the moving panorama as models for the interspace that the poem seeks to create in itself.

When Pound wrote "Moeurs" in December 1917, he was helping Joyce publish *Portrait of the Artist* as a book (it had appeared serially in 1914) and in the middle of rereading all of Henry James. James had died in 1916, and Pound was organizing a commemorative issue of the *Little Review* devoted to the author. Novels and novelists are a theme of the sequence, including references to Charles Nodier, Henry James, and Mary Ward. As Ronald Bush, Perloff, and others have documented, Pound's writing changed radically during these years under the influence of prose.[34] As early as 1913, Flaubert inspired Pound to champion a "prose tradition in poetry."[35] This change in Pound's writing might better be characterized as a modulation toward the novel, the "royal genre" of the period.[36] The influence of prose extends beyond style and rhythm in "Moeurs" to provide a basic narrative framework of multiple characters involved in the life of the central figure, whose disappointment and extinction the sequence documents.

The goal of the novel of development, Moretti writes, is a compromise "between the ideal of *self-determination* and the equally imperious demands of *socialization*."[37] Yet a successful compromise, one that preserves some meaningful self-determination for the protagonist, became increasingly elusive toward the end of the nineteenth century.[38] Rather, the modern novel of development brought out the hostility between the social world and the protagonist's inner reality and development, presenting their "reconciliation" as an arbitrary arrangement or a sacrifice of self rather than a realization of potential. The two works that Pound likely had in mind as models both end with an inconclusive standoff: in James's *Portrait of a Lady,* Isabel Archer's decision to return to Gilbert Osmond may be understood as an ethical choice affirming the value of fulfilling duties toward others, or as a statement about the "social realities" that constrain her actions. In *A Portrait of the Artist as a Young Man,* by contrast, Stephen Daedalus refuses integration altogether and flees Ireland. Though James's and Joyce's *Portraits* conclude in opposite ways (one protagonist accepting social bonds and duties, the other refusing them), in a sense the authors' implications about society are the same: "reconciliation" with "social reality" entails a crushing sacrifice of self. According to Gregory Castle, the outcome of the Modernist novel of development is a "consciousness of nonidentity."[39]

"Nonidentity" accurately describes the central subjectivity whose life runs as a narrative thread through both of Pound's portrait sequences. In "Moeurs," as Fogelman writes disparagingly, the figures are "empty," but this characteristic should not be taken simply as a critique of contemporary life, still less as a failing of the work.[40] Pound had already explored a similar consciousness of nonidentity in poems dating back to "Histrion" of 1908. "Portrait d'une femme" identifies nothingness as a central trait of both the poet and his subject; "Moeurs" tells the narrative of a subject who acquires this trait by giving up his aspiration to social integration. As the narrator relinquishes his role as commentator and judge, he becomes the space in which other figures emerge and speak for themselves. His nonidentity is redefined as the site or occasion of a series of embedded figures, each leading back in time or inward in space to the next.

The first four sections of "Moeurs" establish a world in which individual development and fulfillment seem blocked. The conventional avenues of marriage, family, and profession lead to disappointments, beginning with the marriage of the quasi-autobiographical protagonist and ending in section VI, "Stele," which records his epitaph. In particular, "Mr. Styrax," "Clara," and a section cut from the final version—"On the Marriage of William Hawkins, an imaginative poetaster of Hackney"— protest against marriage as an unsatisfying arrangement for husbands and wives alike.[41] The fictional Hecatomb Styrax combines elements of Pound himself and his father-in-law, Henry Hope Shakespear. Like Hecatomb Styrax, whose initials he shares, Henry Shakespear was a "blue" (a term referring to athletes from elite British schools), and his marriage at the age of 36 to Olivia Tucker had been a disappointment at least to her, leading her to pursue affairs with other men, including W. B. Yeats ("His ineptitudes / Have driven his wife from one religious excess to another").[42] Olivia's involvement in the occult might have led Pound to describe her as a "high-priestess" in the poem. Like many portraits in Pound's previous volume Lustra, "Mr. Styrax" satirizes the deadening effect of Victorian marriages, which trapped women and men alike in loveless financial relationships. The idea that such marriages exchanged, or sacrificed, individuals for money may have inspired the name "Hecatomb."

Although neither Olivia nor Henry married for money, Pound had just married Henry's daughter at twenty-eight (like Styrax), in a union that might have involved financial calculations. Pound is thus present in the portrait through his likeness to Styrax *and* through his role as a son-in-law. As a suitor for Dorothy's hand, Pound had resisted her father's demand for evidence of an income of at least £500 per year. The value of money as a basis for marriage is thus linked with the principle of paternal authority, which together imply the obligation of future husbands to take up profitable jobs such as Henry Shakespear's profession, law. The role of "father-in-law" is to impose this obligation, to which the "son-in-law of Mr. H. Styrax / objects." Yet at the same time, the figure of the son-in-law is complicit with Mr. Styrax in a way that reflects Pound's own involvement in the financial calculations of marriage: "In the parlance of Niccolo Machiavelli: / 'Thus things proceed in their circle'; / And thus the empire is maintained."[43] Empire was the source of the Shakespears' wealth, from both sides of the family, and Dorothy's £150 per year allowance effectively supported the couple for much of their lives.[44] In an irony that probably was apparent to Pound by 1917, the "empire" had provided him with a financial motivation for marrying Dorothy. The introduction of the "son-in-law of Mr. H. Styrax" in the last stanza of the portrait suggests that Pound did include himself in the economic calculus of marriage that had, in his view, ruined "hecatombs" of lives. In some ways, his own marriage with Dorothy would be not unlike Henry and Olivia's, a future that he may have recognized by 1917—a case of "things proceed[ing] in their circle." Indeed, feelings about his own marriage probably underlie the negative representation of marriage throughout "Moeurs Contemporaines," and contribute to the urgency of finding an alternative form of social integration outside of this institution. Pound's autobiographical presence here and at other moments of the sequence, such as "Nodier raconte" and "I Vecchii," make the sequence also a self-portrait; in holding a mirror up to the age, "Moeurs Contemporaines" reflects Pound in his role as the protagonist of the modern narrative of failed development.

"Mr. Styrax" thus responds to the modern novel's exploration of marriage as an institution that limits personal development and agency. Following sections expand this concern to include family and established professions, as in "Clara":

> At sixteen she was a potential celebrity . . . [now]
> Her second husband will not divorce her. . . .
> She does not desire her children,
> Or any more children.

Similarly, "Sketch 48 b. II" is a picture of stunted growth: "At the age of 27/Its home mail is still opened by its maternal parent."[45] "Moeurs" represents the conventional avenues for self-development as dead ends, where the price of social recognition and acceptance is nonidentity. The tone of disillusion cannot be attributed merely to Pound's own situation, for it is an attitude that he learned from Flaubert and Joyce. Flaubert's *Sentimental Education,* one of Pound's favorites, is described by Lukács as the first novel of disillusion, in which "a purely interior reality which is full of content and more or less complete in itself enters into competition with the reality of the outside world . . . and the failure of every attempt to realize this equality is the subject of the work."[46]

The mock epitaph "Stele" announces the protagonist's complete rejection of Edwardian "moeurs" and the institution of marriage: "After years of continence/he hurled himself into a sea of six women."[47] The title

"Stele" suggests Gaudier's *Hieratic Head of Ezra Pound*, which has the look of an Easter Island carving suggested by the term "stele."[48] Pound regarded this sculpture as a phallic symbol, appropriate to his period of extramarital sexual activity in London and coinciding with his work as a proponent of Vorticism. Wyndham Lewis described the statue as "Ezra in the form of a phallus" and Pound declared that "Bzreska is immortalizing me in a phallic column."[49] "Stele" clearly draws on this association between the sculpture and his sexual activity of the same period. Yet if adultery is the comic conclusion to a modern Bildungsroman tale, the figure of Gaudier-Brzeska points to a tragic ending. The conventional epitaphic inscription, "Siste Viator" ("stop, traveler") also commemorates Gaudier-Brzeska and the Vorticist circle. "Moeurs" construes this death as a metaphor for a general state of disappointed hopes and expectations in modern life.

The first, novelistic arc of the sequence thus extends from "Mr. Styrax" to "Stele," portraying an unnamed autobiographical subject in the context of his social milieu and personal relationships. While this narrative closes on a note of failure and extinction, it overlaps with a second arc that describes a different trajectory toward integration in a virtual world of words, images, and sounds suspended in the ether of the protagonist's "nonidentity." "Nodier raconte . . . ," "I Vecchii," and "Ritratto" develop the idea of the self as an empty space traversed by figures of other times, as an echo chamber, performance hall, or picture gallery. This interspace serves as an alternative to the traditional social institutions of marriage, family, and profession. The opening sections of the sequence represent participation in these institutions as a zero-sum game where each attempt at self-development is hemmed in or blocked by others' similar efforts. By contrast, the virtual meeting places developed in "Nodier," "I Vecchii" and "Ritratto" allow figures to overlap and blend in a way that is not negating. Individual subjectivity as such is replaced by a consciousness that occurs among and between figures in these group portraits.

In the second arc of the sequence, references to the visual arts and music proliferate, while also sustaining the theme of novels and novelists. Starting with the section headings "Stele" and "Ritratto," the sequence alludes to painting, sculpture, photography, moving panorama, dance, instrumental music, and opera. Here "Moeurs" seems to aspire to the condition of a *Gesamtkunstwerke,* or total work of art. Albright has described the Pisan Cantos as a "Noh opera," and "Moeurs" also has ambitions in that direction.[50] Pound had already composed a Noh play in 1916 called *Tristan,* featuring a hero based loosely on Gaudier-Brzeska.[51]

In 1919, Pound would begin work on his own opera, setting portions of Villon's *Testament* to music, eventually working with American composer George Antheil to produce his opera *Le testament* in 1923.[52] It is therefore not unlikely that Pound had opera in mind during the composition of "Moeurs," in which the opera house becomes a site of intersection as it is in "les Millwins."

Touching on the arts of music, dance, fiction, and photography, "Nodier raconte . . ." opens the second arc of the sequence and theorizes the relationship among the arts in Pound's emerging conception of avant-garde portraiture. This complex poem is an ekphrastic double portrait: the first half describes a faded photograph of a woman playing a harp with a baby in a basket at her side, and the second half describes a similar harp "in the home of the novelist." The little word "in" marks a difference between this portrait and "Les Millwins." In "Les Millwins," an "X" evokes the clashing perceptions of two audiences, one Edwardian and one avant-garde, who watch the same dance from different places in the theater. Like "Les Millwins," "Nodier raconte . . ." contrasts two figures from different eras, the woman in the photograph and the novelist, who share a look at the same thing, here a harp. While "Les Millwins" construes the relation of past to present as a clashing "X," however, "Nodier" suggests that the earlier image, and the time it evokes, is embedded in the later. Not "X" but "in" describes the relation of the two figures in this portrait.

The title "Nodier raconte . . ." exemplifies the embedded structure of the poem. This title quotes the first words of Théophile Gautier's "Ines de las Sierras" (1852), a poem dedicated to a Spanish dancer Gautier particularly admired, Petra Camara. Gautier's title in turn refers to an 1838 novella of the same name by Charles Nodier. Pound thus alludes to two other texts in his title, each of which concerns the embedding of the past in the present through ghostly resemblances. Nodier's "Ines de las Sierras" is a gothic portrait tale, like Poe's "The Oval Portrait" and Rossetti's unfinished "Saint Agnes of Intercession." It tells the story of two dancers, both named "Ines." The portrait of the earlier Ines hangs in the ruined gallery of an abandoned castle, and bears a striking resemblance to the living Ines, her descendant. Gautier's poem elaborates Nodier's idea that a portrait allows for direct communication between past and present. Comparing Nodier's Ines to the contemporary dancer Petra Camara, Gautier asks "Est-ce un fantôme? est-ce une femme? . . . Un rêve, une réalité."[53] He admires Camara's ability to evoke other characters, other times, and even other modes of representation. In a review of her performance in 1851, Gautier described her dancing as "somnambulistic" and compared her to a woman in a portrait by Velasquez.[54] In the poem, he interprets her dancing as a figure for the Spanish past, murdered by the present.

In "Nodier raconte . . . ," a "faded, pale, brownish photograph" embeds the past in the present, just as the figure of the older Ines is "in" the younger woman, and Nodier's Ines is "in" Gautier's Petra Camara. The photograph records a scene of communication between mother and child, where the child receives and internalizes the smile of the mother:

> And by her left foot, in a basket,
> Is an infant, aged about 14 months,
> The infant beams at the parent,
> The parent re-beams at its offspring.
> The basket is lined with satin,
> There is a satin-like bow on the harp.[55]

The mother "plays" on both her harp and her child as she draws the latter into the realm of expression, signs, and meaning (in an earlier draft of the poem, Pound wrote "Her fingers are placed on the harp-strings").[56] The child learns the language of facial expressions and acquires subjectivity by imitating the mother. The scene documents the moment in which the child inherits and internalizes a sense of self from the parent: just as the child is in the basket, so is the parent in the child, and thus the past is in the present.

This relationship between parent, child, and harp had personal significance for Pound. His 1908 sonnet "Plotinus" asks, "God! Should I be the hand upon the strings?!" The poem continues,

> But I was lonely as a lonely child.
> I cried amid the void and heard no cry,
> And then for utter loneliness, made I
> New thoughts as crescent images of *me*.[57]

In "Nodier raconte . . ." Pound has transposed the image of himself as a child to the photograph, where instead of being "lonely" and hearing "no cry," the infant "beams" at the mother. Pound now represents the image of the smile—or the sound of the harp—as arising from the intersubjective relation between mother, child, and harp rather than issuing in isolation from a subjective interior. This relation of embeddedness is not unlike the mise-en-abîme of mirrors in Whistler's *Little White Girl*. The symbol for this relation is the vortex, a term that first appeared in "Plotinus," beginning "As one that would draw thru the node of things, / Back sweeping to the vortex of the cone." Following Pound's marginal gloss on these lines in "Plotinus," William French and Timothy Materer traced the "vortex of the cone" to the writings of William Atkinson, a.k.a. "Yogi Ramacharaka," author of the popular turn-of-the-century yoga guide *Hatha Yoga*.[58] This book appears again in "Nodier raconte . . ." as one of the objects in the "home of the novelist" along with a harp and "white symbolical cups" of lilies (replicating the shape of the vortex). The presence of *Hatha Yoga* in "Nodier raconte . . ." is not only a nod to "Plotinus" but also a revision of his earlier conception of creativity in isolation. While "Plotinus" represents the poet "alone / In chaos," "Nodier" embeds him in a matrix of figures ("a friend of my wife's," the lady in the photograph, the novelist) and significant objects (a harp, books, lilies), a matrix extending back in time to the earliest moments of consciousness. The term "soul" is employed ironically as a cliché spoken by the novelist at the end of the poem. Both Pound and the novelist (who, like so many of his portrait subjects, is a "crescent image" of himself) exist as a medium for images, sounds, and words, all issuing from elsewhere, not from the "soul."

Pound had developed this concept of the self as a "node" or vortex in collaboration with Wyndham Lewis. A passage from Lewis's novel *Tarr*, serialized in the *Egoist* from April 1916 to November 1917 (the month in which Pound wrote "Moeurs"), offers a very similar account of what a person is. The speaker, Tarr, is a portrait painter:

> A complicated image developed in his mind as he stood with her. . . . It was of a Chinese puzzle of boxes within boxes, or of insects' discarded envelopes. A woman had in the middle of her a kernel, a sort of very substantial astral baby. This baby was apt to swell. She then became all baby. The husk he held was a painted mummy case. He was a mummy case, too. Only he contained nothing but innumerable other painted cases inside, smaller and smaller ones. The smallest was not a substantial astral baby, however, or a live core, but a painting like the rest.=His kernel was a painting. That was as it should be![59]

Tarr's description of himself corresponds closely to the second section of "Nodier raconte . . . ," while his description of the "substantial astral baby" inside a woman dovetails with the first section, the scene of the child's subject formation. The image of "Chinese puzzle boxes" attempts to capture what is inside a person if not a "living core": an infinite regression of representations, of portraits.

"Nodier raconte . . ." articulates a principle of embeddedness that the group portraits "I Vecchii" and "Ritratto" apply to other figures and groups beside Pound himself. These two poems collate fragments of conversation of "old men" and an "old lady" from the literary world of nineteenth-century London. The trope of interiority appears only as physical locations: "in the Row" (Paternoster Row, the literary district of London), "in Rome, after the opera," and in the bedroom of the old lady. Each of these locations is the site of a conversation recalled by the poet, with a figure who reminisces about the past. As in the infinite regressions of "Nodier raconte," each portrait subject is the occasion for a further portrait of an earlier figure. The places where the conversations occur—the "Row," "Rome," and "room"—are metaphors for the fluid medium of language through which these memories are passed down to the present.

"I Vecchii" elegizes Henry James as the champion of the individual, and as the last representative of an era in which "round" subjectivity is possible. At the same time, this elegy deploys James's own technique of free indirect discourse, incorporating elements of James's and others' language without marking it as quotation, and moving from one figure to the next without clear signposts. In doing so, "I Vecchii" hails the passing of Henry James while taking on his mantle and blending the voice of Pound with that of the "Master."

Pound's monumental 1918 essay on Henry James (a "baedeker to a continent") repeatedly describes James as a portraitist, a generic identification that establishes James's work as the model for Pound's own. Together with "I Vecchii," this essay is very much the younger man's homage to the "Master." Pound uses the term "portray" or "portrait" nine times to describe James's writing.[60] In his comments on James, Pound also consistently identifies the American novelist as a "hater of tyranny," an exponent of individual freedom: "[B]ook after early book against oppression, against all the sordid petty personal crushing oppression, the domination of modern life . . . human liberty, personal liberty, the rights of the individual against all sorts of intangible bondage!"[61] "Moeurs Contemporaines" particularly represents the "detestable" forces of family and social pressure in the figure of the "father-in-law," "Mr. Styrax." In "I Vecchi," by contrast, the figure of Henry James quietly mocks the laws of convention, and the portrait pairs him with the crowds of Italian opera-goers who flaunt "the guards" by chanting "Verdi" as an anagram for the name of their exiled king.

The figure of Henry James symbolizes all that has been lost with the onset of modernity. Pound represents James as a complex, many-layered, "rounded" character similar to those he created in his fiction. "He was a great man of letters, a great artist in portrayal, he was concerned with mental temperatures, circumvolvulous social pressures, the clash of contending conventions."[62] The opening of "I Vecchii" associates James's appearance with complexity and depth of character:

> Il était comme un tout petit garçon
> With his blouse full of apples
> And sticking out all the way round;
> Blagueur! "Con gli occhi onesti e tardi."[63]

James's physical shape makes him look like a little boy, while his eyes indicate he is "honest and slow." Thus he seems both young and old, a jokester ("blagueur") and a serious person. James's *rotundity*—"sticking out all the way round"—signifies this capacity to embody contradictions and contain a large interiority.

"I Vecchii" describes and elegizes James's classic individuality, but bids goodbye to it as the subject of contemporary portraiture. Not only is James one among several subjects of this portrait, but what comes out of him when he opens his mouth is a string of names:

> And he said:
> "Oh! Abelard," as if the topic
> Were much too abstruse for his comprehension,
> And he talked about "the Great Mary,"
> And said, "Mr. Pound is shocked at my levity,"
> When it turned out he meant Mrs. Ward.[64]

James's conversation does not reveal his character so much as point to others, in a series of references similar to the heteroglossic phrases that describe his appearance. Pound hails James, and the novelist hails the poet, saying, "Mr. Pound is shocked at my levity." Each exists only to the extent that he is named by the other. This mutual hailing or interpellation can only take place in the poem, for, as Pound begins by explaining, "They will come no more."

The style of this poem contrasts sharply with the "endless sentence" that Pound associated with James (as he describes the author in Canto VII). The historical event of James's death during the war, coinciding with or reflected in Pound's stylistic development toward fragmentation and elision, removes the endless sentence as an option for the poet. This kind of sentence implies a certain security, self-sufficiency, and self-containment that the "round" figure of James reassuringly projects. By contrast, the disjunctiveness of Pound's text reflects a self that is constituted out of echoes and repetitions. This quality of the poem is indebted to Pound's schooling in collage, free-word pictures, and the conversation poem. Yet, at the same time, the poem is not clearly a collage, for it preserves the framework of narration ("he said") and seeks to orient itself in time and three-dimensional space. It is more like another art form that Pound broaches in the same poem: "And he said they used to cheer Verdi, / In Rome, after the opera, / And the guards couldn't stop them."[65] "I Vecchii" has little resemblance to the romantic opera of Verdi, still less the Gesamtkunstwerke of Wagner, but it is like the "after opera" of voices shouting in the hall.

❧

"Ritratto" concludes the sequence. Pound had originally given this title to "Portrait: from 'La Mère Inconnue'" when he first published it in Hueffer's *English Review* in 1909. At fifteen lines, this section of "Moeurs" is in communication with Pound's earlier sonnet by the same name as well as his 1912 "Portrait d'une femme." All three metaportraits represent a female muse figure who gives access to the past. While the earlier portraits express the yearning or judging presence of the poet, his feelings about the subject, in "Ritratto" the poet only reports what "she said," as he listens to the old lady tell her stories about nineteenth-century writers. He becomes the space in which her anecdotes are heard, a space identified with the old lady's bedroom:

> "He stomped into my bedroom. . . .
> (By that time she had got on to Browning.)
> ". . . stomped into my bedroom . . .
> "And said: 'Do I,
> "'I ask you, Do I
> "'Care too much for society dinners?'
> "And I wouldn't say that he didn't.
> "Shelley used to live in this house."[66]

The verbal and thematic center of the portrait is the word "bedroom," placed in the center of the poem at line 8 (the volta line in a sonnet). This room is the scene of the personal exchange between the "old lady" and James Russell Lowell, American "Fireside" poet and ambassador to England in the year of Pound's birth. The fact that the encounter occurred in her bedroom suggests intimacy between them, either invited by the lady or forced by Lowell. This intimacy is reflected in the personal question the poet puts to her, as she recollects their conversation: "Do I care too much for society dinners?" Lowell feels he has a weakness for socializing, for conversation; she refuses to deny it.[67] Their conversation constitutes the "source" of the portrait. Lowell's question, framed by two sets of quotation marks, also represents a textual interiority of embedded utterances. Just as Lowell is "inside" her conversation, Browning is inside her language as the source of the word "stomp," which he coined in "Englishman in Italy." Finally, Shelley was inside her house as its former occupant. The house is a metaphor for the language as shaped and brought to life by a succession of poets; the old lady "inhabits" English, and Browning's word "stomp," just as she inhabits her house. Although a latecomer to the poetic scene ("She was a very old lady. / I never saw her again"), Pound too inhabits this verbal interspace by virtue of conversing with and quoting the old lady.

As the last section of "Moeurs Contemporaines," "Ritratto" concludes the narrative of development with the poet/protagonist's full absorption into a virtual realm of language and letters. While "Mr. Styrax" opens the sequence with the threat of suffocation in contemporary social institutions, "Ritratto" sketches an alternative outcome of *Bildung,* in which the subject is dispersed and absorbed into the "house" of poetry. This outcome presents Pound as the heir of Shelley, Browning, and others, receiving and transforming the nineteenth-century portrait of a lady into a contemporary form. Although the sequence ends on a note of nostalgic finality—"I never saw her again"—in context it is clear that this final portrait affirms a principle of continuity apart from the individual lives of its speakers. In the final section, where the old lady and her memories do all the talking, the poet achieves a "nonidentity" that transforms his social failure at integration into aesthetic success. Such an ending rounds out the double narrative of failed development (beginning at "Mr. Styrax" and ending in "Stele") and the alternative conception of self and portraiture that begins in "Nodier raconte . . ." The old lady is an appropriate counterweight to Mr. Styrax, whose sense of "ownership" repels his wife, brother, and son-in-law; she, in contrast, draws others toward her spacious house in which generations of voices echo.

In its final form, "Moeurs" ends "on" Pound, as the recipient of these voices. Reshaping the portrait poem to accommodate an expanded sense of its subject, Pound pays himself a compliment by reminding us (to paraphrase Rossetti's sonnet) that we who would hear her, must come to him. Yet, the sequence did not originally end with "Ritratto," and where it did end can help us to see what other narratives Pound was considering. When "Moeurs Contemporaines" appeared in the *Little Review* in May 1918, it included a ninth section, "Quis Multa Gracilis." This poem, a free adaptation of Horace's Ode 5, Book I, ended the sequence on a decidedly literary note, and emphasized the temporal correlations between past and present drawn in "Nodier raconte" and "Ritratto." Yet the poem is also about the future, insofar as it expresses anxiety about substitution and replacement.

Quis Multa Gracilis

What youth, abundant Pyrrha,
(Alix, your name is, really);
What blasphemous clear rose,
What sleek black head
Replaces my ragged head?
What upright form,
Owing as much to nature as to Poole,
Is your this fortnight's fool,
Alix (or Pyrrha)?[68]

Horace's Ode concerns a jilted lover who sees his "Pyrrha" with a new amour, and wonders how long it will be before the new one is "replaced" as well. Pound's version extends this anxiety about erotic substitution to a textual level: "Pyrrha" is a fictional name that has been substituted for the "real" "Alix." At many levels the poem struggles with the threat of obsolescence, a theme expressed in the reference to "Poole." This word puns on the name of the English seaside town and the word "pool," thus bringing in Horace's metaphor figuring Pyrrha as the sea. However, the most direct referent for "Poole" is probably "Poole's Myriorama," a moving panorama show popular in the late nineteenth century. Pound's first published version of "Moeurs Contemporaines," then, closed with a reference to a form of popular culture that he treats as a threat to authenticity and masculinity. This conclusion rings a change on the multimedia theme of the sequence, where instances of visual art, literature, and performance complement each other rather than being in competition. Furthermore, "Ritratto" concludes the sequence on a note of achievement and integration, whereas "Quis Multa Gracilis" expresses a mixture of anxiety and defeat. What was "Poole" and why would it have caused Pound any anxiety?

The still panorama of the early nineteenth century was a single long canvas or mural depicting foreign landscapes and architecture, displayed in a round building on a permanent basis. The moving panorama, which developed in the 1830s from this earlier form, consisted of a series of scenes painted on a continuous roll of canvas wound on two cylinders, displayed by turning the cylinders to show a portion of the canvas at a time. The canvas was often painted on both sides and could be backlit to show the thickly painted scene on the reverse. The show would be narrated by a guide and was often accompanied by music and other performed entertainments. Battles and foreign scenes were popular subjects of the panoramas. Naval battles were a particular favorite of Poole's Myriorama, and in 1912 the Poole brothers had produced a show featuring the sinking of the Titanic.[69] The moving panorama was a precursor to the moving picture, which had already upstaged it by 1917.

"Poole" emphasizes the speaker's anxiety about substitution or replacement in a number of ways. As a representation, Poole's show replaces nature. All representation can be accused of this trespass, yet other poems in the sequence do not seem concerned with the ersatz or parasitic nature of representation. Quite the contrary: Pound refers to other media as a way of expanding the range of portraiture. Poole's myriorama would seem an appropriate addition to the intermedial framework of the poem. Like opera, it addresses multiple senses (visual and aural) and takes place both over time and in spatial depth (with figures in the foreground, and moving scenery in the background). However, Pound's tone here seems derogatory and threatened, with his own masculinity at stake in the competition between his "ragged head" and the "upright form" of the Poole-like interloper. The repetition of "head" in two successive lines also calls to mind two other heads that appear earlier in the sequence: the allusion to Gaudier's *Hieratic Head of Ezra Pound* in "Stele" and the description of "the other" old man in "I Vecchii" as "rather like my bust by Gaudier." The second reference to Gaudier's sculpture is an example of embeddedness, in which the earlier work of art returns in a new context as a portrait of another figure. But in "Quis Multa Gracilis," the "sleek black head" that threatens to displace the speaker's "ragged head" is new, not an embedded image of the past.

The threat posed by "Poole" is the youthful appeal of popular visual entertainment, particularly *film*, which looms over "Moeurs Contemporaines" by omission. Film offers an obvious model for his portrait sequence, which combines elements of visual and narrative portraiture. While Pound seems to be able to incorporate any artistic medium—dance, opera, music, photography—in the gradually expanding framework of this sequence, he finally draws the line at the panorama, let alone film. The speaker of "Quis Multa Gracilis" fears not only his replacement by another, sleeker lover but also by a more immediate and popular form of representation. Poole's three-dimensional multimedia show wins the attention of "Alix," threatening to outdo the complex fabric of literary references in "Ritratto."

Pound's writing of "Quis Multa Gracilis" and then his decision to cut it from the final version speak eloquently about the motivations of his avant-garde portraiture. At some level "Moeurs Contemporaines" aspires to the condition of film. The affinities of film and collage have often been noted, as art forms created by cutting and splicing images together. Film renders the human body strangely transparent, cast as light on a screen, so that the figure of the person may be both everywhere (many more places than a living person can be at once) and nowhere at all. It precisely fulfills Lewis's claim (perhaps made with film in mind) that "We all today . . . are in each other's vitals—overlap, intersect, and are Siamese to any extent." On film, the body's qualities of exterior solidity and interior invisibility are dissolved in light and motion. Film operates in "Moeurs" as a repressed metaphor for the gradual dissolution of the individual figure.

Pound already had some personal experience with film's capacity to dissolve the portrait subject. In 1916, he collaborated with Alvin Langdon Coburn to produce "vortographs" created by clipping Pound's shaving mirrors together and taking photographs through them.[70] As well as encouraging Coburn to experiment with abstraction and providing the mirrors, Pound sat for several vortographic portraits that show his profile intersecting with other shapes and with itself from different angles. One print shows a double profile of Pound, janus-faced, looking both right and left. Another combines several overlapping profiles with dark bars that cross the picture. While these works do not portray Pound intersecting with other figures, the technique clearly allows for it. Despite the correlations with his own work, Pound's final assessment of vortography was slighting. In the catalogue to Coburn's exhibition at the Camera Club in 1917, Pound wrote, "Vortography stands below the other Vorticist arts in that it is an art of the eye, not of the eye and hand together." He seemed only interested in making sure that the credit went to himself and Lewis rather than Coburn: "In vortography he accepts the fundamental principles of vorticism, and those of vorticist painting in so far as they are applicable to the work of the camera."[71] Not surprisingly, these comments led to Coburn's falling-out with Pound and the end of vortography. They also show the poet drawing a line at photography (referring slightingly to the intelligence of photographers) just as he drew a line after "Ritratto" to eliminate the final section and its reference to "Poole."

The idea of overlapping, intersecting figures long predated Pound's collaboration with Coburn. The experiment may have had a negative impact, however, in confirming Pound's anxiety about the way that photographic film literally makes the human figure transparent and evanescent, makes it "EXIST much less." By the summer of 1918, Pound had only negative things to say about cinema and photography, calling cinema "the antipodes of Art."

> We hear a good deal about the "art" of the cinema, but the cinema is not Art. Art with a large A consists in painting, sculpture, possibly architecture; beyond these there are activities, dancing, grimacing, etc. Art is a stasis. A painter or a sculptor tries to make something which can stay still without becoming a bore. He tries to make something which will stand being looked at *for a long time.* Art is good in just so far as it will stand a long and lively inspection.[72]

His repetition of the word "stands"—also a word much used in Eliot's portrait poems—evokes the sitter's traditional pose and the appeal of the sustained face-to-face encounter between painter and sitter, viewer and portrait. Pound's critique of film obviously does not apply to still photography, which he finds reason to denigrate on different grounds: "Photography is poor art because it has to put in everything, or nearly everything. . . . It cannot pick out the permanently interesting parts of a prospect."[73] Pound's emphasis on stasis and permanence in art reflects back on the anxiety about substitution expressed, then suppressed in "Moeurs Contemporaines."

"Moeurs Contemporaines" is Pound's most avant-garde work of portraiture, pushing the genre almost to the point where it is no longer recognizable. Ending with "Ritratto" affirmed the generic identity of the sequence and drew back from the threat of modern technologies that might "supplant" Pound's poetry by achieving his goal of interpenetration more effectively than he could himself. Pound's next and most ambitious portrait poem, *Hugh Selwyn Mauberley,* is also a sustained critique of obsolescence and substitution: "The 'age demanded' . . . A prose kinema, not, not assuredly, alabaster / Or the 'sculpture' of rhyme." While "Moeurs" responds to the challenges of avant-garde art by applying its techniques to the portrait poem, *Mauberley* retrenches and takes stock of the genre's achievements. Perhaps "Ritratto" already predicts this direction.

Hugh Selwyn Mauberley

Pound's farewell to London and to the small-scale lyric poem, *Mauberley* is his final work of stand-alone portraiture and summarizes his accomplishments in a dazzling sequence of generic variations and inventions. It is also his longest work of portraiture, almost five times longer than "Moeurs," extending the single-figure portrait to the maximum length it was to achieve in his oeuvre and perhaps for any Modernist poet. As the subtitle "Life and Contacts" indicates, *Mauberley* is a single-figure portrait even as it is also a sequence—a gallery or catalogue—of other portraits.

Though *Mauberley* is usually regarded as a persona poem, textual evidence and publication history suggest that it was written as a portrait sequence. This overlooked generic affiliation makes a significant difference to the meaning of the work. After *Mauberley* appeared in a limited edition volume published by the Ovid Press in 1919, Pound included it in *Poems 1918–1921: Three Portraits and Four Cantos. Mauberley* was the third portrait after "Propertius" and "Langue d'oc" / "Moeurs Contemporaines." Pound himself thus categorized the work as a portrait not long after its composition. He did not publish it in the United States until 1926, when it appeared in his selected *Personae*. That title marked *Mauberley* as a persona poem, a generic label it has retained ever since. Pound's own remarks about the poem in 1922 have often been cited as evidence of the persona method: "Of course, I'm no more Mauberley than Eliot is Prufrock. Mais passons."[74] The comparison of Mauberley to Prufrock suggests that Pound speaks through Mauberley, in the same way that Prufrock, in saying "I," evokes the poet who gives him voice. Yet *Mauberley* is not a first-person dramatic monologue, unlike Pound's other famous "persona" poems, such as "Sestina: Altaforte," "Piere Vidal Old," "The Seafarer," "Lament of the Frontier Guard," and so on. Not only Mauberley, but nearly every other character who appears in the sequence is referred to as "he" or "she." This use of the third person aligns the sequence generically with the portrait, to judge from Pound's previous work and the history of this genre. While Pound's first-person persona poems typically enable the poet to imagine himself as someone he is not (such as a Provençal troubadour), the third person employed in *Mauberley* enables the poet to detach from and objectify his former self as the central figure in a series of portraits of his "contacts."

Many interpretive difficulties can be avoided by understanding the work as a sequence of portraits assembled in a single gallery, similar to "Moeurs Contemporaines" in arrangement. The question of who narrates which section has been the subject of endless critical debate, without satisfying answers (does Mauberley speak in Part I, and Pound in Part II? Or vice versa? And is the final "Medallion" an example of Mauberley's work or of Pound's?).[75] If we see the sequence as a series of portraits,

Mauberley can take his place among the other figures held up for examination, such as Monsieur Verog, Lady Valentine, Mr. Nixon, and Brennbaum. The autobiographical similarities between Pound and Mauberley need not determine the genre of the work. Indeed, Pound's use of the third person shows the greater flexibility of portraiture as a vehicle for representing people, and especially for representing them in a critical or satirical way. As Michael Coyle notes, the poem makes use of Flaubertian free indirect discourse, moving fluidly from one consciousness to another; the unnamed narrator is not the subject of the poem any more than Flaubert is the subject of *Sentimental Education*.[76]

Pound's remark that *Mauberley* was "an attempt to condense the James novel" speaks not only to his conscious use of free indirect discourse but also to its Bildungsroman elements.[77] Like "Moeurs," the sequence concerns a central protagonist who emerges through his interactions with other supporting characters, including male mentor figures from the older generation, a patroness or salonnière, and a female muse. Also like "Moeurs," the sequence has a basic plot of failed or halted development ending in the symbolic or actual death of the protagonist and his diffusion into a fluid medium of language (the "poluphloisboious sea-coast" in "Moeurs" and "phantasmal sea-surge" in *Mauberley*). This narrative of blocked development and social integration through attenuation of self remains consistent through Pound's three major portraits, beginning with *Gaudier-Brzeska*. This memoir is in a sense the prototype for the two sequences, which combine self-portraiture with a homage to Gaudier. The symbolic death of the artist-protagonist mirrors and mourns the death of the young sculptor, treating his premature death as a symbol for the fate of the modern subject. In combining autobiographical elements with features from Gaudier's life, Pound was putting into practice the theory of interpenetration that his metaportraits (such as "Portrait d'une femme," "Nodier raconte . . . ," and "Ritratto") articulate. The central "character" of the sequence is thus himself a composite of two or more figures.

Even as the "James novel" is a major model for *Mauberley*, the sequence also imagines itself as a museum or museum guide. References to the Tate Gallery (in "Yeux Glauques") and Salomon Reinach's illustrated art history *Apollo* (in "Medallion") offer analogues for the sequence as a collection of pictures such as might be found in a museum or a guidebook. Catherine Paul has argued for the relationship between Pound's development as a Modernist and his orientation toward, or within, the museum, particularly the reading room at the British Museum, where he regularly worked between 1908 and 1919.[78] Unlike the London gallery in which Pound places his first meeting with Gaudier, the Tate and Reinach's *Apollo* are repositories of the artworks of the past rather than places to see and buy new art. These models convey the retrospective orientation of the sequence, which preserves "life" in pickling fluid or in amber. Another model for the sequence is Théophile Gautier's "Le Château du Souvenir," an allegory comparing the poet's memory to an ancient portrait gallery where his dead friends are pictured (quoted at the opening of section XII, "Daphne with her thighs in bark"). Again, this gallery of the dead differs from the one where Pound first encountered the living Gaudier-Brzeska, as chronicled in his memoir. Victor Plarr, who appears as Monsieur Verog in "Siena Mi Fe," edited a biographical dictionary of the living (*Men and Women of the Time: A Dictionary of Contemporaries*), but with the passage of time each edition ironically became a catalogue of the dead. As figures enter Pound's poem, they become embalmed as separate objects or artifacts displayed in a museum. Mauberley is an engraver of medallions, an art form suggested to Pound by Théophile Gautier's 1852 *Émaux et Camées*, a collection of quatrain poems describing Gautier's contemporaries in terms derived from the visual arts. Modeled on a museum, biographical dictionary, or collection of medallion profiles—or "pickled foetuses" as suggested in "Siena mi fe"—*Mauberley*'s portraits emphasize their discreteness and materiality rather than their interpenetration.

Mauberley also showcases the techniques and varieties of poetic portraiture, including ekphrasis, epitaph, epigram, multifigure portraits, and quoted speech. Like a curator, Pound "labels" each portrait with a generic identifier of some kind, often by reference to an earlier work in the same form. The sequence thus offers a detailed review of the sources and development of portraiture. The ekphrastic portraits "Yeux Glauques" and "Medallion" anchor the sequence generically and historically, marking the continuity of the genre from the Rossetti circle to Pound himself. The occasion for "Yeux Glauques" is Edward Burne-Jones's *King Cophetua and the Beggar Maid* (1884), one of the icons of Aestheticism. Pound combines the figure of Elizabeth Siddal with the Beggar Maid, referring to the text-image exchanges among Rossetti, Swinburne, Burne-Jones, and Tennyson (whose "Beggar Maid" inspired Burne-Jones's painting) as the precedent for *Mauberley* and Pound's career as a portraitist. "Yeux Glauques" also exposes Pound's conflicted feelings about Rossetti, which date back at least as far as his first documented engagement with the painter in "La Donzella Beata." Commentators on *Mauberley* have observed its ambivalence about Aestheticism, with differing conclusions: Mao argues that Pound links "the virtues of hardness and artistic heroism with an aestheticism that specifically values the thingness of works of the past in opposition to their legibility or transparency," while Beasley disagrees, seeing Pound condemning Aestheticism for its tendency to degenerate into a trade in luxury goods.[79] The difference between Mao and Beasley reflects the internal debate within the sequence itself, and within the poem "Yeux Glauques."[80]

Indeed, the conflict over luxury may be seen in *King Cophetua* itself. The picture of a wealthy, powerful man making a beggar his queen suggests the "symbolical expression of the Scorn for Wealth," as the painter's wife Georgiana Burne-Jones wrote.[81] Yet the painting also pays homage to material luxury, placing the beggar maid on a throne of gold that resembles a gilded cage, flanked by the golden pillars of the frame. The appeal of the picture derives both from its moral message *and* its decorative aspect. In a style made popular by Burne-Jones's mentor Rossetti, the radically foreshortened space of the throne identifies the beauty of the maid, modeled by Georgiana, with that of her sumptuous surroundings, and equates the beauty of both with the surface of the painting itself.[82] The position of the viewer is similar to that of the king, who sits below the beggar maid, appreciating her beauty, as well as the entire effect of the luxurious setting. In other words, the painting leads the viewer to the uncomfortable complicity that troubles Pound's ekphrasis.

"Yeux Glauques" is a composite portrait of the Pre-Raphaelite Beloved, drawn equally from the figure of Burne-Jones's beggar maid and from Elizabeth Siddal, Rossetti's wife and model. Pound focuses on the female subject's "vacant" blue-green eyes, or "yeux glauques," as an index of Rossetti's aesthetic appeal and his ethically problematic treatment of the human figure. The meaning of her eyes is the unanswered question of the poem: "The Burne-Jones cartons / Have preserved her eyes," but what do they tell us?[83] In a few short lines, the poem offers two quite different interpretations of the woman represented in Burne-Jones's painting. On the one hand, as the "pastime for / Painters and adulterers," she is described as the victim of commodification and exploitation. Her "vacant" and "passive" gaze suggests her mental absence; her husband-painter has turned her into a thing. With Elizabeth Siddal in mind, Pound suggests that the Pre-Raphaelite Beloved is literally sold for money when her face and figure are represented in this way, as part of a luxury item. She is compared to "Jenny," the eponymous subject of Rossetti's dramatic monologue that scandalized audiences by sympathetically describing a prostitute from the perspective of her client. Pound calls Rossetti her "last maquero" or pimp. Strangely, Pound's critique of Rossetti places him on the side of Robert Buchanan, whose damaging "Fleshly School of Poetry" review accused the poet of immorality and drove him into seclusion.

On the other hand, the gaze of the Beggar Maid is also "thin like brook-water." The analogy of her gaze to water recalls the aqueous theme—the "distant seas," "Sargasso Sea," "poluphloisboious sea-coast"—that resonates through so much of Pound's portraiture. The analogy also nods to Gautier's "Caerulei Oculi," in which a woman's blue-green, sea-like eyes (hence the title "yeux glauques") seduce and threaten to engulf the speaker in an "abîme."[84] Pound's choice of "brook water" most of all recalls Swinburne's description of himself as "a vein in the heart of the streams of the sea" in "The Triumph of Time," seeking union and oblivion in the "great sweet mother, the sea." The idea of the "stream" or "brook" preserves a sense of the individuality of the figure even as he or she flows toward the all-encompassing sea. Thus, the Siddal/Burne-Jones figure may have a "vacant gaze" but she is also "questing," her gaze "darts out" even though she is "passive." She is not only immobile and thing-like, but also permeable, moving, and in communication with the Rossetti circle and those who now see her eyes "still, at the Tate." In this second reading, "foetid Buchanan" is the villain of "Yeux Glauques," one of several figures in the sequence responsible for suppressing artistic expression and authentic communication, such as "Mr. Nixon." Pound's poem thus worships at the feet of Burne-Jones's beggar maid (like King Cophetua) and also criticizes the work and its entire aesthetic as a kind of prostitution. The painting itself makes both interpretations possible in its mixture of scorn for and appreciation of material luxury.[85] The same work of art may both commodify beauty and also put individuals in contact with one another by "teaching," "questing," "rhapsodizing," and other acts of communication. The portrait in particular may serve either of these ends and sometimes both. *Mauberley* oscillates between condemning the Aesthetic portrait as degenerating into a luxury commodity and hailing it as a heroic gesture of connection. Pound's ambivalence—and the exasperating indeterminacy of the sequence—can be more easily understood and accepted when seen in the context of the genre, which itself negotiates between these possibilities from the 1860s onward.

❧

Mauberley catalogues the subgenres of portraiture and, in doing so, examines how each type operates to reify the subject, or, by contrast, makes him or her an agent of communication. The epitaph recurs throughout the sequence as a sign of the subject's alarming tendency to become an object. Pound's epitaph for himself in "E.P. Ode Pour L'Élection de Son

Sépulchre" opens the sequence, followed by Henri Gaudier-Brzeska's epitaph in "There died a myriad" (V) and Mauberley's epitaph in poem IV of the second part ("I was / And I no more exist; / Here drifted / An hedonist").[86] Indeed, under a looser conception of epitaph, all of the second half could qualify as epitaphic, since each individual lyric ends by summing up and dismissing Mauberley's accomplishments ("Pisanello lacking the skill / To forge Achaia"; "The still stone dogs, / Caught in metamorphosis were / Left him as epilogues"; "Leading, as he well knew, / To his final / Exclusion from the world of letters").[87] Mauberley's vocation as an engraver makes him the fitting subject of many epitaphs, a little ironic joke that links the work of the gravestone-maker with the portraitist.

Closely related to the epitaph is the epigrammatic portrait, found in "Brennbaum" and section XI, "Conservatrix of Milésien." In their contraction, point, and satirical attitude, these sections evoke the portraits of *Lustra,* such as "Phyllidula" or "The Patterns." "Brennbaum," a portrait of the famed caricaturist Max Beerbohm, connects epigrammatic portraiture with Beerbohm's art. In "The Spirit of Caricature" (1901), Beerbohm defined caricature as "the art of exaggerating, without fear or favour, the peculiarities of this or that human body, for the mere sake of exaggeration."[88] Describing Brennbaum's "sky-like, limpid" eyes, Pound subjects the caricaturist to a dose of his own art, suggesting that the caricature and the short satirical portrait are the visual and literary expressions of the same simplifying, reductive impulse. Indeed, the affinities between Pound and Beerbohm extend beyond this short poem. *Mauberley* is affected at its deepest level by the aesthetic of *surface,* which Beerbohm, a member of the Rossetti-Swinburne circle, identified with his own work: "caricature implies no moral judgment on its subject. It eschews any kind of symbolism, tells no story, deals with no matter but the personal appearance of its subject. . . . He portrays each surface exactly as it appears to his distorted gaze."[89] Beerbohm's determination to remain on the surface of the subject reflects the aesthetic of the entire Rossetti circle, and of *Mauberley,* which Pound described as "mere surface."

Mauberley also includes several multifigure portraits: the war poets in part V ("These fought, in any case"), the Rhymer's Club in "Siena Mi Fe," and the poet-patroness relationship in XII ("Daphne with her thighs in bark"). While drawing on strategies developed in "Moeurs Contemporaines" for accommodating multiple figures, these poems emphasize collection rather than intersection. "Daphne with her thighs in bark" is closely modeled on "Nodier raconte . . ."; both concern the poet's place in the contemporary literary salon, and both begin with a quotation from

Gautier. These references evoke different relationships with the past, however. "Nodier raconte" suggests a complicated intertext of embedded figures, while Pound's allusion to "Le Château du Souvenir" suggests a room full of images of the dead, to whom he responds one by one. Rather than a vortex of memories called to mind by the photograph of a mother playing her harp, "Daphne with her thighs in bark" represents a materialistic exchange between the Lady Valentine, who seeks to improve her social standing by patronizing "literary effort," and the poet, who seeks her financial support (a relationship not so different from the "Fleet St." satirized at the end of the poem).

Another group portrait, "Siena Mi Fe," follows the pattern of "I Vecchii" and "Ritratto," portraying an older figure whose recollections frame cameo appearances by other individuals. In "Siena Mi Fe," Monsieur Verog (Victor Plarr) reminisces about Gaston Alexandre Auguste Gallifet, Ernest Dowson, Lionel Johnson, and Selwyn Image. "I Vecchii" presents a similar performance as an opera of voices, but "Siena Mi Fe" has a less flattering metaphor for itself: the "pickled foetuses and bottled bones" where the poet finds Verog. (Lionel Johnson is also described as preserved in alcohol.) The pickled foetuses offer a grotesque variation on the "curious heads in medallion," the "Burne-Jones cartons," "the strait head / Of Messalina," the "still stone dogs / Caught in metamorphosis," and other frozen bodies in the sequence—while also drawing a rather unfavorable parallel between portraiture and taxidermy. Plarr's "catalogue," *Men and Women of the Time,* stands behind these models as a prose genre that resembles a collection of physical objects.

Much of *Mauberley* thus represents portraiture as the reification of living subjects into frozen, pickled, glazed, or sculpted artifacts, which remain mutually impermeable even when gathered together in a group such as the sequence itself. "Yeux Glauques" explicitly traces this conception of portraiture back to Rossetti and his circle, simultaneously adopting and critiquing their aesthetic of surface. By contrast, the second half of the sequence (1920) explores a different set of motifs associated more with Swinburne than with Rossetti: water and sound. Mauberley drifts, listening to the "sea-surge," finally disappearing into "The placid water / Unbroken by the Simoon."[90] Like Swinburne's "sea of time," the sea that swallows Mauberley offers "oblivions," transforming him to "a consciousness disjunct," an "overblotted / Series / Of intermittences."[91] The tale of Mauberley's gradual "anaesthesis" completes Swinburne's narrative of a suffering lover seeking relief in the sound of the sea's waves, suggesting endlessness and nature's indifferent acceptance of all

life. Mauberley's "Olympian apathein / In the presence of selected perceptions" recalls the girl's perspective on herself in Swinburne's "Before the
Mirror": "I cannot see what pleasures / Or what pains were; What pale
new loves and treasures / New years will bear . . . But one thing knows
the flower; the flower is fair."[92] As discussed in chapter 1, "Before the
Mirror" is almost an antiportrait in its vision of art as "the flowing of all
men's tears beneath the sky." Similarly, Mauberley is so "delighted with
the imaginary / Audition of the phantasmal sea-surge" that he, a portraitist, loses "the artist's urge."[93] In "Moeurs," the hearing of the "poluphloisboious sea-coast" (a different translation of the same Homeric phrase)
releases the poet from himself and causes him to dissolve into a medium through which the figures of the "old men" and the "very old lady"
emerge for their final portraits. In *Mauberley,* however, Pound seems as
dissatisfied with fluidity as with solidity. Neither route seems adequate to
the task of representing other people in their full depth and complexity.

Mauberley tries two ways of expanding the portrait poem: by assembling "cameos" together, and by extending a single figure as a medium
containing all the others. While the first way preserves the outlines of
each portrait subject, it flattens him or her to a bas-relief profile, such as
the bronze medallions of Pisanello referred to in part II. Such medallions
may be gathered together, even hoarded, but they remain separate, commodified, and incommunicado. The second way dissolves the outlines of
the individual subject into a formless medium, a "blankness," "incapable
of the least utterance or composition." Pound's frustration with both art
and communication has been understood in terms of his relation to the
literary market, his rejection of art as luxury trade, and his dissatisfaction
with his own poetic productions to date. Yet *Mauberley* also comments
self-reflexively on the history of the portrait poem and its future potential.
In this sequence Pound seeks to elevate the portrait poem as a vehicle
for commenting on history and modern times, as he was also doing in
the early *Cantos.* The character of "Mauberley" is made the antihero of a
narrative that takes its form from the Modernist novel of development:
he emerges and develops in a cast of other characters, and instead of
finding a spouse and a vocation, fails in both, becomes inconsequential,
and dissolves in the sea of these "contacts." But the ambivalence and self-
criticism in this work surely reflect Pound's dissatisfaction with what hap-
pens to the portrait poem as it is expanded and put to work as a vehicle of
social critique and chronicle. The individual figure loses its significance,
and the intersubjective intensity of the best portrait poems from Cowper
to Rossetti is diffused. Rather than a sustained encounter between sit-

ter and portraitist, the expanded portrait becomes medallions clanking against each other in a bag.

The famously ambivalent "Medallion" that concludes the sequence registers the limits of portraiture and, as Pound's farewell to the genre, can hardly avoid mixed feelings. A tour de force of Imagist writing, it also seems to parody the ideal of a concise, "hard," self-contained portrait by rendering it grotesque. The poem records the reification of the female subject, her transformation from a living singer to an inanimate, glazed, "intractable" objet d'art:

> The sleek head emerges
> From the gold-yellow frock
> As Anadyome in the opening
> Pages of Reinach.[94]

Referring to Salomon Reinach's illustrated art history manual *Apollo*, Pound places the singer's transformation in the context of a humanist history of the rise of the subject. "Anadyome" is the "Leconfield Aphrodite," a Roman copy of a work by Praxiteles, whom Reinach credits with bringing a more "meditative" quality to Greek sculpture. Reinach praises the sculpture as "suave," "melting," "freely modeled," and characterized by "a subdued play of light and shadow, which precludes any lingering vestiges of harshness and angularity." He notes that the face is oval, rather than round, and "the eyes, instead of being fully opened, are half closed, and have that particular expression which the ancients described as 'liquid.'"[95] Reinach sees in these visual qualities a response to the school of Plato, which brought "reflection, self-examination . . . depth and subtlety of thought" into Greek culture. Reinach thus uses the Leconfield Aphrodite to tell a history of development toward greater interiority and reflectiveness.

In contrast, "Medallion" reverses this process of development, hardening and freezing the eyes and face:

> The face-oval beneath the glaze,
> Bright in its suave bounding-line, as
> Beneath half-watt rays
> The eyes turn topaz.

Instead of being modeled and shaded, the oval face becomes "glazed," and the eyes lose their naturally "liquid" quality to become stone. As a portrait, "Medallion" tracks the value of the singer from her "clear soprano" to her "sleek head," the "basket-work of braids" that resemble "metal, or intractable amber," and finally to her "topaz" eyes, gradually moving the center of interest from the subject's interior to her exterior, from a living being to an inanimate artifact and from the intangible quality of voice to pure materiality.

Similarly, in describing itself as "Luini in porcelain," "Medallion" offers a condensed history of the decline of portraiture from the representation of interiority into mere commodification. Reinach credits Leonardo da Vinci, like Praxiteles, for using chiaroscuro and modeling to uncover a "profound page of psychology, a study of character and feeling"; he writes that Leonardo's follower Bernardo Luini popularized his master's ideal in "a process . . . not altogether without vulgarity, for his elegance is superficial, his drawing uncertain, and his power of invention limited. His most characteristic trait is a certain honeyed softness that delights the multitude."[96] Pound obviously intends a parallel between Luini and Mauberley on the basis of their "superficial" elegance and limited originality. "Luini in porcelain" suggests an even further decline from the summit of introspective portraiture achieved by Leonardo, however, for porcelain allows only the crudest expression of feeling and belongs more to the realm of knickknacks than art. In contrast to Luini's "honeyed softness," Mauberley uses a "honey-red" glaze to represent the singer's hair. Taking itself as a very late instance in the history of portraiture, "Medallion" embalms the ideals of the genre in glaze and amber to announce their obsolescence.

"Medallion" ends Pound's career as a portraitist both in a blaze of glory—for it is one of his most widely read and closely analyzed lyrics—and on a dark note. Beyond his own personal farewell to portraiture and the era of his life captured by *Mauberley,* the sequence seems to pronounce the "death" of the genre, a judgment also reflected in his decision to collect this and all other poems "worth keeping" in a volume entitled *Personae.* At any rate, that title has certainly reinforced *Mauberley*'s history of portraiture ending in decline and obsolescence. However, in the larger context of the genre, including its continued viability for other poets, perhaps we can see *Mauberley* not as the end of portraiture but as one of its high points, both as an artistic achievement and as the moment at which the genre found its limit in scale. In this form, at least, it could be stretched no farther nor made more comprehensive. And, in Pound's own work, portraiture had an afterlife in the *Cantos,* where portraits appear as insets (like the "Lilith" inset in *The Waste Land*) from the cameo of Henry James to full-length official portraits of Malatesta and Mussolini.

SIX

Pastoral Mode

WILLIAM CARLOS WILLIAMS AND NATIVIST PORTRAITURE

I N 1914, WILLIAM CARLOS WILLIAMS sent a sequence of "Pastorals and Self-Portraits" to his friend Viola Baxter. Like Eliot's "On a Portrait" and Pound's "La Donzella Beata" and "Portrait: from 'La Mère Inconnue,'" these poems were the first in a series of portraits that Williams would write in the nineteen-teens, before moving on to more expansive forms in the 1920s. The group of eight poems included two "Self-Portraits," two "Pastorals," and two "Idyls." As these titles suggest, Williams saw an affinity between pastoral and portraiture in the sense that the natural world, specifically landscape, was his subject in both genres. Many of Williams's subsequent portraits focus on the body of the subject and liken it to soil, trees, flowers, and even clouds and weather. At this time Williams felt "very much attracted by the pastoral mode," as he commented later.[1] Williams used pastoral to shape his portraiture and distinguish it from the nineteenth-century tradition as well as from Eliot's and Pound's work in the same genre. This chapter looks at three stages of Williams's portraits: the 1914 "Pastorals and Self-Portraits" sequence, the portraits of *Al Que Quiere!* (1917), and his "Portrait of a Lady" as it was published in a sequence of landscape poems in *The Dial* in 1920. Each employs pastoral in a different way. Although his use of the pastoral mode began as a way of connecting to an ancient literary tradition, Williams gradually turned the pastoral portrait into a vessel for his Nativist politics, seeking a form of poetry that was independent from European culture.

In modulation, a work of one genre adopts an incomplete set of traits from another genre (a "mode") without changing its basic form and identity. One of the most common modes is the pastoral, which appears almost always in its adjectival form conferring its attributes on another genre (pastoral elegy, eclogue, play, etc.). The pastoral mode can take many different forms, including representing nature, contrasting rural and urban life, and treating the subjects of work and working-class lives.[2] As more than one critic has noted, Williams used pastoral traits for social and political critique. Focusing primarily on *Al Que Quiere!*, John Marsh argues that Williams invented a modern counter-pastoral by "cast[ing] a spotlight on the rural poor and working class . . . to intervene in his hometown (Rutherford, New Jersey) and its politics, which suffered from their own 'unreal, prettified, [and] remote' tendencies."[3] For Marsh, Williams's move to pastoral was motivated both by the desire to distinguish himself as a poet and by sympathy for the working poor. In contrast, Maria Farland claims that Williams's pastoral in *Spring and All* of 1923 engages with a "newly anti-rural strain in early twentieth-century American thought," a discourse that treated rural and agrarian America as degenerate and in need of scientific expertise.[4] The divergence between these two interpretations has something to do with the difference in Williams's own beliefs between 1916, when many of the poems of *Al Que Quiere!* were written, and 1923. Williams was swept up in the Nativist movement that exploded in both art and politics at the end of World War I.[5] The focus of Progressive politics shifted around 1920 from aiding and improving the underprivileged to promoting Americanness and purifying American "stock," both racially and culturally. As Walter Michaels has argued, Williams's emphasis on the "American thing"—as in his famous slogan, "No ideas except in things"—participates in a larger Nativist discourse of racial purity and anti-immigration politics, which fully emerged in the 1920s.[6] As Williams became involved in this movement, switching his allegiance from a transatlantic literary tradition to a nationalist loyalty, he readjusted the meaning of pastoral from an ancient poetic mode to an affirmation of the physical body.

Williams's connection to the Nativist movement in the visual arts is well known. In the first study of Williams's ties to the contemporary art scene, Bram Dijkstra emphasized Williams's involvement in Alfred Stieglitz's program for the renewal of American arts.[7] Following Dijkstra, Schmidt observed that Williams's poetry shares many elements of Precisionist painting and photography, especially as seen in the works of Stieglitz, Charles Demuth, Paul Strand, and Charles Sheeler. A loosely organized movement under Stieglitz's mentorship that emerged after World War I, Precisionism "saw itself as rediscovering an autonomous cultural tradition, one that, for the first time, would allow America to create fine arts that could rival those of Europe."[8] In particular, Schmidt shows that Williams, like the Precisionists, combined still life with pastoral in representations of American cities and technology. In fact, Williams was drawn to pastoral before the Precisionist movement began. The appeal of representing the American landscape in a Modernist idiom extended beyond this movement to painters such as Marsden Hartley, who was connected to the Stieglitz circle but not a Precisionist. Williams combined pastoral traits with his many portraits written between 1914 and 1920 as he negotiated his relationship with poetic tradition and his status as an American poet. The rise of Nativism and Williams's contacts with Hartley and Demuth changed his relationship to the land and to poetic tradition, and consequently changed how he used both portraiture and pastoral.

In this chapter I begin by looking at Williams's 1914 "Pastorals and Self-Portraits." Predating the Nativist movement, these poems are mainly concerned with the poet's relationship to tradition, imagining the poet "in" the earth as well as "in" the pastoral tradition. The eight poems of the sequence experiment with different pastoral contrasts—between the country and the city, the outdoors and the indoors, earth and sky, the humble laborer and the aristocrat, nature and culture—as the poet seeks ways of placing himself in a tradition without being imitative or artificial. Williams shared this goal with both Pound and Eliot, as we have seen in previous chapters. References to Theocritus suggest that Williams was using a strategy that had proved effective for the Imagists: making an end-run around the nineteenth century by hearkening back to ancient models. In this group of poems, Williams combines portraiture with traits of an even older genre, pastoral, and aligns his loyalties with poetic tradition and against the commercialism of American culture.

Following "Pastorals and Self-Portraits," I turn next to a group of portraits in *Al Que Quiere!* that begin to show the impact of Nativist ideas. These portraits explore the primacy of the physical body as a person's defining attribute, in contrast to culture. In particular, Williams identifies the female body with nature, as in "Woman Walking." In developing the metaphor of body to land, Williams was probably influenced less by Precisionism than by Marsden Hartley, one of the foremost spokesmen of artistic Nativism, who advocated a return to "authentic" representation. At the same time, this turn places Williams surprisingly in line with Rossetti, who also privileged the female body as the source of meaning and value. Like the Rossettian portrait, Williams's portraits of women-as-nature, such as "Sympathetic Portrait of a Child," "Portrait of a Woman in Bed" and "Portrait in Greys," create a division between the poet and the body of the subject—a division that the poem also attempts to undo.

Williams recasts this problematic division between the poet and his subject, and between culture and nature, in his 1920 "Portrait of a Lady," discussed in the last section of this chapter. "Portrait of a Lady" is an explicitly Nativist response to Eliot's and Pound's earlier poems by the same name; it is also in dialogue with Williams's friend, the painter Charles Demuth, who similarly struggled to reconcile the internationalism of Modernist art with Nativist goals. "Portrait of a Lady" seems to respond to Demuth's 1918 watercolor illustration for Walter Pater's "A Prince of Court Painters," one of Pater's *Imaginary Portraits* of 1887. Demuth's watercolor is a composite portrait of Watteau and himself, reflecting both on the gender issues raised by Pater's story and on the question of his own national loyalties as a painter. Williams answers Demuth's melancholic self-representation in a portrait of the female body as national landscape, urging Demuth to forgo European conventions for an art of unmediated physical presence.

As each of these thumbnail sketches suggests, Williams tended to structure his portraits using a series of oppositions.[9] Opposition is a major trait of the pastoral mode, perhaps one of the reasons that it appealed to Williams. Scholars of pastoral literature frame this trait in different ways, such as between the urban and the rustic (Frank Kermode), "the machine and the garden" (Leo Marx), nature and culture, or simply between reality and the imagination (Harold Toliver).[10] For Williams, the terms of the opposition changed as his purposes shifted from inserting himself into the poetic tradition to promoting an all-American art. Yet even as his oppositional technique proved serviceable, the poems also express a longing for union, a desire to eliminate their own dualism. Williams imagines—but obviously cannot achieve—an Arcadia of poetry without culture, without language.

Theocritus in "Pastorals and Self-Portraits"

The *Idyls* of Theocritus are considered the first pastoral poems, and Williams often professed his passion for this poet. "The Idyls of Theocritus have always been a dream, an obsession of mine. I love everything that's pastoral."[11] "I don't know any Greek but the pastoral mode fascinates me. Theocritus . . . adopted a mode which was the Idyl . . . no one did it as well as Theocritus."[12] These remarks date from the 1950s, when Williams reencountered Theocritus and composed a version of Idyl 1. At this time he also looked back at his early work in *I Wanted to Write a Poem*

(1956), claiming Theocritus as the inspiration for much of *Al Que Quiere!*
Speaking of the proem of that collection, "Sub Terra," Williams wrote:

> I thought of myself as being under the earth, buried in other words,
> but as any plant is buried, retaining the power to come again. The
> poem is Spring, the earth giving birth to a new crop of poets, showing
> that I thought I would some day take my place among them, telling
> them that I was coming pretty soon. . . . Without knowing Greek I
> had read translations of *The Odes of Theocritus* and felt myself very
> much attracted by the pastoral mode. But my feeling for the country
> was not as sophisticated as the pastorals with their picturesque shep-
> herdesses. I was always a country boy, felt myself a country boy. To me
> the countryside was a real world but nonetheless a poetic world. I have
> always had a feeling of identity with nature, but not assertive; I have
> always believed in keeping myself out of the picture. When I spoke of
> flowers, I *was* a flower, with all the prerogatives of flowers, especially
> the right to come alive in the Spring.[13]

In this passage, Williams acknowledges the history of pastoral in both its
ancient and baroque phases ("picturesque shepherdesses"), while claiming to have a more authentic relationship to the earth than other, more
"sophisticated" pastoral poets. His feeling of identity with nature seems
to offset a sense of belatedness and ignorance ("without knowing Greek")
by authorizing himself as one in a "new crop of poets" to come out of the
(American) earth.

Though uttered in the 1950s, Williams's remarks on pastoral capture
quite closely the mix of ideas and motives present in his earliest experiments in this mode, the "Pastorals and Self-Portraits" sequence of 1914.
In particular, Williams suggests that his initial interest in pastoral concerned his relationship to a poetic tradition and his identity as a poet.
Thus, the poems that he combined with his first pastorals and idyls were
self-portraits—not, as in *Al Que Quiere!*, portraits of the inhabitants of
Rutherford. Williams's need to place himself in a poetic tradition has
to be understood in the context of his earliest efforts to enter the vocation. According to Paul Mariani and other biographers, around 1908 Williams burned a large amount of verse written in the Keatsian manner,
including many sonnets.[14] Even so, his first two books—*Poems* of 1909
and *The Tempers* of 1913—clearly exhibited his continuing dependence
on nineteenth-century models, as indicated by the mottoes on the cover
of *Poems:* "So All My Best is Dressing Old Words New" and "Spending
Again What Is Already Spent."[15] In 1913, following the publication of *The*

Tempers, Williams again underwent an artistic crisis.[16] It was time for him to make a fresh start. The 1914 poems experiment with pastoral as a way to connect with poetic tradition while distinguishing themselves as new and original. Indeed, this double aim typically underwrites the transformation of genre; the poet doesn't do away with a genre but rather inhabits it in an original way. Williams vividly expresses his desire to inhabit pastoral when he states, "I *was* a flower."

Williams's recourse to ancient Greek poetry as an antidote to the English tradition was a strategy that had worked well for Imagism and that Pound in particular had played for all it was worth: "making it new" by returning to the origins of Western culture. Theocritus played a similar role for Williams as Sappho and the *Greek Anthology* did for H.D., and Catullus for Pound's portraits. Theocritus's reputation in the nineteenth century was supported by echoes in Wordsworth's *Prelude* and Tennyson's many "Idyls," and by John Addington Symonds's influential *Studies of the Greek Poets* (1873).[17] Symonds represented Theocritus as a belated figure in Greek literature who invented a new and durable poetic genre by drawing on memories of rural life in his native Sicily. The contrast between Theocritus and the decadent Alexandrian court where he lived probably appealed to Williams if he read Symonds's essays: "Theocritus was the most brilliant ornament of that somewhat artificial period of literature; he above all the Alexandrian poets carried the old genius of Greece into new channels, instead of imitating, annotating, and rehandling ancient masterpieces."[18] In the introduction to his prose translations of Theocritus—issued multiple times between 1880 and 1913—Andrew Lang drew explicit parallels between the poet's time and the end of the nineteenth century: "Our own age has often been compared to the Alexandrian epoch, to that era of large cities, wealth, refinement, criticism, and science; and the pictorial *Idylls of the King* very closely resemble the epico-idyllic manner of Alexandria."[19]

Into this decadent, imitative, and "sterile" atmosphere, Theocritus brought a sensibility that excluded nothing on the basis of a false sense of decorum, according to Lang. "There was scarcely a form of life he saw that did not seem to him worthy of song, though it might be but the gossip of two rude hinds, or the drinking bout of the Thessalian horse-jobber, and the false girl Cynisca and her wild lover Aeschines."[20] Lang attributes this sensibility to the poet's rural background and his training in Cos, a city renowned for its medical school; another translator claims that Theocritus was trained in medicine.[21] Thus both Lang and Symonds represent Theocritus as a down-to-earth, creative poet at a time and place when these qualities were in short supply—a characterization that likely appealed to Williams. In addition, both Symonds and Lang define the Idyl as a "little picture." Symonds writes, "They ought to affect us in the same way as the bas-reliefs and vases of Greek art, in which dramatic action is presented at one moment of its evolution, and beautiful forms are grouped together with such simplicity as to need but little story to enhance their value."[22] Indeed, Theocritus's first Idyl consists primarily of a long ekphrasis describing a cup carved with scenes from rural life. Pastoral poetry thus began its existence as a modulation of ekphrasis, perhaps suggesting to Williams an affinity between these genres.

Theocritus renovated an existing tradition by broadening the scope of lyric poetry to include rural matters treated in a pictorial style. These were also Williams's aims as a young poet, a "country boy" with ambitions to "come pretty soon" to take his place among a "new crop of poets." Williams adopted Theocritus as the mentor and model for his 1914 "Pastorals and Self-Portraits" sequence, where he imagines himself renewing a debased pastoral mode by returning it to its original, Theocritan immersion in the earth and in nature. "Pastoral 1" and the first of two "Idyls" imply that the pastoral mode has been corrupted by delusions of grandeur, by being elevated and blown out of proportion. "Pastoral 1" contrasts "The old man who goes about / Gathering dog lime" with the "Episcopal minister / Approaching the pulpit."[23] This contrast follows the pastoral convention of oppositions between the simple laborer and the sophisticated aristocrat, emphasized by the figures' relative positions "in the gutter" and "approaching the pulpit." Another word for "minister" is "pastor," and one meaning of the term "pastoral" refers to the church's spiritual care of its "flock." The true, down-to-earth pastoral of the old man in the gutter and the sparrows on the pavement dramatizes and decries the artifice and emptiness of the establishment pastoral mode associated with wealth and social position, perhaps with the former poet laureate Tennyson specifically in mind.

Williams's first "Idyl" performs a more specific and extended critique of this overblown aristocratic pastoral. The poem opens with pastoral's most cherished contrast: the country versus the city. The poet is refreshed by "wine of the grey sky" and "invisible rain," whereas the day before,

> I was in the city
> I stood before
> The new station
> Watching

> The white clouds
> Passing
> The great Hermes
> And flying,
> Flying toward Greece.[24]

This "new station" is almost certainly Grand Central Terminal, which was completed in 1913. The building's chief external ornament is an enormous sculpture of Hermes, messenger and god of commerce, flanked by Hercules and Athena, representing strength and wisdom respectively. Williams's description of this sculpture might at first seem to associate the industrial achievement of the new station with the cultural accomplishments of Greece, putting his ekphrasis in parallel with Theocritus's description of the prize cup in Idyl 1. The comparison is ironic, however. In Theocritus's poem, a shepherd sings about Daphnis dying for love after various figures have tried to comfort him, including his father Hermes. Theocritus's Hermes is the father of song, but New York's Hermes is the god of commerce. Williams then emphasizes the difference between the two epochs by noting that the "fluted columns" of Grand Central are "Not ground / Piece into piece / But fitted with plaster." He also notes the "frieze of acanthus" decorating the building, another detail from Theocritus's Idyl 1, in which the prize cup is decorated with acanthus. The new station symbolizes the way that American aspirations to greatness are founded on the values of speed, efficiency, and vastness of scale, all serving the god of commerce; in contrast, the poet is refreshed by the sky and clouds, and he thinks back to "Phidias" and "his Parthanon." In Williams's "Idyl," it is significant that the poet is not specifically placed anywhere; rather, he imagines traveling back to Greece on the "White and formless" clouds. Three years later, Williams would reject such an affinity to European tradition. In *Al Que Quiere!*, the poem "History" concludes a long visit to the antiquities collection at the Metropolitan Museum of Art by enjoining the reader to go outside and leave the dead: "Come! / Life is good—enjoy it! / A walk in the park while the day lasts. . . . The world is young, surely!"[25] But in the 1914 "Idyl," a renewal of the pastoral mode is more important to Williams than an affirmation of American life. Grand Central is impressive, but it represents the wrong values, cheapening the meaning of Greek art. "Idyl" likens two sets of contrasts: Williams superimposes "Ancient Greece vs. America" on the conventional pastoral opposition between "country vs. city."

"Self-Portrait 1" opens Williams's sequence by announcing the poet's relationship to the pastoral tradition that "Pastoral 1" and "Idyl" then explicitly engage. The portrait places the poet literally "in" this tradition by placing him in the ground:

> You lie packed,
> Dark:
> Turned sluggishly
> By plough.
> Wheels stir you—
> Up behind them!
> You tissue out
> You drink light
> And go in clouds![26]

While other poems in the sequence variously place the poet before Grand Central Station, alone in a room, outside talking to the plants, outside in the rain, and in his bed, this first location is the most fundamental. It is less a physical place than a metaphorical identification. Moreover, his poetic awakening is imagined as a movement from the ground to the sky and clouds. These are the same clouds that later, in "Idyl," carry the poet's thoughts back to ancient Greece. The poems that follow "Self-Portrait 1" imagine various ways of being close to or inside pastoral. Without committing the poet to a specific relationship to the land, the sequence adopts the core Theocritan traits of a low-style treatment of rural life presented in a series of "little pictures." This modulation reflects a poetic project rather than a political motivation. In later pastorals, Williams returns often to the idea of being in the ground, proposed in "Self-Portrait 1" and repeated in "Pastoral 2," but with a difference: he subsequently imagines the earth as female or identifies it with women's bodies. This subtle shift, as I argue in the next section, reflects Williams's awakening Nativism and contact with the Stieglitz circle, especially Marsden Hartley and Georgia O'Keeffe.

Nativism in *Al Que Quiere!*

In the winter of 1914, when Williams sent his "Pastorals and Self-Portraits" to Viola Baxter in a self-deprecating note, Americans were barely conscious of the war.[27] The Nativist movement that would burgeon with the American entry into this war hardly rippled the surface of national life.[28] By 1917, however, Williams's loyalties had shifted from

Theocritus to Whitman as the source or origin of his own work. In this year, Williams published his first critical article, "America, Whitman, and the Art of Poetry," announcing a nationalistic poetic project:

> In America to speak of the art of poetry is pure imbecility unless there be an art in America. And if I cannot speak of that which exists here where I can know it, it stands to reason that I cannot speak of the art anywhere.
>
> Whitman created the art in America. But just as no art can exist for us except as we know it in our own poetry even our own art cannot exist but by grace of other poetry. Nothing comes out of the air, nor do we know whence anything comes but we do know that all we have receives its value from that which has gone before.[29]

Williams claims that he cannot speak of art unless it already exists in "America" and in his own poetry, but also that such native art "cannot exist but by grace of other poetry." Thus, Whitman's poetry occupies a pivotal role here, as a single example of art that is distinctively American while also standing in the past, as a source. Williams's emerging Nativism is here qualified and restrained by the idea that poetry is inherently a matter of literary reception and tradition; but, as he explains in the essay, he really has no use for Whitman as a poetic model, only as a reassurance of the validity of "art in America." Soon, Williams would decide that poetry need not, indeed should not, depend on any tradition.

As Williams's essay suggests, by 1917 the Nativist movement in the arts had found its goal, if not precisely its means. The painter Marsden Hartley was one of the first to articulate these means, in terms that were soon adopted by other artists and by Waldo Frank, whose *Our America* became the manifesto of artistic Nativism in 1919. Williams became acquainted with Hartley around 1916 through the Arensberg circle, and they remained friends and correspondents until Hartley's death in 1943.[30] A protégé of Alfred Stieglitz and frequent exhibitor at the 291 gallery, Hartley had spent time in Paris and Berlin between 1912 and 1915, absorbing avant-garde ideas and gaining "a reputation in European art circles as one of America's leading modernists."[31] During this time he also began incorporating Native American motifs into his Berlin work with the Blaue Reiter group (including some of his most famous paintings). His 1917 essay "A Painter's Faith"—later collected in *Adventures in the Arts*—is considered the earliest expression of Nativism among the Stieglitz circle.[32] Hartley declared, "The artist is being taught by means of war that there is no longer a conventional center of art, that the time-worn fetish of Paris as a necessity in his development has been dispensed with. . . . It is having its pronounced effect upon the creative powers of the individuals in all countries, almost obliging him to create his own impulse upon his own soil."[33] Hartley's interest in autochthonous American culture took him to New Mexico in 1918, where he focused on the desert landscape. Because of its proximity to indigenous culture, the Southwest appealed to Hartley as closer to the "origin" of America than his more European-ized home state of Maine. At this time, Hartley's ideal as a painter was to create an authentic American art by representing the desert landscape without the least use of painterly conventions.[34]

In "Aesthetic Sincerity" (December 1918), Hartley admonished American artists to treat the New Mexico landscape with "genuineness" and "authenticity," to represent the "soil" in its own terms, without "apply[ing] the convention of Paris or Munich or Dresden."[35] "Soil" was a favorite Na-tivist buzzword even before the war, as in the title of the little magazine *Soil* that celebrated modern American culture. Hartley repeatedly refers to "soil" or "ground" as the literal subject of landscape painting, and as a metaphor for reality treated in a direct, unmediated way: "We as painters will have to get 'on the ground,' and 'into' the subject." Hartley means that painters will have to go to New Mexico to see it for themselves; he also means that their method should avoid "convention" or "application" of European techniques—or indeed of any techniques at all. This idea of rejecting European conventions was also becoming a cornerstone of Williams's poetic project. Hartley concludes,

> We are now finished with 'à la mode' esthetics. . . . the return to nature
> will show a greater audacity in consulting the rhythms of nature as
> they exist. . . . the war has demanded originality [of the painter]. It
> has sent him back to his own soil to ponder and readjust himself to a
> conviction of his own and an esthetics of his own.[36]

Advocating a naturalistic treatment of the landscape, Hartley suggests that the artist himself should become an extension of the land. In "America as Landscape," published the same winter, Hartley urges "first-hand contact" with American landscape, claiming "We are becoming native," but cautioning, "there must be a stouter connection established, a verity of emotion between subject and observer."[37] Later, in the 1920s, Hartley would carry out these ideas by painting landscapes with human features, thus fusing the body with the land in a way that his essays of 1917 and 1918 already envision. Though much of Hartley's Nativist writing was published after 1917, when it could not have influenced *Al Que Quiere!,* it shows the drift of the two friends' thinking, as they began to focus on the nationalistic significance of landscape and its connection to American bodies.

By 1919, Waldo Frank's *Our America* had made a public cause of artistic Nativism, calling for a home-grown Modernist movement among American artists. Frank conceived of America as a body struggling to speak:

> America is a turmoiled giant who cannot speak. The giant's eyes wander about the clouds: his feet sunk in the quicksands of racial and material passion. One hand grasps the mountains, and the other falls bruised and limp upon the lowlands of the world. His need is great, and what moves across his eyes is universal. But his tongue is tied.[38]

Frank urged American artists to speak for this body, which may be understood both as landscape and as the physical body of the native-born American. His analogy shows how landscape and portraiture came together in the artistic project to represent "America."

Diverging from Hartley, whose landscapes often suggest male bodies, Williams more conventionally represented the land as female, revisiting the ancient myth of Kora or Persephone, whose descent to the underworld in the winter brought desolation to the earth, and whose return in the spring brought life. The significance of this myth was a matter of firm belief for Williams throughout his career, as exemplified by his avant-garde manifesto of 1920, *Kora in Hell*.[39] Williams's gendering of the landscape brought myth and poetic convention into the service of his political program. The male-female opposition fit easily into Williams's existing framework of pastoral contrasts. In a letter to Dora Marsden published in *The Egoist* in August 1917, Williams defined the female principle as that of earthly contact and physical maintenance:

> Female psychology . . . is characterized by a trend not away from, but toward the earth, toward concreteness, since by her experience the reality of fact is firmly established for her. Her pursuit of the male results not in further chase, at least not in the immediate necessity for further chase, but to definite physical results that connect her indisputably and firmly with the earth at her feet by an unalterable chain, every link of which is concrete. Woman is physically essential to the maintenance of a physical life.[40]

The figure of "woman" doubles or intensifies the Nativist analogy of person to soil, earth, or landscape.

The trope of landscape as female body and vice versa was popular in Nativist writing and especially in the Stieglitz circle. When Georgia O'Keeffe came to New York in 1917 at Stieglitz's insistence, he and Hartley immediately interpreted her work as representations of female anatomy.[41] Stieglitz exhibited her drawings in 1916 and presented her first one-woman show in 1917, the last exhibit at the 291 gallery before it closed. In a review of the 1916 show he commented, "'291' had never seen a woman express herself so frankly on paper."[42] In response to a request for his thoughts on "Woman in Art" in 1919, Stieglitz wrote that the art of women and men was "differentiated through the difference in their sex make-up . . . The Woman receives the World through her Womb. That is the seat of her deepest feeling."[43] Influenced by the new ideas of Freud, Stieglitz continually implied or stated that O'Keeffe expressed an *un*repressed sexuality through the imagery of female anatomy.[44] Soon after he began living with O'Keeffe in 1918, Stieglitz put this interpretation to work in a series of eroticized portrait photographs of O'Keeffe, many of them in the nude. The exhibition of these photographs in 1921 made O'Keeffe famous overnight and reinforced the idea of her painting as an extension of her body. Thus, at O'Keeffe's next one-woman show of paintings and sculpture in 1923, the reviews "implied that O'Keeffe was a sexually obsessed woman . . . and described her art as if it were an extension of the forms of her body."[45] O'Keeffe would labor to change this perception of her work for the next decade. The widespread interpretation of O'Keeffe's abstract canvases as representations of her sexual anatomy reflected not only the sexism of the time but also artists' and critics' eagerness to find a new "native" subject matter in American bodies and landscapes. In particular, the sexualizing or anatomizing of her paintings drew on the conventional symbolism of the American nation as a powerful woman. "Georgia IS America," Stieglitz often remarked.[46] Stieglitz and other members of the circle regarded O'Keeffe as the personification of the promise of America, and their reduction of her work to representations of her body followed this Nativist conception.

Written between 1914 and 1917, the poems of *Al Que Quiere!* reflect the impact of Cubism, Futurism, and Vorticism and the reception of these movements in the work of other American artists.[47] They also show Williams working out the metaphor of the body that became so important to the Nativist movement. The high concentration of portraits in this volume suggests the pivotal role played by this genre as Williams shifted his sights from literary to visual models, and from a transatlantic to a nationalistic perspective. The poems specifically called portraits include "Sympathetic Portrait of a Child," "Portrait of a Woman in Bed," "Portrait of a Young Man with a Bad Heart," and "A Portrait in Greys," published in this order between 1916 and 1917. Other poems that exhibit portrait-like traits include "Woman Walking" (1914), "The Ogre" (1915), "M.B." (on Maxwell Bodenheim), "K. McB.," and "The Young Housewife" (1916). As this list shows, Williams intensified his use of the title "portrait" over this period; "Sympathetic Portrait of a Child" was first printed under the title "Touché" and changed for its book publication in 1917. Williams's preference for the portrait in this volume reflects his transition from a primarily literary frame of reference to that of the Nativist movement in the visual arts. In this transition, the portrait—particularly representing the female body—became the ground where poetic genre intersected with Williams's emerging artistic and ideological concerns. As a genre of both painting and poetry, the portrait was well suited for exploring the differing demands and values of these two media. Whereas "Pastorals and Self-Portraits" negotiated the poet's position within a set of pastoral oppositions (keyed to a literary source), the portraits of *Al Que Quiere!* seek ways of representing the subject's physical materiality. In focusing on the human body, Williams engages both with the visual immediacy of painting and photography, and with the emerging Nativist discourse of bodies and soil.

The number of portraits in *Al Que Quiere!* also probably reflects Williams's amicable competition with his college friend Ezra Pound. Pound had dedicated his 1912 *Ripostes* to Williams, the volume that included "Portrait d'une femme" as well as the shorter portraits "An Object," "Phasellus Ille," "A Girl," and "Quies." Williams more subtly indicated that *Al Que Quiere!* was a reply to Pound by including a poem by the title of "Riposte." Williams's portraiture is a definite "riposte" to Pound in several ways. In contrast to Pound, whose 1912 collection cultivated a critical, detached perspective on his subjects, Williams sympathizes with, identifies with, and desires his subjects. The poem "Riposte" heralds love ("Love is like water or the air . . . it cleanses, and dissipates evil gases") as the poet's proper attitude, rather than detachment, still less scorn.[48] While Pound turns his attention to the subject's mind ("Your mind and you are our Sargasso Sea"), Williams focuses intently on her physical body. Finally, whereas "Portrait d'une femme" suggests that a person is composed of received memories, ideas, and possessions, Williams's portraits programmatically analogize the person to earth, nature, and weather, suspiciously avoiding culture as a source of subjectivity. As seen in Hartley's essays, the Nativist associates culture per se with Europe and idealizes—or hopes for—an American art that is an extension of the uncultivated land.

Al Que Quiere!'s proem "Sub Terra" combines pastoral with a call for a like-minded audience to rise up out of the earth. The poet confesses "earthy tastes" and seeks a "band" of "grotesque fellows" to share his tastes, such as the "seven year locusts" who come up from the ground where they have been buried, to "go with me a-tip-toe, / head down under heaven."[49] The proem sets the stage for a series of portraits of individuals with "earthy" qualities that attract the poet's desire and sympathy. The earliest of Williams's portrait-like poems in this volume is "Woman Walking," which Marling identifies as his first engagement with Cubism.[50] The poem opens in a flat, grey, mist-covered landscape described as if it were a painting ("To the right, jutting in, / a dark crimson corner of roof"). From this landscape the poet sees a Kora-like "powerful woman" walking toward him with "supple shoulders, full arms / and strong, soft hands."[51] The woman, carrying a basket of eggs, is obviously associated with the land as a principle of fertility. Yet Williams also contrasts her with the "dead hillside," suggesting that her warm, three-dimensional body is more powerful and appealing than the mere picture of the landscape. "Woman Walking" suggests a merging of pastoral and portrait—both imagined specifically as visual genres—while distinctly privileging the female body over the landscape. In this poem, the woman herself emerges as the subject of the poem, with the soil as background and metaphor. Williams makes this metaphor explicit in "K. McB.," which compares the subject, Kathleen, to the soil: "You exquisite chunk of mud / Kathleen— just like / any other chunk of mud!"[52] Carefully avoiding the derogatory word "dirt," the portrait seeks to elevate the subject (noting her "dignity") while keeping her, as it were, on the ground.

Like "K. McB.," "Portrait of a Woman in Bed" claims the subject's physical body as the source of her identity. As a dramatic monologue, it also adds an important formal element to Williams's Nativist project. When the woman speaks, the poem issues ostensibly from her body. This choice of form nods both to Pound, whose 1909 *Personae* had distinguished him as a writer of dramatic monologues, and to Browning, thus placing Williams in conversation with an international poetic tradition. But Williams's use of dramatic speech also anticipates what would be an important component of Nativism: the idea of a speaking earth. "America is a turmoiled giant who cannot speak," Waldo Frank would write in 1919, exhorting artists to interpret the giant body of the continent and its mute inhabitants.

Hartley imagined a speaking earth by integrating Nativist ideas with Wassily Kandinsky's theory of expression. Hartley had originally been drawn to Berlin and the Blaue Reiter group through his interest in Kandinsky.[53] In Berlin, Kandinsky mentored the young artist, who was profoundly influenced by his ideas.[54] Kandinsky's book *Über das Geistige in der Kunst* (*On the Spiritual in Art*), which Hartley had first read in Paris, argued for the "inner necessity" of art: the artist's need to express himself, his own age, and what is universal in art. Kandinsky's work became the basis of a revived theory of expression that was used to justify abstraction, not as a distortion of reality, but as a true representation of the feelings of the artist: "the artist can employ any forms (natural, abstracted or abstract) to express himself, if his feelings demand it."[55] Yet Hartley seems to have imagined the artist more as a conduit for communicating his subject matter than expressing himself. In "Aesthetic Sincerity," Hartley warns, "Until the artists who come to New Mexico take upon themselves this esthetic sincerity there is little hope of arriving at an art expression which will be in any way expressive of the facts at hand." By "facts," Hartley seems to mean, not the painter's emotional state, but rather the landscape: "America extends the superb invitation to the American painter to be for once original."[56] Hartley combines the essentially Romantic call for original expression with a Nativist mandate for representation of American landscape unmediated by inherited forms or techniques. His call for painters to get "'on the ground,' and 'into' the subject" is literal: his ideal for painting is a direct transfer of landscape into paint.

Williams similarly uses dramatic speech in portraiture in order to emphasize the physical presence of the speaker. Pound's dramatic monologues demonstrate his concept of a fungible identity by combining features of fictional or historical characters, sometimes including his own in the mix. Williams, by contrast, insists on the concrete particularity of the speaker's body as the source of his or her identity. The speakers describe their own physical appearance and bodily traits, unlike Pound, who reserves visual description for third- and second-person descriptive portraits. The speaker in "Portrait of a Woman in Bed" insists on her physical presence by constantly evoking her body and her immediate material surroundings, such as the bed and her clothes. "There's my things / drying in the corner: / that blue skirt / joined to the grey shirt—" she begins.[57] The visual element lies not only in the speaker's concrete description of her clothes, but also the suggestion of a physical gesture of pointing or nodding at them: "There's my things." Yet these "things" are not essential to her identity. The speaker lies naked under the bedclothes: "Lift the covers / if you want me / and you'll see / the rest of my clothes— / though it would be cold / lying with nothing on!"[58] The poem moves gradually closer to defining the speech-making power as itself physical. Beginning by gesturing at her clothing, then referring to her concealed naked body, the speaker now refers to her head, from which her speech issues:

> But I've my two eyes
> and a smooth face
> and here's this! look!
> it's high!
> There's brains and blood
> in there—
> my name's Robitza![59]

The portrait reaches its "high" point when the speaker reaches the origin of speech ("brains and blood") and identity ("my name's Robitza!"). With a brilliant, deceptively simple move, Williams evokes the trope of interiority that drives the nineteenth-century portrait poem, repurposing it as *physical* interiority: brains and blood. Robitza's identification of herself by gesturing at her head—rather than identifying her memories or anything in her consciousness—conveys a physicalist ontology: the mind may be conscious, but it is still a physical thing. "Portrait of a Woman in Bed" thus elaborates the view that Williams explains in his letter to Dora Marsden and develops in "Shadow," "K. McB.," "Portrait in Greys," and other poems where he likens or identifies woman to matter and to the earth. Robitza's gesture toward her head—"look!"—links Williams's physical conception of identity with the dramatic monologue form, as embodied speech.

In "Portrait of a Young Man with a Bad Heart," Williams extends the same treatment to a male subject. In this poem, the male speaker's life is limited by and identified with his "bad heart," "this / damned pump of mine / liable to give out."[60] The inverse of Robitza, he derives not strength but weakness from his body. Knowing of his weak heart, he refrains from courting the girl he loves. While his feelings—his "heart" in the clichéd poetic sense—lead him toward the girl, the physical fact of his "damned pump" draws him back. The young man speaks "from the heart" in the sense that his internal organ determines his speech and actions. The realistic course that he pursues is dictated not by conventions of romance (which would urge him to court his beloved despite his infirmity), but rather by the physical limitations of his body. Though feeble, he is every bit as embodied as Robitza. In both cases the portrait subject's interiority defines him or her as a person, but it is a physical interiority in contrast to the intangible soul attributed to the sitter in the nineteenth-century portrait poem, or the ideas and received notions of Pound's "Portrait d'une femme."

"Portrait of a Woman in Bed" and "Portrait of a Young Man with a Bad Heart" propose to push language toward the natural body and away from culture. The demonstrative pronoun "this" grounds the speaker's utterance explicitly in his or her body, although in the context of the poem, "this" is singularly vague. The word only makes sense with reference to a physically present body, in contrast to Pound's literary references, which generate his speakers out of allusions to older texts. Robitza scorns all things social and cultural: "Corsets / can go to the devil—/ and drawers along with them!"; "The county physician / is a damned fool / and you / can go to hell!"[61] Her suspicion of culture pushes her use of language toward physical matter, with the poem imagining a kind of poetry founded on the body—or, as Williams would later claim, in things.

The project of uniting the body with its representation entails some internal contradictions that Williams confronts in "A Portrait in Greys," the last in the group to be published as well as the final portrait in the volume. This poem rehearses the pastoral contrast between nature and culture on which Williams had superimposed the opposition between female and male. It is intensely personal; according to Williams's later recollection of this poem, it portrays his wife, Florence.[62] He represents her as undifferentiated from a "grey-brown landscape" through which she moves, "weighted down with me," the poet who "stand[s] upon your shoulders touching / a grey, broken sky."[63] She inhabits the realm of earth, matter, and uninspiring fact ("level and undisturbed"), both holding him down ("gripping my ankles") and supporting him in his futile attempt to escape into the sky. The division that marks their separate spheres of activity also creates a situation in which the male striving for transcendence burdens the earth-bound female. Even a poem that celebrates the physical and material is still a cultural production that separates itself from pure matter. The autobiographical content of this poem represents poetic composition as a burden supported by woman's body and her labors. The poem, which is this burden, tries to rehabilitate itself by representing *both sides* of the divide between the poet and his wife (and all that each figure represents: man and woman, portraitist and portrayed, imagination and body, sky and earth).

"A Portrait in Greys" asks, "Must I always be moving counter to you?" This question applies to more than Williams's relationship with Flossie.

It is the poet's frustrated address to matter, to the human body and the land. The poet's use of language pushes him away from "earth" even as he attempts to get closer to it by describing or ventriloquizing it. Williams's difficulty is caused both by the basic divide between things and language, and also by his emerging project of speaking for America without using the cultural mediation of Europe. Just as Rossetti attempted to describe a unified body and soul in dualistic language that kept them separate, Williams here aims for a union between principles that he can only articulate by describing them as different from each other. In the portraits of *Al Que Quiere!*, Williams clarified the physical body as the focus of his portraiture, and more generally of much of his poetry to come. This choice was shaped both by his exposure to the visual arts and by his emerging artistic Nativism, as well as, no doubt, his day job as a doctor. Yet as "Portrait in Greys" demonstrates, the rejection of culture for nature—a classic pastoral opposition—could create problems for the poet as well as making an opening for his work. Williams's next poem in this genre treats this problem more consciously and also with a sense of humor. "Portrait of a Lady" asks what steps a poem can take to remove itself from the realm of culture—now presented specifically as European culture—without falling mute.

Demuth in "Portrait of a Lady"

By the time Williams published "Portrait of a Lady" in *The Dial* in 1920, artistic and political Nativism were in full swing. Waldo Frank's *Our America* had appeared in 1919, as had Williams's Nativist manifesto, the prologue to *Kora in Hell*, first published in Pound's *Little Review* in 1919. In *Kora* as well as in "Portrait of a Lady," Williams treats Eliot and Pound as the chief offenders against the cause of American poetry. Attacking them both for playing into the English sense of superiority over American writers, Williams calls their work "rehash, repetition" of their European "masters."[64] He demands true innovation that doesn't depend on stale imitation: "Nothing is good save the new. If a thing have novelty it stands intrinsically beside every other work of artistic excellence. If it have not that, no loveliness or heroic proportion or grand manner will save it. It will not be saved above all by an attenuated intellectuality."[65] "Portrait of a Lady" also joins in the attack on Eliot and Pound, who had written similar poems by the same title almost a decade before.

Ironically, Williams's call for originality is founded on allusions to their work, an irony not lost on Pound in 1933, when he refused this poem for his planned *Active Anthology*. Acknowledging receipt of Williams's poems, Pound wrote back, "Noo poems to hand and a damn fine set," but singled out "Portrait of a Lady" as "the least interesting simply in *confronto* with yr / other stuff. The theme HAS been treated before."[66] "Portrait of a Lady" is extremely conscious of pastoral, pictorial, and poetic precedents. The poem contemplates how to be authentically American in view of the traditions it rests on. Picking a quarrel with Eliot and Pound, and more important, engaging in dialogue with his friend Charles Demuth, turn out to be part of the answer to this question. Insofar as these artists are American, like Whitman, referring to their work does not mean slavish dependence on European tradition. All three "portrait of a lady" poems—Pound's, Eliot's, and Williams's—triangulate through the "lady" to a generic source, but in Williams's case he triangulates to Eliot, Pound, and Demuth, rather than to the Victorians. This is his solution to the dilemma of writing American poetry.

"Portrait of a Lady" first appeared in the *Dial* in 1920 as the first of six poems that mix portraiture and landscape. The pastoral quality of "Portrait of a Lady" stands out more in the context of this sequence than when read alone. The six poems follow the seasons, beginning and ending in spring. Each one identifies an aspect of nature with a person or a feeling: "Your thighs are appletrees" ("Portrait"); "Old age is / a flight of small / cheeping birds" ("To Waken an Old Lady"); love is a "vast and grey" sky ("The Desolate Field," which Williams identified as a "tribute" to his wife). "Blizzard" compares snow falling to a man's "years of anger," and "Spring Storm" resolves the sequence with, "The sky has given over / its bitterness."[67] "Portrait of a Lady" compares the lady successively with apple trees, a southern breeze, a gust of snow, tall grass, and the seashore. There are no built environments in these poems, no social institutions, just human figures and feelings compared to weather and landscapes bare of cultivation. The sequence is an experiment in composing poetry without culture, an ideal suggested by the figure of the lone man in "Blizzard": "The man turns and there— / his solitary track stretched out / upon the world."[68] The ideal of poetry as the individual poet's "solitary track" dovetails with the Nativist theme of the sequence, which locates all human experience in unpeopled landscapes.

"Portrait of a Lady" differs from the other poems in the sequence, however, in that "nature" answers back, albeit indirectly. The poem consists of a series of statements followed by questions ("Which sky?"), either spoken by the female subject of the portrait, or else by the male poet / portraitist in response to her interruptions of his monologue. Her questions raise or cause the speaker to raise the issue of artistic precedents:

"Watteau" and "Fragonard," but also by implication, the tradition of portraiture and the more recent "track" of modern "portrait of a lady" poems.
The work is thus also a conversation about the Nativist project that drives
the rest of the sequence, a conversation about the possibility of an authentic and original American art. There are more than two sides to this
conversation. In addition to the general principles of male and female,
culture and nature, language and things that Williams addressed in his
other portrait poems, this work engages specific American artists who,
like Williams, have tackled the challenge of making art in a culture predominantly derived from Europe.[69]

The question "Which shore?" that is repeated four times at the end of
"Portrait of a Lady" is a way of asking where the American poet and artist
should live. This was a question that many in his generation had asked:
Eliot, Pound, H.D., Gertrude Stein, Robert Frost, Mina Loy, and other
writers had crossed the Atlantic in order to find better working condi-
tions and a more receptive audience. "I praise those who have the wit
and courage, and the conventionality, to go direct toward their vision of
perfection in an objective world where the signposts are clearly marked,
viz., to London," wrote Williams in the prologue to Kora in Hell, somewhat pettishly, "But confine them in hell for their paretic assumption that
there is no alternative but their own groove."[70] The issue was a live one
for Williams, who would pack up and move to Paris for a "sabbatical" in
1924. More pertinently, the question "Which shore?" also asks where the
sources of the poet's work should be: here or across the Atlantic. The answer, "I said petals from an apple tree," gestures to the Edenic apple (the
original source of knowledge), and to the iconic significance of apples as
a national symbol ("American as apple pie"). This apple tree signifies an
origin that is natural and American rather than artificial and European.
The apple is not dictated by Fragonard's painting The Swing, as I will soon
explain, for the tree in that painting is too large to be an apple and is probably not found in nature at all. Rather, the poem directs the American
poet to the landscape of his origin.

Both Hartley and Demuth studied painting in Europe and then returned to the States to struggle with adapting their newly acquired avant-
garde techniques to a specifically American subject matter. "Portrait of a
Lady" is also in dialogue with both of them. As a fellow Nativist, Hartley
shared similar aims with Williams, and he denounced European influence in harsh terms that probably affected his friend. Demuth, by contrast, absorbed thematic and stylistic elements of Decadence and the
techniques of Cubism, and "came to be aligned with the anti-naturalism

which sprang from the Symbolist movement in Europe."[71] Williams had been friends with Demuth since his second year in medical school (1903–4), in a close relationship that lasted to Demuth's death. Williams commemorated this relationship by dedicating *Spring and All* (1923) and his long elegy "The Crimson Cyclamen" (1935) to the painter. Williams's 1921 poem "The Great Figure"—composed in Marsden Hartley's studio—in turn inspired Demuth's famous poster-portrait of Williams by the same name (1928). Demuth also represented Williams as "Uncle Billy" in *The Azure Adder,* a 1913 play about the role of the "little magazine" in the contemporary art world. From these significant homages, it is safe to assume that they discussed their work and ideas with each other whenever Demuth was in residence in New York.

"Portrait of a Lady" appears to be in dialogue with a work of Demuth's that Williams very likely saw and/or discussed with the painter. Between 1915 and 1919, as he was working toward a synthesis of Cubism and Nativist Modernism, but before he achieved his mature style, Demuth composed a series of watercolor illustrations of nineteenth-century authors including Walter Pater, Henry James, Emile Zola, Honoré de Balzac, and Frank Wedekind. He chose texts that dealt with sexuality, including coded references to homosexuality, and used his illustrations to work out issues of both personal and artistic identity. He apparently intended these works as "private entertainments" to be circulated among friends.[72] One, *A Prince of Court Painters* of 1918, illustrates Walter Pater's fictionalized portrait (by the same name) of the eighteenth-century painter Antoine Watteau (fig. 10). Pater's story was first published in 1885 and collected in *Imaginary Portraits* (1887), an important document of Aestheticism. Demuth's painting refers to a series of portraits, both literary and visual: Pater's fictional portrait, a painting by Watteau thought to be a self-portrait, and a nineteenth-century wooden sculpture of one of Demuth's ancestors. Williams's allusion to Demuth thus taps into a complex chain of portraits reaching back to the eighteenth century via Aestheticism.

Demuth's painting ostensibly represents Watteau in his studio, dressed in eighteenth-century costume, pensively holding a woman's shoe. The text for the illustration is the last line of Pater's story: "He was always a seeker after something in the world that is there in no satisfying measure, or not at all."[73] The wistful dissatisfaction on Watteau's face is mirrored in a painting that stands on an easel in the background: Watteau's famous picture of the Commedia dell'Arte figure Pierrot (often referred to as "Gilles"). The sadness on the clown's face contrasts with his elaborate white costume. (The representation of Pierrot in fin de siècle literature as a dandy would make him a natural object of interest for Demuth, who also assumed this role.) Watteau's *Pierrot* was until recently thought to be a self-portrait. Its presence in Demuth's painting suggests autobiographical elements in his picture of Watteau, just as Watteau incorporates himself in his painting of Pierrot.

Many aspects of Watteau's life as told in Pater's story apply to Demuth himself: lifelong loneliness, illness, and a sense of social alienation from his wealthy patrons.[74] The penultimate line of Pater's portrait is "He has

FIG. 10. Charles Demuth (1883–1935), *A Prince of Court Painters*, 1918. Watercolor on paper, 20.3 x 27.9 cm (8 x 11 in.). (Private collection, used by permission)

been a sick man all his life." In Demuth's painting, a cane leans against the chair behind Watteau, signifying not only Watteau's illness but also Demuth's lameness (this cane tellingly appears in several other water-colors). As Pamela Allara has fascinatingly shown, even the appearance of the main figure refers to Demuth himself. The position and dress of the Watteau figure exactly reproduce those of a small wooden statue that was a Demuth family heirloom. In 1770, the Demuths had founded the first tobacco shop in the United States. In the nineteenth century, to commemorate the origins of the business, a family member carved "The Snuff-taker of Revolutionary Days," a wooden sculpture that stood out-side the shop for many years.[75] By incorporating the stance and costume of this statue into his painting, Demuth assimilated these two eighteenth-century figures, one a painter (like himself), the other a family icon. His representation of Watteau/Demuth thus elides the distinction between the European tradition of painting and his own native heritage, traced back to "Revolutionary Days." Demuth's painting interprets his own situ-ation as a modern American artist attempting to synthesize European traditions and avant-garde innovation in the context of American culture. The work suggests the painter's isolation and longing, surrounded by the artifacts of culture but without human company. This isolation obviously speaks both to Demuth's personal isolation as a gay man in a repressively heterosexual culture and also his sense of being out of time and place as a European-trained Modernist painter working in the United States.

The Watteau/Demuth figure conveys his isolation most of all by the shoe he holds in his hand. A detail introduced by Demuth—it does not appear in Pater's story—the shoe symbolizes femininity or its absence.[76] The woman's shoe enters Demuth's painting via a specific iconographic tradition exemplified by the very painting that Williams alludes to in "Portrait of a Lady": Honoré Fragonard's *The Swing*. In eighteenth-century visual iconography, a woman's lost shoe was a common symbol of lost chastity.[77] Thus, in Fragonard's painting the woman's shoe flies off as she swings through the air (a symbol of sexual pleasure), to be caught by her appreciative lover hiding in the bushes and staring up at her legs. This famous painting encodes many elements of eighteenth-century French court culture, celebrating the woman's intended (or actual) liaison with her lover, while her unsuspecting husband or guardian pushes the swing in the background. Fragonard's masterpiece of frivolity contrasts mark-edly with the sober tone of Watteau's *Pierrot* as well as Demuth's self-representation in his *A Prince of Court Painters*. While Fragonard cel-ebrates erotic love, Demuth and Pater both emphasize loneliness and absence in their portraits of Watteau. The woman's shoe seems to have flown through the air from *The Swing* to *A Prince of Court Painters*. There, the shoe no longer signifies the eroticized female body but the trappings, equipment, and artifacts of femininity. It becomes the focal point of an array of other "props" in the painting: a woman's dress draped over the chair, elaborate rococo furniture, the painted screen (even the cane), and most of all Watteau's painting of himself in clown costume. All of these artifacts have the air of substitutes about them, given the main figure's despondency. The "seeker" is after something that is not represented in the picture.

Demuth's portrait of Watteau draws all its artifacts together in a representation of lack and dissatisfaction: costume, furniture, the cane (an ersatz leg), and painting itself. In fact, Demuth's treatment of the shoe as a focal point of culture in the painting brings to mind his friend Hartley's exhortation in "A Painter's Faith," published the previous year: "The artist is being taught by means of war that there is no longer a conventional center of art, that the time-worn fetish of Paris as a necessity in his development has been dispensed with. . . . It is having its pronounced effect upon the creative powers of the individuals in all countries, almost obliging him to create his own impulse upon his own soil."[78] Jonathan Weinberg interprets the shoe as a fetish object; yes, it is, but not only sexual.[79] The shoe is the painter's "time-worn fetish of Paris" that the Watteau/Demuth figure desires while knowing it can't entirely satisfy him. *A Prince of Court Painters* is, in a sense, the obverse of Hartley's paintings of landscapes as bodies. Whereas Hartley aspires to paint presence, to paint the source of the American body in the southwestern landscape, Demuth follows an infinite regression through a series of absences in search of a cultural origin—a structure not unlike Pound's embedded figures in "Moeurs Contemporaines."

A Prince of Court Painters is one statement on the problem of presence, a problem that Demuth explored in several genres. In 1916 during a trip to Bermuda with Marsden Hartley, Demuth began painting glowing still-lifes of flowers and fruit. Demuth would continue to paint in this genre until his death, including such works from the 1920s as *Yellow Calla Lily Leaves, Bowl of Oranges, Flower Study: White Tulips*, and *Calla Lilies (Bert Savoy)*. His still-lifes were some of his most popular paintings during his lifetime. The paintings are obviously representational (in a way that the more abstract poster portraits are not), but in focusing on objects from nature which are prized for their beauty and as symbols of vitality, Demuth diminished the problem of absence raised by his representation of costume in *A Prince of Court Painters* (and in many watercolors of vaudeville performers and nightclubs). While *A Prince* emphasizes a lack inherent in representation, Demuth's flower paintings offer representation as an enhancement of aesthetic pleasure, both enlarging the size of the actual flower and preserving it from decay. In *A Prince,* costume indicates the ways that society shapes or enforces gender roles, and the painter's longing gaze suggests the difficulty of satisfying desire. By contrast, Demuth's flowers emphasize the physical, anatomical aspect of sexuality, in focusing on the reproductive part of a plant (as O'Keeffe would also do in large-scale flower paintings beginning in 1924). The flower paintings naturalize and celebrate human sexuality, emphasizing the capacity of paint to render presence. These works might thus be considered analogous to Hartley's Nativist landscapes, where features of the human body may be discerned in the shapes of the hills and valleys that are otherwise devoid of the marks of human habitation or culture. Individually and together, the friends Williams, Hartley, and Demuth debated how to represent American life without recourse to imported styles and techniques. Their answers varied but all experimented with representing the human body through "nature," particularly landscape, plants, and weather. In 1918–1920 this question was very much in the air for all three.

Williams and Hartley aimed to reduce, and ideally eliminate, artistic mediation. Williams's portraiture, as we have seen, gravitated toward the physical body and away from tradition and culture. By contrast, Pound sought to detach portraiture from bodies altogether and instead represent the way ideas and language constitute a person and link him or her to a rich historical past. Demuth's shifting styles and subjects interrogated these options for American Modernist art. "Portrait of a Lady" seems to be in conversation with Demuth, directly contradicting the conclusions of *A Prince of Court Painters,* but affirming the flower and fruit still lifes. Understanding this poem as a dialogue with Demuth helps to clear up much confusion that the references to Watteau and Fragonard have created.

W. J. T. Mitchell and others have assumed from the references to Watteau and Fragonard that the work is "an ekphrastic poem that may be an address to a woman who is compared to a picture, or a woman in a picture."[80] The problem with this reading may be seen in Mitchell's double formulation: is the woman *compared* to a picture, or is she *in* a picture? The poem is only ekphrastic in the usual sense if she is in a picture, making the poem a representation of this picture. But she can't be in the picture if she is correcting his attribution of *The Swing* to Watteau:

Your thighs are appletrees
whose blossoms touch the sky.
Which sky? The sky
where Watteau hung a lady's
slipper. Your knees
are a southern breeze—or
a gust of snow. Agh! what
sort of man was Fragonard?
—as if that answered
anything.[81]

In fact, the speaker doesn't seem to have much interest in any painting; he produces "The sky / where Watteau hung a lady's slipper" as an answer to her question "Which sky?" She asks him to justify his metaphor of her thighs to appletrees, and he dutifully names a famous precedent in the European tradition. But his lack of knowledge and interest in this tradition may be gauged by the fact that he gets the artist wrong, and when corrected by her, dismisses the painting altogether with an *ad hominem* attack: "Agh! what / sort of man was Fragonard?" It is impossible to imagine this utterance coming from the lover in *The Swing*, who, as Fragonard's creation, would not be in a position to comment on the artist. The speaker's next remark, "Ah, yes—below the knees," indicates that he has quickly moved on from the question of precedent to the more important matter of examining and praising her body. Whereas the female addressee would seem to welcome a conversation about painting, the speaker is more interested in her physical presence, to which he devotes the rest of the poem. His references to "tall grass" and "sand" have nothing to do with Fragonard's painting, although they may have everything to do with the national landscape (prairies and shores) that Williams consistently invoked in earlier portraits and that accompanied this poem in the *Dial* sequence.

In Fragonard's painting, the flying slipper symbolizes erotic pleasure, but the speaker of "Portrait of a Lady" connects the shoe with Watteau. This "mistake" makes sense in the context of Demuth's *A Prince of Court Painters*, which literally puts the slipper in Watteau's hands, as the central European cultural artifact among several, including the painting of *Pierrot* in the background. Williams associates the slipper with the European tradition that Demuth's painting also considers, taking that slipper as a symbol of lack. Again, Williams seems to be thinking of Hartley's remark about the need to discard the "time-worn fetish of Paris." To look at Demuth's painting instead of at an embodied woman is to feel her absence. Perhaps to look at any painting in the European tradition (particularly the representational style, such as Watteau and Fragonard), is to experience lack. Williams connects the European cultural heritage with absence, and from a Nativist perspective, this is logical: the European tradition is *not here*, it can only be experienced second hand, from a distance, like a lost slipper. Yet, unlike the Demuth/Watteau figure who dwells on this lack, Williams's male portraitist moves on quickly to redefine the female figure as a national landscape: "Your knees / are a southern breeze—or / a gust of snow." Though the frothy white skirts of the woman in Fragonard's painting might suggest snow, the work as a whole projects the feeling of mild temperature. Williams, by contrast, identifies the weathers of the upper and lower regions of the largely *intemperate* United States, comparing them to his lady's volatile emotions. Thus "snow" and "southern breeze" mark the northern and southern states, the "tall grass" indicates the Great Plains, and "shores" demarcate the east and west coasts. The poem is saturated with geographical and topographical references. In effect it rejects cultural artifacts, as associated with the slipper and the complicated genealogy of Demuth's painting, instead offering a metaphor generated from the landscape of North America itself. Like Hartley, Williams has "create[d] his own impulse upon his own soil."

The poem has already answered the question "Which shore?" by the time the speaker asks it. The answer is the east coast and the west coast—but not the other side of the Atlantic. The lady, with Fragonard on her mind, presumably prompts him on this point because there is no seashore in the painting. Though he pretends to be interested in what she has to say about painting, his real motivation is erotic access to her body. His answer,

> Agh, petals maybe. How
> should I know?
> Which shore? Which shore?
> I said petals from an appletree

returns to his original conceit of thighs as apple blossoms, emphasizing his determination to stay on this side of the Atlantic in his thoughts and speech. In the end, his utterance breaks down as he apparently succumbs to the excitement of the encounter with her body. The suggestion of physical contact between "my lips" and hers at the end of the poem works to cut out language as much as possible, suggesting that words are no longer necessary for communication. In a sense, the ending of "Portrait of a Lady" tries to realize the project of Williams's earlier portraits: to complete the identification of self and earth, so as to eliminate the mediation of culture (language, poetry, painting) altogether. The poem is a portrait of presence and erotic union, in contrast to the mirror images and fluid interspaces of Eliot's and Pound's portraits, and the longing and absence of Demuth's *A Prince of Court Painters*. Williams is with Hartley in rejecting "'à la mode' esthetics" and returning "to nature" and "to his own soil."[82]

The irony of the poem, and perhaps what held Williams back from including it in *Sour Grapes*, is that the soil itself remains mute, as it must, and the poem remains in the domain of culture. The union of the poet and the earth (or the woman) seems metaphysically impossible. Not only is the poem a linguistic artifact, but it engages with culture by responding to Eliot and Pound, Demuth and Hartley, and alluding to Watteau and Fragonard. These pairs constitute a system of symbolic exchanges between men that substitute for erotic union with a woman. Perhaps the greatest irony of the poem is that while engaging in a Nativist discourse (about the body as ground of American art, about staying on "this shore"), the poem actually refers to two French painters. In addition, the poem exhibits one of the most established traits of pastoral, found in both Theocritus and the Renaissance poets: dialogue, particularly carried on as a witty exchange between sparring lovers or would-be lovers. Whether on purpose or despite itself, the poem proves the impossibility of exiting culture for a world of pure physical presence—at least while remaining in poetry, in language.

In its most extreme form, Williams's poetic project is an impossibility. Even as he makes the case for a native aesthetics, the many ties between his poem and European art and literature place this work in a transatlantic tradition of portraiture. Eliot and Pound both struggle, too, with their perception of themselves as stepsons to the mother culture. Their portraits specifically deal with this perception by imagining the self as an empty space through which pass the images and figures of the past. Williams's quite different strategy is to represent the self as purely, deeply physical. In elevating the female body and erotic love as the subject of portraiture, Williams returns, perhaps inadvertently, to an earlier conception of the genre: Rossetti's. As discussed in chapter 1, Rossetti expressed his theory of the fundamental unity of body and soul in ways that seemed to privilege body, indeed to suggest a thoroughgoing materialism. It was the sheer physicality of the Rossettian female, from the Blessed Damozel to the Beloved of the *House of Life* sequence, that shocked his contemporaries and became his lasting contribution to Aestheticism and its followers. Williams's revival of this physicality in a completely different style underscores the continuity of genre: finally, there are not an infinite number of ways to develop a portrait.

❧

Coda

ROSSETTI AND E. E. CUMMINGS

I N FOCUSING ON ONLY a few poets, this study has excluded many portrait poems that deserve attention. Before ending, I turn here briefly to one such group of portraits that point both forward to the rest of the twentieth century, and backward to the nineteenth.

The name E. E. Cummings has been synonymous with Modernist formal experimentation since the publication of his first book, *Tulips and Chimneys*, in 1923. Unlike Pound and Eliot, whose work seems weighted by the past and by tradition, Cummings addressed contemporary topics in a fresh style that assimilated "high" Modernist fragmentation with down-to-earth language and frank treatments of ordinary life and the human body. Despite his significant differences in theme and style from Eliot and Pound, the portrait was also a central genre for him. In the original 1922 manuscript of *Tulips and Chimneys,* a group of twenty-nine "Portraits" assembled under this heading is the largest single category in the collection. Written between 1916 and 1919, the poems in this manuscript were published in three volumes: the much-abridged collection called *Tulips and Chimneys* (1923), a second book entitled *&* (1925), and *Poems* (also 1925). Cummings distributed the original group of portraits over these three volumes, in each case retaining the heading "Portraits." They include some of his most famous poems, such as "Buffalo Bill's" and "5," a group portrait of men in a restaurant. In each of Cummings's first three volumes, a section headed "Portraits" proclaims the importance of this category, surpassed in length only by Cummings's other favorite kind, the sonnet. Exhibiting Cummings's characteristic formal play with typography, these portraits also experiment with a wide range of new topics, preferring outdoor urban scenes with prostitutes and indigents to Eliot's and Pound's indoor encounters with older literary figures.

In these works, Cummings struck out in a new direction that was nevertheless predicated on Rossetti, one of his main influences.

In 1913, when T. S. Eliot was finishing up his Ph.D. at Harvard under the direction of Josiah Royce, the philosopher also played an important role in Cummings's life when he introduced Rossetti's *House of Life* to the 19-year-old aspiring poet who was his neighbor in Cambridge. As Cummings said of this encounter with Rossetti, "And very possibly (although I don't, as usual, know) that is the reason—or more likely the unreason— I've been writing sonnets ever since."[1] Rossetti's influence explains not only Cummings's preference for the sonnet form, but also for the theme of erotic love and focus on the body of the beloved. Because Cummings addressed these subjects with a graphic explicitness that was unprecedented even among the avant-garde, his affinities with Rossetti have not received critical attention. In gravitating toward the portrait and the sonnet as his favored genre and form, respectively, Cummings was taking a page from Rossetti. Indeed, these two categories often overlap, as in Rossetti's sonnet "The Portrait" and in Cummings's "the Cambridge ladies who live in furnished souls," "goodbye Betty, don't remember me," "'kitty', sixteen, 5'1", white, prostitute." Cummings's sonnets exemplify his direct relationship to Rossetti, for they explicitly remain in the tradition of the *House of Life* both in terms of form and content.

Like Rossetti, Cummings takes the theme of erotic love, only updated to reflect the changed sexual mores of the 1920s. Cummings's frank representation of prostitutes is one of his distinctive topics in this manuscript, and here again the impact of Rossetti may be felt. Rossetti's "Jenny" shocked contemporary readers not so much for his treatment of prostitution but for the complicity of the male speaker, apparently one of her customers, and for the poet's nonjudgmental sympathy toward both figures. Cummings similarly places himself or the reader in this complicit role, variously celebrating the prostitute and her customers (Portrait XVI, "Between the breasts") or accusing himself of being responsible for her condition (as in Portrait XIV, "the young / man sitting / in Dick Mid's Place"). The portraits of prostitutes share Rossetti's mix of objectification and sympathy, inviting the reader to acknowledge his own complicity in the commodification that takes place in the poem.

Like Rossetti, Cummings was a painter, and his knowledge and practice of visual art informed his poetic portraiture just as Rossetti's did. The major influences on Cummings's painting were the works of Cézanne, Synchromism (Morgan Russell and Stanton MacDonald-Wright), Cubism (primarily Picasso and Gleizes), and Futurism (particularly the Amer-

icans Joseph Stella and John Marin).[2] Referring to Picabia, Picasso, Kandinsky and Cézanne, the proem of his 1922 "Portraits" sequence frankly
acknowledges this mixture of Modernist influences at work on his
writing:

> of my
> soul a street is:
> prettinesses Pic-
> cabian tricktrickclickflick-er
> garnished
> of stark Picasso
> throttling trees[3]

The array of artists mentioned in this poem signals Cummings's intention to write portraits in the context of Modernist visual art. It also signals
that their primary contribution to his aesthetics is *multiplicity*. Cummings
uses plural nouns to describe each painter's technique or subject matter: "prettinesses," "trees," "prisms of sharp mind," "Matisse rhythms,"
"Kandinsky gold-fish." In turn, Cummings's poem incorporates their
multiplicity by referring to not one or two but five modern painters. "Of
my / soul a street is" announces one of Cummings's main interventions
in the portrait poem: his incorporation of multiple figures. This interven-
tion is similar to Pound's response to Futurism and Vorticism in "Moeurs
Contemporaines" and *Hugh Selwyn Mauberley*.

"Of my / soul a street is" also indicates the predominant setting or
medium for Cummings's multifigure portraits: the urban street. This
setting differs from Pound's group portraits, which typically are set indoors (the novelist's house, the house of the very old lady, the opera in
"Moeurs"). "As usual i did not find him in cafés" (III), "the skinny voice"
(IV), "the / nimble / heat" (VIII), "i walked the boulevard" (XII), "but
the other / day I was passing a certain / gate" (XVII), "inthe, exquisite;"
(XVIII), "spring omnipotent goddess" (XX), and "somebody knew Lincoln somebody Xerxes" (XXIV) are group portraits set in the street or
other open spaces of the city. A number of portraits are set in cafés that
share the anonymity of the street, such as "it's just like a coffin's" (X),
"5/derbies-with-men-in-them" (XIII), and "one April dusk" (XV). A third
group are set in brothels or strip clubs, a setting that combines the anonymous interactions of street and café life with the erotic theme that also
runs through the sequence: "between nose-red gross" (XI), "the young /
man sitting" (XIV), "between the breasts" (XVI), and "the waddling /
madam star" (XXVI), which seems to move between nighttime street life

and the brothel. Indeed, the setting of these portraits seems nearly as important as the figures in them, each of whom is reduced to a simple description or formula: "the leatherfaced / woman with the crimson nose" (IV), or, in "5 / derbies-with-men-in-them," to an algebraic sign, "x and y play b" (XIII). As in Pound's multifigure portraits, reduction goes hand in hand with combination and intersection: the reduction of the individual figure means that the aggregate acquires more significance.

A number of the poems focus on individual women, offsetting the multifigure portraits and anchoring the sequence in the traditional single-figure orientation of the genre. Women and girls are the subjects of most of these portraits, specifically focused on their erotic appeal, whether to the poet or to others: "being / twelve / who hast merely / gonorrhea" (II), "Babylon slim- / ness of / evenslicing / eyes" (V), "the dress was a suspicious madder, importing the cruelty of roses" (VI), "of evident invisibles / exquisite the hovering / at the dark portals / of hurt girl eyes" (VII); "ta / ppin / g / toe" (IX), "Cleopatra built" (XXII), "her / flesh" (XXVII), and "raise the shade" (XXVIII), the dramatic utterance of a woman in the act with her lover. Whether the female subject is celebrated, as in "Cleopatra"; mourned, as in "the "Oldeyed / child" of II; or viewed with distaste, as in "the dress was a suspicious madder" ("Her gasping slippery body moved with the hideous spontaneity of a solemn mechanism"), the portrait always emphasizes lost innocence. This theme is expressed and generalized in portrait XIX, "the rose / is dying," which addresses Rossetti's archetypal symbol of female beauty and sexuality. "Motionless / with grieving feet / and wings," the rose ascends while "the lips of an old man murder / the petals."[4] The rose is both the body of a girl desecrated by the lascivious old man—a theme developed in "being twelve" (II), "i walked the boulevard" (XII), and "the young/man" (XIV)—and the love poem that the old man has cheapened and turned to a cliché by repeating it. The "prose faces" of the mourners seem to be the antithesis of "the symbol of the rose," which "mounts / against the margins of steep song," suggesting that the misuse of language is somehow involved in the murder of the rose.

Do Cummings's portraits seek to document the loss of innocence and the reduction of the "rose" into "prose," or to renew the "steep song" of the Rossettian portrait by celebrating and representing the Beloved in a more immediate, contemporary, and realistic way? The answer must be, of course, both. Cummings's poem "the rose" acknowledges and regrets the loss of many qualities that are present in Rossetti's portrayal of women: their idealized beauty, the reverential attitude of the poet toward his Beloved, the celebration of erotic love as the union of body and soul. His own portraits of prostitutes and twelve-year-old girls with gonorrhea frontally assault, puncture, and deflate the ideal of female beauty and erotic love that Rossetti elevates to an aesthetic principle. Yet these poems also raise their own "steep song" about how life is lived in the body and be-tween bodies. The song is uneven; some celebrations of sex seem merely coarse (such as "her / flesh"), and other portraits of women are misogy-nist ("the dress was suspicious madder," "between nose-red gross"). The uneven tone is part of the process of experimentation, and Cummings's most successful love poems are probably among the sonnets rather than portraits. In both kinds, however, Cummings aims to translate Rossetti's commitment to the body into a contemporary idiom and subject matter, while carrying on Rossetti's spirit of truth-telling about human sexuality.

Rossetti's presence in "high" Modernist portraits by Eliot, Pound, and Cummings is not a defining trait of the genre, for it flourished before his contributions, and many subsequent twentieth-century examples do not allude to him. Yet it is striking that Rossettian motifs continued to provide generic definition for the portrait, even as Pound bade farewell to the lyric in *Mauberley*, Eliot announced modernity in a genre-defying collage of voices and styles in *The Waste Land*, and Cummings undid the very conventions of language and writing on which centuries of poetry were predicated. Rossetti is both part of the past that the poets sought to shed, and also their model for modernization within the poetic tradition. "Rossetti" means many things as a model for modern poetry: his free adaptation of a much earlier, historically discontinuous poetic tradition to inform his own poetry; the intermedial exchanges between word and image in his work; his rejection of a religious dualism that privileges the intangible soul over the physical body; an aesthetic of flatness, sur-face, and decoration; his willingness to affront the norms of propriety by speaking frankly about sexuality; and his elevation of the work of art as a self-sufficient object of value and beauty. The modern poets chose freely from among these traits as they brought new life to the portrait poem. Far from being a constraint from which they sought to escape, the genre as they found it was a resource for poetic invention in another nation and a new century.

Notes

Introduction

1. Two important works of criticism whose titles very well express this widely accepted argument include Dasenbrock's *The Literary Vorticism of Ezra Pound and Wyndham Lewis: Towards the Condition of Painting* (see pp. 6–7), and Perloff's *The Futurist Moment: Avant-Garde, Avant Guerre, and the Language of Rupture.*

2. Corbett, *The World in Paint: Modern Art and Visuality in England, 1848–1914,* Prettejohn, *Art for Art's Sake: Aestheticism in Victorian Painting,* and Prettejohn's edited collection *After the Pre-Raphaelites: Art and Aestheticism in Victorian England* particularly influenced this book; see also Kate Flint, *The Victorians and the Visual Imagination* (New York: Cambridge University Press, 2000) and Carol Christ and John O. Jordan, ed., *Victorian Literature and the Victorian Visual Imagination* (Berkeley: University of California Press, 1995).

3. According to Ford Madox Hueffer [Ford], Whistler said on his deathbed in 1903, "You must not say anything against Rossetti. Rossetti was a king." Ford, *Memories and Impressions: A Study in Atmospheres* (New York: Harper and Brothers, 1911), 33. Quoting this remark, McGann assigns the dates of 1848 to 1912 as the period of Rossetti's ascendancy, in *Game That Must Be Lost,* 2.

4. Casteras, *English Pre-Raphaelitism and Its Reception in America,* 143.

5. Jackson, *Early Poetry of Ezra Pound,* 28; Eliot, *Selected Essays,* 223.

6. In 1957, Frank Kermode acknowledged Rossetti as a conduit for passing the "Romantic image," epitomized in the figure of a beautiful woman, from Keats to Yeats. Kermode, *Romantic Image,* 61–67. Carol Christ opened a new chapter in Modernist studies by examining the similarities between the Victorian theory of the picturesque and the Modernist concept of the image. Christ, *Victorian and Modern Poetics,* chapter 3. Cassandra Laity drew attention to Rossetti and Swinburne's images of powerful female figures as influences on H.D.'s Modernism. Christ and Laity both argued that Eliot, Pound, and Yeats repressed this female figure in order to forge a more masculine poetic style. Christ, "Gender, Voice, and Figuration," 23; Laity, *H.D. and the Victorian Fin de Siècle,* chapter 1. In *Game That Must Be Lost* and various articles cited in chapter 2, note 3, Jerome McGann has identified Rossetti as the precursor of many aspects of modern poetry, including the visual and material orientation of Imagism and Pound's theory of translation and bookmaking practices. Credit is also due to McGann's digital *Rossetti Archive* for assem-

bling Rossetti's complex oeuvre of visual and literary works in one accessible place for the first time. Jessica Feldman connects Rossetti's "domestic sublimity" with Modernist aesthetics, and Celia Marshik places Rossetti at the start of a series of celebrated censorship cases that shaped Modernism. Feldman, *Victorian Modernism: Pragmatism and the Varieties of Aesthetic Experience* (New York: Cambridge University Press, 2002), chapter 3; Marshik, *British Modernism and Censorship* (New York: Cambridge University Press, 2006), chapter 1.

7. Robert Langbaum's study of dramatic monologue, *The Poetry of Experience*, established this line of interpretation; more recently, full-length studies of Pound's debt to nineteenth-century poetry continue to deprecate Rossetti while elevating Browning. Thomas Grieve argues that it was Browning who facilitated Pound's "objectivity," referring to Rossetti's influence only as the cause of his "preliminary flirtation with the subjective mode" (*Ezra Pound's Early Poetry and Poetics*, 29). See also Gibson, *Epic Reinvented: Ezra Pound and the Victorians* (Ithaca: Cornell University Press, 1995), chapters 2 and 3.

8. The myth of the breakdown of genre in Modernism was launched in 1902 by Benedetto Croce's claim that "every true work of art has violated some established kind," was promoted by Rene Wellek who wrote that modern writers have "called into doubt . . . the very concept" of genre, and has remained a consistent starting point for discussions of Modernism. Croce, *Aesthetic as Science of Expression and General Linguistic*, trans. Douglas Ainslie (London: Macmillan, 1922), 37; Wellek, *Discriminations: Further Concepts of Criticism* (New Haven: Yale University Press, 1970), 225. Jahan Ramazani's defense of the relevance of genre in Modernist poetry has shaped my own methods; see his introduction to the *Poetry of Mourning*, 23–25, 374.

9. Laity, *H.D. and the Victorian Fin de Siècle*, chapter 1.

10. Sborgi, "Between Literature and the Visual Arts: Portraits of the Self in William Carlos Williams, Marianne Moore, and Fernando Pessoa," in *Stories and Portraits of the Self*, ed. Helena Carvalhao Buescu (New York: Rodopi, 2007), 267–79. The idea that portraiture from the turn of the century increasingly reflected the identity of the painter rather than the subject is widely found, for example in Rubin, *Picasso and Portraiture*, 21.

11. See, for example, Howard Fulweiler, *"Here a Captive Heart Busted": Studies in the Sentimental Journey of Modern Literature* (New York: Fordham University Press, 1993), 3.

12. Rossetti, *Collected Poetry and Prose*, 129.

13. The scholarship on the history of the self is vast; aside from Taylor, discussed below, see also Roy Porter, ed., *Rewriting the Self: Histories from the Renaissance to the Present;* Michael Carrithers, Steven Collins, and Steven Lukes, ed., *The Category of the Person: Anthropology, Philosophy, History* (New York: Cambridge University Press, 1985); Jerrold Siegel, *The Idea of the Self: Thought and Experience in Western Europe since the Seventeenth Century* (New York: Cambridge University Press, 2005); and Raymond Martin and John Barresi, *The Rise and Fall of Soul and Self: An Intellectual History of Personal Identity* (New York: Columbia University Press, 2006), including a useful bibliography on pp. 5–7.

14. The popularity of the portrait as a literary form in the late nineteenth and early twentieth centuries was not limited to poetry, as a few of the outstanding examples demonstrate: Henry James's *The Portrait of a Lady*, Oscar Wilde's *The Picture of Dorian Gray*, James Joyce's *A Portrait of the Artist as a Young Man*, and Gertrude Stein's prose portraits. Anne Herrmann's *Queering the Moderns: Poses/Portraits/Performances* (New York: Palgrave, 2000) and Jamie Hovey's *A Thousand Words: Portraiture, Style, and Queer Modernism* (Columbus: Ohio State University Press, 2006) examine Modernist prose portrai-

ture (memoir and fiction), emphasizing the role of gender and the differences between male and female, straight and queer writers in their approaches to this genre.

15. My understanding of the "thing-tradition" in modern poetry draws on Douglas Mao's *Solid Objects: Modernism and the Test of Production;* see also the very different account in Jerome McGann's *Black Riders: The Visible Language of Modernism* (Princeton: Princeton University Press, 1993).

16. Taylor, *Sources of the Self,* 172.

17. Ibid., section 24.3.

18. Ibid., 476.

19. The work of Henry James in particular has yielded the concept of intersubjectivity or shared consciousness, as explored by Sharon Cameron: "James's fiction records the outrageous triumph in which the mind and the world, the self and the other, consciousness and the things it appropriates . . . converge or are even interpenetrated." *Thinking in Henry James* (Chicago: University of Chicago Press, 1989), 30.

20. A rich literature on visual portraiture has contributed to this study, including West, *Portraiture,* Woodall, ed., *Portraiture: Facing the Subject,* and Schneider, *The Art of the Portrait.* Soussloff's *The Subject in Art: Portraiture and the Birth of the Modern* (Durham: Duke University Press, 2006) examines the practice of portraiture in turn-of-the-century Vienna, and McPherson's *The Modern Portrait in Nineteenth-Century France* examines the impact of photography on mid-nineteenth-century French portraiture. Cynthia Freeland's *Portraits and Persons: A Philosophical Inquiry* examines some of the philosophical issues entailed in portraiture (New York: Oxford University Press, 2010).

21. McPherson, *The Modern Portrait in Nineteenth-Century France,* 4; Woodall, *Portraiture,* 10.

22. The secular portrait is said to have emerged in the figures of donors painted into the devotional scenes for which they paid, figures who are distinguished by a heightened attention to the details of their facial features, including flaws and irregularities, that mark them as unique individuals (West, *Portraiture,* 14–15; Woodall, *Portraiture,* 1.) The documentation of physical appearances as the function of portraiture seems to have preceded any exploration of the psychological or spiritual dimension. Toward the end of the fifteenth century, portraiture "focused increasingly on inward states, the evocation of atmosphere and the portrayal of mental and moral attitudes" (Schneider, *The Art of the Portrait,* 14–15, 6).

23. Peter Burke, among others, links this development of interiority to changes in portraiture; see his "Representations of the Self from Petrarch to Descartes" in Porter, *Rewriting the Self,* 17–28. Woodall's *Portraiture* is premised on the idea that the history of portraiture reflects the emergence of a bourgeois, Protestant subject (10).

24. Taylor, *Sources of the Self,* 201.

25. Fried introduces these concepts in *Absorption and Theatricality* and discusses Manet in relation to these approaches in *Courbet's Realism* and *Manet's Modernism.* Here I am drawing on the definitions offered in the introduction to *Courbet's Realism,* especially pp. 6–13.

26. Fried, *Courbet's Realism,* 13.

27. Ibid., 200–201; *Manet's Modernism,* 404–7.

28. This widely used definition appears in Heffernan, *Museum of Words,* 3. The studies of ekphrasis consulted for this book include Jean Hagstrum's *The Sister Arts,* Murray Krieger's *Ekphrasis,* Heffernan's *Museum of Words,* W.J.T. Mitchell's *Picture Theory,* John

Hollander's *The Gazer's Spirit*, Elizabeth Bergmann Loizeaux's *Twentieth-Century Poetry and the Visual Arts*, and Stephen Cheeke's *Writing for Art*. While most of these books do not deal specifically with portraiture, they address issues of gendering, reflection, and temporality that also arise in portrait poems.

29. Claire Pace, "'Delineated Lives': Themes and Variations in Seventeenth-Century Poems about Portraits," *Word and Image* 2.1 (1986): 1–17, 3. See also Brian Steele, "In the Flower of Their Youth: 'Portraits' of Venetian Beauties ca. 1500," *Sixteenth Century Journal* 28.2 (Summer 1997): 481–502.

30. Loizeaux, *Twentieth-Century Poetry and the Visual Arts*, 3–4.

31. The intersection of the "sister arts" has a distinguished history, in which the ungainly term "intermediality" is a latecomer. Nevertheless, it usefully denominates an area or process of exchange not just between painting and writing but more generally among many possible media. I have chosen the term "intermedial" over "interart" since it has slightly more currency, but the two seem interchangeable. Peter Wagner defines intermediality as the intertextual use of one medium in another medium (*Icons, Texts, Iconotexts*, 17), thus covering more than the term "ekphrasis"; my use of intermediality includes the stylistic, formal, and generic influences flowing from other arts into poetry, which may not take the form of explicit allusions.

32. On the importance of titles as generic indicators, see Fowler, *Kinds of Literature*, 92–98, as well as Hollander, *Vision and Resonance* (New Haven: Yale University Press, 1985), 212–26, and Gérard Genette, *Paratexts: Thresholds of Interpretation*, trans. Jane Lewin (New York: Cambridge University Press, 1997), chapter 4, esp. 56–57.

33. Fowler, *Kinds of Literature*, 55.

34. Ibid., 48–52.

35. Ibid., chapters 10 and 11.

36. Schneider, *The Art of the Portrait*, 10; see also William A. Ewing, *About Face: Photography and the Death of the Portrait* (London: Hayward Gallery Publishing, 2004), 9–15.

37. Steiner, *Exact Resemblance to Exact Resemblance*, 12.

38. McGann, "Medieval versus Victorian versus Modern," 109.

1 Portraiture in the Rossetti Circle

1. "About Portraits," 417.

2. McGann, *Game That Must Be Lost*, 44.

3. "About Portraits," 412.

4. Ibid., 519.

5. Haley, *Living Forms*, 101.

6. Albert Franklin Blaisdell, *Outlines for the Study of English Classics: A Practical Guide for Students of English Literature* (New England Publishing Company, 1878), 163.

7. Stopford Brooke, *Theology in the English Poets: Cowper, Coleridge, Wordsworth and Burns* (New York: D. Appleton, 1875), 61.

8. William Cowper, *The Works of William Cowper: Comprising His Poems, Correspondence, and Translations*, ed. Robert Southey, vol. X (London: Baldwin and Cradock, 1835–37), 65. English Poetry Full-Text Database.

9. Ibid., 67–68.

10. Bernard Barton, *Household Verses* (London: George Virtue, 1845), 150. English Poetry Full-Text Database.

11. Ibid., 150, 149, 151, 152.

12. Elizabeth Barrett Browning, *Poetical Works* (New York: Thomas Y. Crowell, 1882), 383.

13. Frederick Locker-Lampson, *London Lyrics, 1857* (London: Macmillan, 1904), 131. English Poetry Full-Text Database.

14. John Stuart Blackie, *Messis Vitae: Gleanings of Song from a Happy Life* (London: Macmillan, 1886), 73. English Poetry Full-Text Database.

15. Ibid., 74.

16. Francis Palgrave, *Amenophis and Other Poems Sacred and Secular* (London: Macmillan, 1892), 174. English Poetry Full-Text Database.

17. Haley discusses the background of this poem and offers a different interpretation in *Living Forms*, 102–4.

18. William Wordsworth, *Yarrow Revisited, and Other Poems* (New York: R. Bartlett and S. Raynor, 1835), 208.

19. Heffernan's discussion of "My Last Duchess" in *The Museum of Words* (139–45) introduced the category of ekphrasis to the discourse on this famous poem. It has typically been regarded as a paradigm-setting example of the dramatic monologue.

20. Prettejohn, *Rossetti and His Circle*, 6–7, 29.

21. Greenberg, "Modernist Painting," 194.

22. Prettejohn, *Art for Art's Sake*, 29–30.

23. See Barlow, "Facing the Past and Present: The National Portrait Gallery and the Search for 'Authentic Portraiture,'" in Woodall, *Portraiture*, 234–36.

24. M. S. Watts, *George Frederic Watts: His Writings* (London: Macmillan, 1912), 3:35.

25. Corbett, *The World in Paint*, 146.

26. Ross, *Modernist Impulses in the Human Sciences, 1870–1930* (Baltimore: Johns Hopkins University Press, 1994), 1.

27. John Stuart Mill, *An Examination of Sir William Hamilton's Philosophy* (Boston: William Spencer, 1865), 1:255.

28. The practice of portraiture flourished throughout the nineteenth century but was consistently denigrated by the Royal Academy and art critics. On the status of the portrait in England, see Elizabeth Fay, "Portrait Galleries, Representative History, and Hazlitt's *Spirit of the Age*," in *Nineteenth-Century Contexts* 24.2 (2002): 152; Marcia Pointon, *Hanging the Head: Portraiture and Social Formation in Eighteenth-Century England* (New Haven: Yale University Press, 1993), 38–40; Haley, *Living Forms*, 85–86; Barlow, "Facing the Past and Present," in Woodall, *Portraiture*, 224.

29. Rossetti, *Correspondence*, 2:269–70 (letter 59:35).

30. Letter from Arthur Hughes to William Allingham, Feb. 1860. *Letters to William Allingham*, ed. H. Allingham (London: Longmans, Green, 1911), 67.

31. Swinburne, *Swinburne Letters*, 1:27.

32. Quoted in Surtees, *Paintings and Drawings*, 1:69.

33. Prettejohn, "Beautiful Women with Floral Adjuncts," in Treuherz, Prettejohn, and Becker, *Dante Gabriel Rossetti*, 58.

34. Shefer, "A Rossetti Portrait," 10.

35. On Rossetti's frames, see Alastair Grieve, "The Applied Art of D. G. Rossetti— I. His Picture-Frames," *Burlington Magazine* 115.838 (1973): 16, 18–24.

36. Surtees, *Paintings and Drawings*, 69; Prettejohn, *Art for Art's Sake*, 39; Shefer, "A Rossetti Portrait," 4.

37. Fried, *Manet's Modernism*, 195–96.

38. McGann, *Game That Must Be Lost*, xvi.

39. See Riede, *Limits of Victorian Vision*, 53.

40. Helsinger, *Poetry and the Pre-Raphaelite Arts*, 52.

41. Rossetti, *Collected Poetry and Prose*, 161.

42. Rossetti, *Correspondence*, 4:450 (letter 70.110).

43. Swinburne, *Major Poems and Selected Prose*, 372.

44. Pater, *Three Major Texts*, 150.

45. Kermode, *Romantic Image*, 61–67.

46. Archibald MacLeish, "Ars Poetica," paraphrased in Kermode, *Romantic Image*, 66.

47. Rossetti, *Collected Poetry and Prose*, 132.

48. Helsinger, *Poetry and the Pre-Raphaelite Arts*, 161.

49. Riede and Helsinger both discuss the influence of the gothic portrait tale on Rossetti, including Walpole's *Castle of Otranto*, Radcliffe's *Mysteries of Udolpho*, Poe's "The Oval Portrait," and Hawthorne's "Prophetic Pictures." In these tales, a portrait typically exerts some influence over its subject or the viewer, and may come to life at the expense of the living sitter. Wilde's later *Picture of Dorian Grey* is another example of this subgenre. Rossetti's unfinished tale "Saint Agnes of Intercession," probably intended as a frame for "On Mary's Portrait," employs the devices of the gothic portrait tale. Helsinger, *Poetry and the Pre-Raphaelite Arts*, 122–28.

50. Riede, *Limits of Victorian Vision*, 35–37.

51. McGann, *Game That Must Be Lost*, 10.

52. Rossetti, *Collected Poetry and Prose*, 70.

53. Ibid.

54. McGann, *Game That Must Be Lost*, 26.

55. Prettejohn, *Art for Art's Sake*, 109.

56. Fried, *Manet's Modernism*, 229.

57. Edward Burne-Jones's 1877 painting *The Mirror of Venus* elaborates and amplifies the theme of reflection seen in *The Little White Girl*. For a discussion of this painting in the context of interiority, see Kate Flint, "Edward Burne-Jones's *The Mirror of Venus*: surface and subjectivity in the art criticism of the 1870s" in Prettejohn, ed., *After the Pre-Raphaelites*, 152–64.

58. J. Hillis Miller suggests *Nocturne in Blue and Silver* or *Harmony in Grey and Green*, but Whistler began both of these works in 1872 or later. Miller, "Whistler/Swinburne: 'Before the Mirror,'" in *Haunted Texts: Studies in Pre-Raphaelitism in Honour of William E. Fredeman*, ed. David Latham (Toronto: University of Toronto Press, 2003), 141. On "Brown and Silver" and "Nocturne in Blue and Silver," see Dorment and MacDonald, *James McNeill Whistler*, 100, 128, respectively.

59. Dorment and MacDonald, *James McNeill Whistler*, 100.

60. Ibid., 307.

61. Swinburne, *Swinburne Letters*, 1:118–20.

62. Swinburne, *Major Poems and Selected Prose*, 118.

63. Ibid.

64. Whistler resisted this approach, becoming increasingly vocal about the status of his paintings as nonnarrative "symphonies," "nocturnes," and "arrangements" during the 1860s and 1870s; however, he did not retitle the "white girl" series as "symphonies in white" until 1867, after Swinburne's poem had been composed and publicly displayed on the picture. Dorment and MacDonald, *James McNeill Whistler*, 78.

65. Swinburne, *Major Poems and Selected Prose*, 118.

66. Ibid., 373.

67. Ibid., 118.

68. Fried, *Manet's Modernism*, 228.

69. Swinburne, *Poems and Ballads: First Series*, 14 (lines 87–88).

70. Swinburne, *Major Poems and Selected Prose*, 269 (lines 117–20). Charlotte Ribeyrol draws attention to the term "interspace" in connection with "Before the Mirror." Ribeyrol, "Swinburne-Whistler: Correspondances," 68.

71. Taylor, *Sources of the Self*, 476.

72. Pound, *Literary Essays*, 292–93.

73. Swinburne, *Major Poems and Selected Prose*, 83 (lines 56–60), 89 (lines 287–88).

74. Ibid., 89 (lines 301–4).

75. Ibid., 118–19 (lines 47–49; 54–56; 61–63).

76. Interpretations of the poem typically avoid commenting on this final section, which seems to add little to the poem as an ekphrasis. Wilson reads the final section as expressing "an antithesis between art and life," in which the White Girl remains isolated and frozen in her aesthetic world. Wilson, "Behind the Veil, Forbidden: Truth, Beauty, and Swinburne's Aesthetic Strain," *Victorian Poetry* 22.4 (1984): 435.

77. On Swinburne's musical aesthetic, see Thomas E. Connolly, *Swinburne's Theory of Poetry* (Albany: SUNY Press, 1964), Robert L. Peters, *The Crowns of Apollo: Swinburne's Principles of Literature and Art* (Detroit: Wayne State University Press, 1965), and Jerome McGann, "Wagner, Baudelaire, Swinburne: Poetry in the Condition of Music," *Victorian Poetry* 47.4 (2009): 619–32.

78. Pater, *Three Major Texts*, 156.

79. Prettejohn, *Art for Art's Sake*, 110–12.

80. The significance of Whistler's musical titles has been much discussed. Spencer comments that Whistler would have found this idea in Ruskin's *Modern Painters*, vol. 5, "Of Invention Formal." Ruskin also discusses the motif of mirroring in the following section, "The Dark Mirror." Spencer, "Whistler, Swinburne, and Art for Art's Sake," in Prettejohn, *After the Pre-Raphaelites*, 64. Prettejohn notes that Whistler's "Symphony in White" paintings shared their musical analogy with Albert Moore's *Musicians* (1867) and Frederick Leighton's *Spanish Dancing Girl* (1867); all three paintings "order their compositions on principles of rhythm or proportion that can be seen as analogous to the proportional relationships of musical intervals and chords. Thus the idea of an analogy with music can suggest a compositional method based on spatial measurements, as music is based on quantifiable acoustic vibrations." Prettejohn, *Art for Art's Sake*, 111.

2 Ezra Pound

1. H.D., *End to Torment*, 39.

2. Pound, introduction to *Sonnets and Ballate*, dated 1910; *Pound's Cavalcanti: An Edition of the Translations, Notes, and Essays*, ed. David Anderson (Princeton: Princeton University Press, 1983), 14.

3. Though a number of other critics have acknowledged Pound's debt to Rossetti, there remains no book-length analysis of this relationship. My retracing of it was guided by De Nagy and Jackson, who observe many specific points of contact between Pound and Pre-Raphaelitism. De Nagy attributes Pound's medievalism to Rossetti's influence (*The Poetry of Ezra Pound*, 54–68); Jackson identifies a number of similarities between their approaches, especially in contrast to the Decadents, whom he finds less impor-

tant to Pound: significant "moments of complete awareness," of vision or revelation; the importance of myth to both; and a number of stylistic affinities (*The Early Poetry of Ezra Pound*, 17–28, 40–46, 149–62). While detailing this influence, de Nagy and Jackson both conclude with the familiar judgment that Pound used up and went beyond his model. McGann has examined several areas of Rossetti's impact on Pound, including translations, the design of the first printing of *Mauberley* and the 1925 and 1928 editions of the *Cantos*, and the influence of the Rossettian picture-poem on Imagism. See McGann, "A Commentary on Some of Rossetti's Translations from Dante," *Journal of Pre-Raphaelite Studies* 9 (2000): 25–38; "Pound's Cantos: A Poem Including Bibliography"; and "Medieval versus Victorian versus Modern." Peter Faulkner states that "Of the Pre-Raphaelites, Rossetti was to be the strongest influence on Pound," in "Pound and the Pre-Raphaelites," *Paideuma* 13 (1984): 229–44, 231. T. Wilson West ("D. G. Rossetti and Ezra Pound") and Banerjee ("Dante through the Looking Glass") also comment on aspects of Rossetti's influence on Pound.

4. The most thorough analyses of Pound's relation to Whistler can be found in Rebecca Beasley's "Ezra Pound's Whistler" and chapter 1 of her book *Ezra Pound and Visual Culture*, on which I draw here.

5. Beasley, "Ezra Pound's Whistler," 491.

6. Pound, *Gaudier-Brzeska*, 119–20.

7. Beasley, "Ezra Pound's Whistler," 495–98.

8. De Nagy discusses Swinburne's influence on Pound in *Poetry of Ezra Pound*, 68–80; Jackson in *Early Poetry of Ezra Pound*, 68–72, 123–28.

9. H.D., writing as Delia Alton, also pairs herself with Elizabeth Siddal and Richard Aldington with Rossetti; the title of her novel refers to Swinburne's "Before the Mirror." *White Rose and the Red*, ed. Alison Halsall (Gainesville: University Press of Florida, 2010).

10. The sestinas include "Sestina: Altaforte" and "Sestina for Ysolt"; the quotation from Swinburne in "Elegia" is "I have put my days and dreams out of mind." Pound, *Poems and Translations*, 166.

11. Pound, *Literary Essays*, 292–93.

12. See Grieve, *Ezra Pound's Early Poetry and Poetics*, chapter 3; Diggory, *Yeats and American Poetry*, chapter 3; Litz, "Pound and Yeats: The Road to Stone Cottage"; and Ellmann, *Eminent Domain: Yeats among Wilde, Joyce, Pound, Eliot, and Auden* (Oxford: Oxford University Press, 1967), chapter 4.

13. Diggory, *Yeats and American Poetry*, 37; Litz, "Pound and Yeats: The Road to Stone Cottage," 129.

14. Loizeaux, *Yeats and the Visual Arts*, 19.

15. Rossetti, "Severed Selves," *Collected Poetry and Prose*, 145.

16. Jackson, *Early Poetry of Ezra Pound*, 28; foreword to reissue of Pound's *A Lume Spento* (New York: New Directions, 1965), 7.

17. Kenner, *The Pound Era* (Berkeley: University of California Press, 1971), 80.

18. Grieve, *Ezra Pound's Early Poetry and Poetics*, 29; Banerjee similarly comments that Pound's "Donzella Beata" personifies "Pound's rejection of the passive sensuality and the mood of longing embodied by the Damozel in Rossetti's poem." Banerjee, "Dante through the Looking Glass," 142.

19. McGann, "Pound's Cantos: A Poem Including Bibliography," 58.

20. Casteras, *English Pre-Raphaelitism and Its Reception in America*, 143.

21. Such as an illustrated "Waistcoat-pocket" edition of "The Blessed Damozel" published in Philadelphia in 1905 by Henry Altemus, or William Michael Rossetti's edition

of *The Poems of Dante Gabriel Rossetti with Illustrations from His Own Pictures and Designs* published in Boston by Little, Brown in 1904. By 1904, H. C. Marillier's *Dante Gabriel Rossetti: An Illustrated Memorial of His Art and Life* (London: G. Bell and Sons) was already in its third edition. WorldCat figures indicate that over 900 books by or about Dante Gabriel Rossetti were published between 1880 and 1905, with production peaking in 1900 with over 140 publications in that year, as well as 40 or more in each of the years 1902–5.

22. Pater, *Three Major Texts*, 530.

23. Rossetti, *Collected Poetry and Prose*, 3.

24. Shefer, "A Rossetti Portrait: Variation on a Theme," 10.

25. Rossetti, *Collected Poetry and Prose*, 129.

26. Riede, for example, observes that the poem's "religious sentiment and symbolism can sometimes ring ludicrously false." Riede, *Limits of Victorian Vision*, 22.

27. Rossetti, *Collected Poetry and Prose*, 129.

28. Buchanan, "The Fleshly School of Poetry," 335.

29. Ibid., 337.

30. Pound, *Poems and Translations*, 4.

31. Laity, *H.D. and the Victorian Fin de Siècle*, 15.

32. Pound, *Poems and Translations*, 9.

33. Ibid., 148.

34. Pound, *Ezra Pound's Poetry and Prose: Contributions to Periodicals*, 1:17 (hereafter cited as *Periodicals*, by volume).

35. Pound, *Poems and Translations*, 169.

36. Ibid., 142.

37. Ibid., 168; Rossetti, *Collected Poetry and Prose*, 106, lines 478–80. This allusion is noted in West, "D. G. Rossetti and Ezra Pound," 66.

38. McGann, Rossetti Archive commentary for *Sancta Lilias*, http://www.rossetti archive.org/docs/s244c.rap.html.

39. Pound, *Poems and Translations*, 168.

40. Eric Homberger, ed., *Ezra Pound: The Critical Heritage* (Boston: Routledge and Kegan Paul, 1972), 61.

41. Pound, *Poems and Translations*, 80.

42. Yeats, *Collected Poems*, 33.

43. Diggory, *Yeats and American Poetry*, 37; Jackson, *The Early Poetry of Ezra Pound*, 129.

44. Quoted in James Hamilton's *Arthur Rackham: A Life with Illustration* (London: Pavilion Books, 1990), 89.

45. Shakespeare, *A Midsummer Night's Dream*, Act III, scene 2.

46. Pound, *Poems and Translations*, 113.

47. Swinburne, *Major Poems and Selected Prose*, 119.

48. Pound, "To La Mère Inconnue," Beinecke YCAL MSS 43, Box 112, Folder 4743. All subsequent citations of "To La Mère Inconnue" refer to this manuscript.

49. Ibid., 2.

50. Yeats, *Collected Poems*, 39, 360, 365, 386, 46.

51. Swinburne, *Major Poems and Selected Prose*, 83 (lines 57–58), 89 (lines 287–89), 88 (lines 257–58).

52. Pound, *Poems and Translations*, 50.

53. Swinburne, *Major Poems and Selected Prose*, 89 (lines 301–5).

54. Ibid., 90 (lines 321–28).

55. Pound, "To La Mère Inconnue," 7. The second "thy" in the last line is unclear and could also read "only."

56. Pound, *Poems and Translations*, 113. All quotations of this poem are from the same page.

57. Rossetti, *Collected Poetry and Prose*, 132.

58. Pound, "To La Mère Inconnue," 7–8.

59. Schneidau, *Ezra Pound: The Image and the Real*, 6.

60. Pound, *Poems and Translations*, 233.

61. Ibid., 234.

62. Mao similarly comments, "the descriptions of exotic treasures threaten to over-whelm by their splendor the theme that generates them" (Mao, *Solid Objects*, 153).

63. "Dim" is one of Pound's early favorite words, appearing twenty-eight times in his work before 1912, and only three times afterward, including here in "Portrait d'une femme."

64. Pound, *Ezra Pound and Dorothy Shakespear: Letters*, 130–32.

65. See Josephine Johnson, *Florence Farr: Bernard Shaw's "New Woman"* (Totowa, NJ: Rowman and Littlefield, 1975) on Farr's relationship with Shaw (chapter 4), the Golden Dawn and her relationship with Yeats (chapter 5); psaltery and poetic chanting (chapter 6).

66. Pound, *Ezra Pound and Dorothy Shakespear: Letters*, 115.

67. DuPlessis, "Propounding Modernist Maleness," 399.

68. As discussed in chapter 1, Charles Taylor offers Pound's poetry as an example of the "interspatial epiphany" that Modernists substituted for Romantic interiority. See Taylor, *Sources of the Self*, 476, and discussion in chapter 1, p. 43.

69. Pound, *Poems and Translations*, 234.

70. See Thomas Dilworth, "The other 'person of some interest' in Pound's 'Portrait d'une femme,'" *Paideuma* 25.1/2 (1996), 221.

71. DuPlessis, "Propounding Modernist Maleness," 400.

72. "Portrait d'une femme" must have been composed in or before January 1912, when it was rejected by the *North American Review*, on the basis of the three repeated "r"s in the first line. Pound sent the manuscript of *Ripostes* to his publisher Stephen Swift and Co. in February 1912. Thus, although the poem did not appear until October 1912, the poems were all composed before Marinetti's appearance in London. Pound, *Patria Mia and the Treatise on Harmony* (London: Peter Owen, 1962), 29–30; *Poems and Translations*, 1239. DuPlessis hangs her argument on Pound's August 1912 note to Harriet Monroe referring to two poems he can offer her for *Poetry*: an "over-elaborate post-Browning Imagiste affair" and "a note on the Whistler exhibit." DuPlessis claims that Pound's deprecating remark about the "Imagiste affair" reveals his self-critical feelings about "Portrait d'une femme" and his own work in general. However, "Portrait d'une femme" was already in press at this time, and Monroe published "To Whistler, American" along with the dramatic monologue "Middle-Aged: A Study in an Emotion" in *Poetry* 1 (Oct. 1912), so presumably it was the latter, a rather mediocre work, to which Pound referred in his letter.

73. Pound was away from London from June 1910 to February 1911, thus missing not only the publication of excerpts of the first Futurist Manifesto in *The Tramp* in August 1910, but also Roger Fry's exhibit of Manet and the post-Impressionists and the extensive debates in the press about this event (Beasley, *Ezra Pound and Visual Culture*, 69–78).

His first exposure to Marinetti would have been in March 1912, when the Futurist gave an uproarious lecture to the public on the same day that Pound lectured to a select, by-invitation-only audience on Arnaut Daniel; he must have noted the difference in press coverage between Marinetti's famous performance and his own, as Litz and Rainey observe ("Ezra Pound," 69). Pound's first allusion to Futurism and Marinetti appears in "Patria Mia III," published in September 1912 in *The New Age*.

74. Pound, *Periodicals*, 1:102.

75. Ibid., 103.

76. Ibid.

77. James, *Portrait of a Lady*, 280.

78. Pound, *Selected Letters*, 10.

79. Pound, *Poems and Translations*, 608.

80. Beasley, "Ezra Pound's Whistler," 505; she remarks that Pound might have discussed the more abstract nocturnes rather than these portraits, but Pound specifically notes that these were not shown in the exhibition to which his article and the poem "To Whistler" respond. Rather, he viewed the portraits and the nocturnes as part of the same Aesthetic project.

81. Pound, *Periodicals*, 1:103.

82. Barbara Weinberg, "Late-Nineteenth-Century American Painting: Cosmopolitan Concerns and Controversies," *Archives of American Art Journal*, 23.4 (1983): 22.

83. Elizabeth Chang, *Britain's Chinese Eye: Literature, Empire, and Aesthetics in Nine-teenth-Century Britain* (Palo Alto: Stanford University Press, 2010), 101.

84. Fried, *Manet's Modernism*, 229.

85. Alexander Sturgis, *Rebels and Martyrs: The Image of the Artist in the Nineteenth Century* (London: National Gallery/Yale University Press, 2006), 128.

86. Described in a letter to Fantin-Latour, 16 Aug. 1865, quoted in Andrew McLaren Young, ed., *The Paintings of James McNeill Whistler* (New Haven: Mellon Centre/Yale University Press, 1980), 1:37.

87. Beasley observes that the poem is about "personality, both Whistler's and Pound's," and she associates it with the persona poem/dramatic monologue. However, in terms of genre, "To Whistler" exhibits more traits of portraiture than dramatic lyric, since it is addressed *to* the painter and describes him in the second person rather than adopting his voice. Beasley, "Ezra Pound's Whistler," 506.

88. Pound, *Poems and Translations*, 608.

3   T. S. Eliot

1. Eliot, *Selected Essays*, 223.

2. On Norton's role in creating Rossetti's American reputation, see Casteras, *English Pre-Raphaelitism and Its Reception in America*, 28–29, 126–27.

3. As Ronald Bush observes, much Eliot criticism since the 1980s (including books by Ann Ardis, Colleen Lamos, and Cassandra Laity) has focused on Eliot's ties to Decadence and his politically and personally motivated suppression of these ties as he became an "elder statesman" of letters after the publication of *The Waste Land*. Overemphasizing that act of suppression risks "replicating the modernist myth of a break from the 1890s rather than clarifying [the modernists'] genuinely conflicted relations with aestheticism." For an overview of the criticism about Eliot's engagement with the 1890s, see Bush's "In Pursuit of Wilde Possum: Reflections on Eliot, Modernism, and the Nineties," *Modernism/Modernity* 11 (2004): 469–86. I see Eliot's relationship to Rossetti in terms

similar to those Bush maps out between Eliot and Wilde, though perhaps less charged with sexual anxiety: a complex ambivalence rather than a politically motivated suppression. See also Laity's "T. S. Eliot and A. C. Swinburne: Decadent Bodies, Modern Visualities, and Changing Modes of Perception," *Modernism/Modernity* 11 (2004): 425–49.

4. Julia Cartwright, "Edward Burne-Jones" in *Eclectic Magazine of Foreign Literature (1901–1907)* (July 1905): 145. American Periodicals Series Online.

5. Not every detail in Eliot's poem matches Burne-Jones's painting; for example, Eliot refers to a "fountain," which Burne-Jones did not include, although it is possible to view the falling drops of potion from Circe's hand as a kind of fountain. The subject of Circe was a popular one in fin de siècle art, including multiple works by John William Waterhouse. Burne-Jones was the only artist to include panthers, a New World animal, as far as I can tell. Maxfield Parrish's 1907 *Circe's Palace* represents the figure of Circe pouring her potion into a fountain at the center of the painting. It is possible that Eliot combined the fountain from Parrish's image with the flowers, panthers, and python of Burne-Jones's. However, Parrish's painting probably would not have been available to Eliot in 1908; it was published as an illustration to Hawthorne's *Tanglewood Tales* in 1910. Thanks to Can Kantarci for pointing out Parrish's painting.

6. John Ruskin, *Munera Pulveris: Six Essays on the Elements of Political Economy* (New York: John Wiley and Son, 1884), 78.

7. In the painting, which was only recently reproduced in color for the first time, Circe's hair has tints of red that harmonize with her robe; the darkest elements of the painting are her carved throne and the panthers. Both Rossetti and Eliot play freely with the details of the picture to bring out what interests them.

8. Rossetti, *Collected Poetry and Prose*, 185.

9. In contrast, Stephen Cheeke sees these opposites as "incommensurable," and the sonnet structured "around the threat of mistaking one for the other." Cheeke, *Writing for Art*, 78.

10. Rossetti, *Collected Poetry and Prose*, 337–38.

11. Eliot, *Poems Written in Early Youth*, 20.

12. Swinburne, *Major Poems and Selected Prose*, 119, 121.

13. Helsinger, *Poetry and the Pre-Raphaelite Arts*, 48–49.

14. Wollheim, *Painting as an Art*, 160.

15. Powel, "Notes on the Life of T. S. Eliot," 90.

16. Greenberg, "Modernist Painting," 194.

17. Pater, *Three Major Texts*, 149.

18. A similar look appears in many of Manet's other single-figure portraits: *The Absinthe Drinker* (1858–59), *Madame Brunet* (1860), *La Prune* (1877), and most famously in his last major work *Bar aux Folies-Bergère* (1882).

19. Spuller, "M. Edouard Manet et sa peinture," 1867, quoted in Fried, *Manet's Modernism*, 284.

20. Fried, *Manet's Modernism*, 282.

21. Ibid., 17.

22. Ibid., 339. Focusing on *Olympia* and *Bar aux Folies-Bergère*, T. J. Clark claims, in contrast, that the women-for-hire represented in these paintings look back at us with consciousness of their commodified condition, which they passively resist. *The Painting of Modern Life: Paris in the Art of Manet and His Followers* (New York: Alfred A. Knopf, 1985), 253, 254.

23. Theodore Reff discusses Manet's use of this book in "Manet and Blanc," *Burlington Magazine* 112 (1970): 456–58.

24. Elaine Shefer, "Deverell, Rossetti, Siddal, and 'The Bird in the Cage,'" *Art Bulletin* 67.3 (1985): 438.

25. Arden Reed, *Manet, Flaubert, and the Emergence of Modernism: Blurring Genre Boundaries* (New York: Cambridge University Press, 2003), 119.

26. Mona Hadler, "Manet's Woman with a Parrot of 1866," *Metropolitan Museum Journal* 7 (1973): 122.

27. The nosegay of *violets* and the half-peeled *orange* are not only accessories but they also self-referentially name their own colors (in French as well as in English). Armstrong, *Manet Manette*, 166.

28. Armstrong, *Manet Manette*, 168.

29. Fried, *Manet's Modernism*, 24.

30. Blanc, *Histoire des peintres de toutes les écoles* (Paris: Librairie Renouard, 1861–76) 2:3 (translation mine).

31. Wollheim, *Painting as an Art*, 149.

32. Carol Christ, among others, argues that Pater formulated the problem of epistemological isolation for both Victorian and Modernist literature (Christ, *Victorian and Modern Poetics*, 30–32).

33. Pater, *Three Major Texts*, 218.

34. Ibid., 74.

35. Eliot, *Poems Written in Early Youth*, 21.

36. The expression is echoed in Eliot's 1914 notebook poem "The Burnt Dancer" (as "circle of my brain") and generally points forward to his consistent attention to problems of perspective in "Prufrock," "Portrait of a Lady," his dissertation on F. H. Bradley, and *The Waste Land*. Indeed, "circle of our thought" is not so far from the expression "finite centers" that he uses in *Knowledge and Experience* to describe the problem of perspective and the difficulty of making contact with any reality outside one's own mind. "How do we yoke our divers worlds to draw together?" Eliot asks in this work. "How can we issue from the circle described about each point of view? and since I can know no point of view but my own, how can I know that there are other points of view, or admitting their existence, how can I take any account of them?" (Eliot, *Knowledge and Experience*, 141). "Circle of thought," "finite center," and "point of view" all imply a horizon, however broad, that bounds the mind and cuts it off from others.

37. Eliot, *Poems Written in Early Youth*, 21.

38. Rossetti, *Collected Poetry and Prose*, 161.

39. Swinburne, *Major Poems and Selected Prose*, 131.

40. Powel points out the correspondence with this passage from Swinburne in "Notes on the Life of T. S. Eliot," 90.

41. Eliot, *Poems Written in Early Youth*, 21.

42. Coleridge, *The Notebooks of Samuel Taylor Coleridge*, ed. Kathleen Coburn (Princeton: Princeton University Press, 1973), 3:4176.

43. "Immaterial" may also echo Swinburne's "immortal" in the first stanza of "The Garden of Proserpine," discussed below: "Who gathers all things mortal / With cold immortal hands."

44. Powel, "Notes on the Life of T. S. Eliot," 88.

45. A. D. Moody, *Thomas Stearns Eliot: Poet* (New York: Cambridge University Press, 1979), 17.

46. I am relying on Ricks's chronology in Eliot, *Inventions of the March Hare*, xxxix–xxxx.

47. Fried, *Manet's Modernism*, 111–12, 160–62.

48. For the Fine Arts 20B final exam of spring 1910, see the Papers of Edward Waldo Forbes, 1856–1971, at the Harvard University Archives, HUG FP 139.62 box 1. During his college days, Eliot made the acquaintance of Okakura Kakuzo, the curator of Asian art at the Boston Museum of Fine Arts. Eliot mentions Kakuzo in a letter to Isabella Gardner in 1915 (Eliot, *Letters*, vol. 1, 93), and the editor claims that Kakuzo took Eliot to meet Matisse in 1910. In 1907 Kakuzo made a large acquisition of Chinese paintings, including a stunning set of twelve eighteenth-century hanging scrolls entitled *Elegant Gathering in a Secluded Garden*. These are landscapes, but it is possible that they inspired Eliot's poem, or that he saw other works in the same collection to which "Mandarins" refers. Thanks to John Morgenstern for drawing my attention to Eliot's connection with Kakuzo and with Matthew Prichard, who served as secretary to the director of the MFA and contributed to the design of the new museum building (Eliot, *Letters*, vol. 1, 23). Nancy Hargrove also observes that Eliot's copy of Baedeker's *London and Its Environs*, which he used on his October 1910 and/or April 1911 trips to London, contains notes on Asian art at the British Museum and the South Kensington Museum. Nancy Duvall Hargrove, *T. S. Eliot's Parisian Year* (Gainesville: University Press of Florida, 2009), 131–32.

49. "Ohio and the Shijo School," Museum of Fine Arts Bulletin 8 (August 1910): 31; see also "Special Exhibition of Japanese Screens by Three Artists of the Kano School—Yeitoku, Sanraku, and Sansetsu," Museum of Fine Arts Bulletin 10 (February 1912): 6–10.

50. Eliot, *Inventions of the March Hare*, 19. The new MFA galleries were designed to encourage such spectatorship by featuring a few important works in spacious surroundings that allowed crowds to gather around them, rather than filling rooms with cases of objects. Eliot's friend Matthew Prichard advocated vocally for the new design, as did Kakuzo. Anne Nishimura Morse, "Promoting Authenticity: Okakura Kakuzo and the Japanese Collection of the Museum of Fine Arts, Boston," in *Okakura Tenshin and the Museum of Fine Arts, Boston*, ed. Nagoya Bosuton Bijutsukan (Boston: Museum of Fine Arts, 1999), 145.

51. Eliot, *Inventions of the March Hare*, 19, 21.

52. Ibid., 21, 22.

53. Eliot, *Complete Poems and Plays*, 20.

54. Denis Donoghue follows this lead in his interpretation of "La Figlia," which he praises as a beautiful poem. "Beauty," of course, is a key term of Aestheticism and Rossetti in particular, suggesting that this poem arose not just out of Eliot's love of Virgil. *Words Alone: The Poet T. S. Eliot* (New Haven: Yale University Press, 2000), chapter 3.

55. Roper, "T. S. Eliot's 'La Figlia Che Piange,'" 223.

56. Ibid., 224–26.

57. Eliot, *Complete Poems and Plays*, 20.

58. Roper, "T. S. Eliot's 'La Figlia Che Piange,'" 229.

59. Eliot, *Complete Poems and Plays*, 20; Rossetti, *Collected Poetry and Prose*, 161.

60. Eliot, *Complete Poems and Plays*, 20.

61. Roper, "T. S. Eliot's 'La Figlia Che Piange,'" 231.

62. John Xiros Cooper, "Thinking with Your Ears: Rhapsody, Prelude, Song in Eliot's Early Lyrics," in *T. S. Eliot's Orchestra: Critical Essays on Poetry and Music*, ed. Cooper (New York: Garland Publishing), 92, 91.

63. Matthew Arnold, *Poems: Second Series* (London: Longman, Brown, Green, and Longmans, 1855), 184.

64. Ibid., 188.

65. Eliot, *Complete Poems and Plays*, 9.

66. Shakespeare, *Twelfth Night*, Act I, Scene 1, lines 4, 7–8.

67. In *The Matrix of Modernism*, Sanford Schwartz diagnoses the instability of the male speaker in the terms of "half-objects" that Eliot would employ in *Knowledge and Experience* (Princeton: Princeton University Press, 1985), 193. Yet, as Donald Childs has noted, the philosophical discourse in which Eliot learned to articulate and manage his skeptical problems is not the one where he first encountered them; "Portrait" and "Prufrock" were composed before reading Bradley. Childs, *From Philosophy to Poetry: T. S. Eliot's Study of Knowledge and Experience* (New York: Palgrave, 2001), 73–84. The influence of Bergson provides a more likely explanation for the conflicts that seem inherent in the male speaker—particularly, Bergson's distinction between an "outer" or "social" self shaped by things and environment, and an inchoate, inexpressible "inner and individual existence." Henri Bergson, *Time and Free Will: An Essay on the Immediate Data of Consciousness*, trans. Pogson (London: George Allen, 1913), 130. Childs also notes the appearance of the "pure self" in "Portrait of a Lady" as prompted by images and smells that release nonverbal memories. However, Eliot wrote section II, the part most engaged with Matthew Arnold, in February 1910, before the onset of his Bergsonism. Rather than informing the poem from the start, Eliot's explicit philosophical interests might be said to arise out of a context of artworks (literary and visual) that indirectly address similar questions of the self's constitution and relationality.

68. Eliot, *Complete Poems and Plays*, 9.

69. "Salvation is to be sought in a return to the jungle. It is the tom-tom that convinces the reader that the young man is, potentially at least, capable of being saved from the genteel hell in which he is immured." Robert Crawford, *The Savage and the City in the Work of T. S. Eliot* (Oxford: Clarendon, 1987), 77.

70. Claude Rawson, "Tribal Drums and the Dull Tom-Tom: Thoughts on Modernism and the Savage in Conrad and Eliot," in *Rethinking Modernism*, ed. Marianne Thormälen (New York: Palgrave, 2003), 107.

71. The primitive, for Eliot, was all about a state of mind that is inaccessible to Europeans, a case that tests our assumptions about what we can know of other people. In a paper written for Josiah Royce's philosophy seminar, 1913–14, Eliot argues, as summarized in Costello's notes, "How can we be sure we are correctly interpreting the mental life of a savage when the savage could not verify our interpretation if we could present it to him, because he could not understand it?" The record of this seminar suggests that the case of the "savage" was one which Eliot raised entirely on his own initiative, on two separate occasions, as a counter example to Royce's pragmatist-influenced theory of interpretation by community (worked out in *The Problem of Christianity*, 1913). The philosophical virtue of the "savage," for Eliot, is as an example of a mind whose contents we could not possibly imagine. Harry T. Costello, *Josiah Royce's Seminar, 1913–1914: As Recorded in the Notebooks of Harry T. Costello*, ed. Grover Smith (New Brunswick, N.J.: Rutgers University Press, 1963), 85.

72. Eliot, *Complete Poems and Plays*, 11.

73. Ibid., 8.

74. Eliot, *Inventions of the March Hare*, 11.

75. Symons, *Symbolist Movement*, 154.

76. Though following Eliot's connection with Manet on the point of marionettes would take us too far afield, it is worth noting two etchings by Manet that represent Edmond Duranty's *Théâtre de Polichinelle*, a commedia dell'arte puppet theater established in the Tuileries in 1861. According to Fried, Manet thought of these theatrical scenes as capturing "essential aspects of his art" (*Manet's Modernism*, 53).

77. Swinburne, *Major Poems and Selected Prose*, 119.

78. Eliot, *Complete Poems and Plays*, 11.

79. Sandra Gilbert and Susan Gubar, *No Man's Land: The Place of the Woman Writer in the Twentieth Century* (New Haven: Yale University Press, 1996), 60–76; Christ, "Gender, Voice, and Figuration," 27.

80. Fowler, *Kinds of Literature*, 179–80.

81. Eliot, *Complete Poems and Plays*, 39.

82. Ibid., 40.

83. Milton, *Paradise Lost*, bk. 4, line 140.

84. Rossetti, *Collected Poetry and Prose*, 162.

85. Milton, *Paradise Lost*, bk. 4, lines 69–75.

86. Eliot, *Complete Poems and Plays*, 41, 11.

87. Ibid., 40.

4   Contraction

1. See, among others, Jean-Michel Rabaté, *1913: The Cradle of Modernism* (Oxford: Blackwell Publishing, 2007).

2. Fowler, *Kinds of Literature*, 23, 191–212.

3. Ibid., 62–64.

4. Schneidau, *The Image and the Real*, 188. Peter Davidson discusses the influence of the Catullan epigram on Pound, in *Ezra Pound and Roman Poetry: A Preliminary Survey*, 53–58.

5. Fowler observes in passing that the Modernist short poem "would be unintelligible" without the elegiac modulation of epigram. *Kinds of Literature*, 210. I am making the somewhat different argument that the lyric portrait of the nineteenth century was modulated by epigram in Modernism—but the effects are, I think, the same. On the decline of epitaph, see Scodel, *English Poetic Epitaph*, p. 10 and chapter 12; on the decline of epigram, see Hamilton, *English Verse Epigram*, 31, 38.

6. Hagstrum, *The Sister Arts*, 23.

7. Krieger, *Ekphrasis*, 15.

8. Fitzgerald points out two conflicting associations with epigram: its "lapidary compression and closure point to inscriptional uses," implying permanence, but its "one-dimensional brevity and compressing wit" imply the "ephemeral, the improvised, and the spoken." William Fitzgerald, *Martial: The World of the Epigram* (Chicago: University of Chicago Press, 2007), 3.

9. Holmes, *Dante Gabriel Rossetti and the Late Victorian Sonnet Sequence*, 3.

10. Colie, *Resources of Kind*, 67; Fowler, 137–38; 183–84.

11. Hamilton, *English Verse Epigram*, 31; on elegiac modulation, see Fowler, 206–12.

12. Mackail, *Select Epigrams from the Greek Anthology*, 4.

13. Ibid., 51.

14. See Ivor Winters, *Edwin Arlington Robinson* (Norfolk, CT: New Directions, 1946), 25, 100; Wallace Anderson, *Edwin Arlington Robinson: A Critical Introduction* (Boston:

Houghton Mifflin, 1967), 108, 141; Hoyt Franchère, *Edwin Arlington Robinson* (Boston: Twayne, 1968), 38, 39, 114.

15. Scodel, *English Poetic Epitaph*, 64.

16. Robert Frost, introduction to E. A. Robinson, *King Jasper: A Poem by Edwin Arlington Robinson* (New York: Macmillan, 1935), x–xi.

17. In the February 1897 issue of *Bookman*, reviewer Harry Thurston Peck wrote that Robinson's "humour is of a grim sort, and the world is not beautiful to him, but a prison-house." This was Robinson's reply, in a letter published in the March 1897 issue of *Bookman*. Peck, "Chronicle and Comment," *Bookman* 4 (February 1897): 510. American Periodicals Online.

18. Robinson, *Collected Poems*, 86.

19. Ibid., 88.

20. Ibid., 94.

21. Ibid., 93.

22. Fowler, *Kinds of Literature*, 207.

23. Robinson, *Collected Poems*, 82.

24. Peter Sacks, *The English Elegy: Studies in the Genre from Spenser to Yeats* (Baltimore: Johns Hopkins Press, 1985).

25. Scodel, *English Poetic Epitaph*, 409.

26. Ramazani, *Poetry of Mourning*, 14–22.

27. Robinson, *Collected Poems*, 230, 225, 227, 228.

28. Ibid., 229–30.

29. Ibid., "The Happy Man," 225; "The Dust of Timas," 228; "An Inscription by the Sea," 230.

30. William Pratt, *Modern Poetry in Miniature* (New York: E. P. Dutton, 1963), 13.

31. Ayers, *Modernism*, 3.

32. Ibid., 2.

33. Laity, *H.D. and the Victorian Fin de Siècle*, 34, 79.

34. H.D., *Asphodel*, ed. Robert Spoo (Durham: Duke University Press, 1992), 53.

35. Mackail, *Select Epigrams*, 165.

36. As printed in *Poetry* 1.4 (January 1913): 122. See H.D., *Collected Poems*, 309.

37. Ayers, *Modernism*, 4.

38. Swinburne, *Major Poems and Selected Prose*, 92.

39. Rossetti, *Collected Poetry and Prose*, 191; Lowell, *Complete Poetical Works*, 15.

40. Lowell, *Complete Poetical Works*, 205.

41. Ibid., 226.

42. Rossetti, *Collected Poetry and Prose*, 191; Lowell, *Complete Poetical Works*, 210.

43. Lowell, *Complete Poetical Works*, 567.

44. Ibid., 569. Thanks to Can Kantarci for drawing my attention to interesting aspects of this poem.

45. Ibid.

46. Ibid., 73; Richard Aldington, *Complete Poems* (London: Allan Wingate, 1948), 66.

47. Pound, *Poems and Translations*, 148.

48. Pound, *Literary Essays*, 7.

49. Colie, *Resources of Kind*, 67.

50. Pound, *Poems and Translations*, 234.

51. Ibid., 236.

52. Ibid, 231.

53. Mao, *Solid Objects*, 154.

54. Poems of thirteen, fourteen, and fifteen lines dominate *Ripostes* (eleven of this length out of a total of twenty-seven), yet many are sonnets only in length and not in rhyme scheme.

55. Davidson, *Ezra Pound and Roman Poetry*, 53.

56. E. T. Merrill, editor, *Catullus* (Cambridge, MA: Harvard University Press, 1903), xxviii.

57. Hookham Frere, *The Works of the Right Honorable John Hookham Frere in Verse and Prose* (London: Pickering, 1874), 383–84.

58. Pound, *Poems and Translations*, 235.

59. Buchanan, "Fleshly School," 338.

60. Pound, *Poems and Translations*, 235.

61. G. W. Cronin, "Classic Free Verse" in Homberger, *Ezra Pound: The Critical Heritage*, 126.

62. *Poetry* 2.6 (1913): 191–99.

63. Davidson, *Ezra Pound and Roman Poetry*, 55–57.

64. Pound, *Poems and Translations*, 278.

65. Ibid., 281.

66. Davidson, *Ezra Pound and Roman Poetry*, 56.

67. Pound, *Poems and Translations*, 281.

68. Hamilton, *Ezra Pound and the Symbolist Inheritance*, 12.

69. Hamilton explains that Pound's representation of Gautier combined three different strains of French influence: the "Parnassian" (or Romantic), Symbolism (the more recent descendant of French Romanticism), and the "satirical realism" of Flaubert (Hamilton, *Ezra Pound and the Symbolist Inheritance*, 14). It is difficult to treat any one line of influence in Pound's work because it crosses with so many others, as in this poem, where the satire of Flaubert intersects with the epigrammatic wit of Catullus and Martial, and feelings about Rossetti's *Lady Lilith*, another woman in white, are projected onto Gautier's lady.

70. Eliot, *Complete Poems and Plays*, 17.

71. Ficke, "Swinburne," *Poetry* 1.5 (Feb. 1913): 137–44.

72. Ficke, *Twelve Japanese Painters* (Chicago: Alderbrink, 1913), 17.

73. Ficke, "Portrait of an Old Woman," *Poetry* 1.5 (Feb. 1913): 146.

74. Ibid.

75. Ficke, "Sonnets of a Portrait-Painter: A Sequence," *Forum* (Aug. 1914): 255, 251, 263.

76. The text of the original volume of *Spectra* and information about the movement is collected in Smith, *The Spectra Hoax*.

77. Smith, *Spectra Hoax*, 77.

78. Ibid.

79. Smith, *Spectra Hoax*, 94, 108, 120, 105.

80. Marjorie Seiffert, *Others* 3.5 (Jan. 1917): 11.

81. Smith, *Spectra Hoax*, 142.

82. Bynner, *Pins for Wings*, 9, 14, 16, 25.

83. Masters (under pseudonym of Ford), *Songs and Sonnets* (Chicago: Rooks Press, 1910), 84.

84. Hallwas discusses Masters's friendship with Dreiser and his naturalism in the introduction to *Spoon River Anthology*, 14–15, 28–29; his reading of Swinburne, 13.

85. Masters, *Spoon River Anthology*, 134.

86. Masters gave a lecture in St. Louis entitled "The Rat Trap and How to Get Out of It," according to a report of the event ("The Origin of 'Spoon River'") in the *St. Louis Dispatch*, March 29, 1918, p. 21. He had "thrown out the Bible as revelation and the miracles as nonsense," Masters wrote in *Across Spoon River: An Autobiography* (Urbana: University of Illinois Press, 1991), 81.

87. Masters, *Toward the Gulf* (New York: Macmillan, 1918), vii. The edition was, again, Mackail's *Select Epigrams*.

88. Ibid., viii, ix, xi. Willis Barnstone discusses the influence of the *Greek Anthology* in his introduction to Masters's *New Spoon River*, xix–xxii.

89. Masters, *Spoon River Anthology*, 90, 95.

90. Ibid., 113.

91. Pound, "Our Contemporaries," *Poetry* 5 (Oct. 1914): 42.

92. Bell, "In the Real Tradition," *Criticism* 23.2 (1981): 141–54.

93. Barnstone, introduction to *New Spoon River*, xx.

5 Expansion

1. Pointon, "Kahnweiler's Picasso; Picasso's Kahnweiler," in Woodall, ed., *Portraiture*, 190.

2. The synergy between modern art and poetry has been one of the most fruitful avenues of criticism for decades. Some of the major studies that contributed to this chapter include Timothy Materer's *Vortex: Pound, Eliot, and Lewis* (1979), Reed Way Dasenbrock's *The Literary Vorticism of Ezra Pound and Wyndham Lewis* (1985), Marjorie Perloff's *The Futurist Moment* (1986), and Daniel Albright's *Untwisting the Serpent* (2000).

3. Pierre Daix, *Picasso, The Cubist Years, 1907–1916: A Catalogue Raisonné*, trans. Dorothy Blair (New York: New York Graphic Society, 1979), 255–92.

4. See William Rubin's "Reflections on Picasso and Portraiture" and other essays in Rubin, ed., *Picasso and Portraiture: Representation and Transformation*.

5. Steiner, *Exact Resemblance*, 25.

6. Apollonio, *Futurist Manifestos*, 26.

7. Ibid., 28.

8. Dasenbrock, *Literary Vorticism*, 37.

9. Michel, *Wyndham Lewis: Paintings and Drawings* (Berkeley: University of California Press, 1971), 55; Cork, *Vorticism and Abstract Art*, 1:330.

10. Lewis, "The New Egos," *BLAST* 1: 141.

11. Perloff, *Dance of the Intellect*, 33, 56.

12. Another important example of a turn-of-the-century novel of development is Oscar Wilde's *Picture of Dorian Gray*, which itself may respond to James, and is an important piece of the relationship between Aestheticism and Modernism, though I have not seen its direct influence on Pound. See Michèle Mendelssohn, *Henry James, Oscar Wilde, and Aesthetic Culture* (Edinburgh: University of Edinburgh Press, 2007) for a discussion of Wilde's response to James in *The Picture of Dorian Gray*.

13. Moretti, *The Way of the World*, 10.

14. Other literary models that have been proposed for *Gaudier-Brzeska* similarly offer to impose continuity on a fragmented surface. Christine Froula proposes elegy in her

essay "*Gaudier-Brzeska:* Abstract Form, Modern War, and Vorticist Elegy" in *Ezra Pound and Referentiality*, ed. Hélène Aji, 119–31. In "From Epitaph to Obituary: The Death Politics of T. S. Eliot and Ezra Pound," Marysa Demoor calls the work a biographical essay (*Biography* 28.2 [2005]: 255–77). Finally, Lynne Hinojosa identifies *Gaudier-Brzeska* as a typological history based on Vasari and Burckhardt, in her "Modern Artist as Historian, Courtier, and Saint: Typology and Art History from Vasari to Pound," *Clio* 35.2 (2006): 201–24.

15. Pound, *Gaudier-Brzeska*, 17.

16. Pound's early reference to Futurism here has gone virtually unnoticed in the critical literature, despite wide recognition of Marinetti's influence on the poet. On Pound's reception of Futurism, see Perloff, *The Futurist Moment*, 171–77; and Litz and Rainey, "Ezra Pound," 68–70.

17. Pound, *Ezra Pound and Dorothy Shakespear: Letters*, 190.

18. Pound, *Poems and Translations*, 273.

19. Albright, *Untwisting the Serpent*, 38.

20. Propert, *The Russian Ballet*, 21. Propert's eyewitness accounts of Russian Ballet performances in Europe are an important source of information about the ballet's work and the impression it made on contemporaries.

21. Ibid., 76; see also MacDonald, *Diaghilev Observed*, 75–85.

22. Propert, *The Russian Ballet*, 78.

23. MacDonald, *Diaghilev Observed*, 78.

24. Koritz, *Gendering Bodies/Performing Art*, 127.

25. Cork, *Vorticism and Abstract Art*, 2:392.

26. Edwards, *Wyndham Lewis: Painter and Writer*, 85.

27. Ibid., 99.

28. MacDonald, *Diaghilev Observed*, 94.

29. "The futurists had a good painter named Severini," Pound acknowledged in a 1914 review of Edward Wadsworth. *Ezra Pound and the Visual Arts*, 191.

30. Perloff, *The Futurist Moment*, 175.

31. Lewis's later choice of the name "Group X" for the short-lived gathering of former Vorticists after the war, who exhibited together in 1920, also suggests that the letter had particular significance for him.

32. Pound, *Poems and Translations*, 273.

33. Koritz, *Gendering Bodies/Performing Art*, 121.

34. Studies of the impact of prose on Pound's poetic development include Schneidau, *Ezra Pound: The Image and the Real*, 3–37, 74–109; Bush, *The Genesis of Ezra Pound's Cantos*, 142 ff.; and Perloff, *The Futurist Moment*, 162–93.

35. Pound, "The Approach to Paris V," *Periodicals*, 1:180–82.

36. Polish formalist Ireneusz Opacki proposed the concept of a "royal genre" that contributes its traits to other genres during the period of its dominance. "Royal Genres," translated in David Duff, *Modern Genre Theory* (New York: Longman, 2000), 118–26. Bakhtin claims such status for the novel throughout the period of its ascendancy.

37. Moretti, *Way of the World*, 15.

38. Moretti classifies Flaubert's *Sentimental Education* of 1869 as the last masterpiece of the genre (*Way of the World*, 9); Lukács identifies it as the first "Romantic novel of disillusion (*Theory of the Novel*, 112).

39. Gregory Castle, *Reading the Modernist Bildungsroman* (Gainesville: University Press of Florida, 2006), 162.

40. Fogelman, *Shapes of Power: The Development of Ezra Pound's Poetic Sequences* (Ann Arbor: UMI Research Press, 1988), 80.

41. The typescript of this poem, including two unpublished sections, may be found in the Ezra Pound papers at the Yale Beinecke Library, YCAL MSS 43, folders 5207–13.

42. Pound, *Poems and Translations*, 522.

43. Ibid.

44. John Harwood, *Olivia Shakespear and W. B. Yeats: After Long Silence* (New York: St. Martin's Press, 1989), 16–17.

45. Pound, *Poems and Translations*, 523.

46. Lukács, *Theory of the Novel*, 112.

47. Pound, *Poems and Translations*, 525.

48. The title does not refer to Wyndham Lewis's portrait of Pound, which he described in a later review as a "classic *stele*," since Lewis did not paint it until 1919.

49. Cork, *Vorticism and Abstract Art*, 1:183; Horace Brodzky, *Henri Gaudier-Brzeska* (London: Faber and Faber, 1933), 62.

50. Albright, *Untwisting the Serpent*, 84.

51. Ibid., 78.

52. Pound rewrote this work for radio in 1931 and also composed a further opera, *Cavalcanti*, that was only recently resurrected and produced for the first time. Albright examines the music to the 1923 *Le testament* in *Untwisting the Serpent*, 141–48, and Margaret Fisher has recovered Pound's work with the BBC for the 1931 radio productions in *Ezra Pound's Radio Operas: The BBC Experiments, 1931–1933* (Cambridge, MA: MIT Press, 2002).

53. "Is it a ghost? is it a woman? . . . a dream, a reality" (translation mine). Gautier, *Selected Lyrics*, 120.

54. Théophile Gautier, *Gautier on Dance*, edited and translated by Ivor Guest (London: Dance, 1986), 59.

55. Pound, *Poems and Translations*, 524.

56. Pound, "Moeurs Contemporaines," Beinecke YCAL MSS 43, folder 5209.

57. Pound, *Poems and Translations*, 46.

58. Pound wrote in the margin of "Plotinus": "the 'cone' is I presume the 'Vritta' whirlpool, vortex-ring of the Yogi's cosmogony. . . . the sonnet ["Plotinus"] . . . is in accord with a certain Hindoo teacher whose name I have not yet found." Pound, *Poems and Translations*, 1258; William French and Timothy Materer, "Far Flung Vortices & Ezra Pound's 'Hindoo' Yogi," *Paideuma* 11.1 (1982): 39–42.

59. Wyndham Lewis, *Tarr* (New York: Alfred A. Knopf, 1918), 60.

60. Such as "the major conflicts that he portrays," "the portrayal of these forces," "portrayal of a character," "the faculty for a portrait in a paragraph," and others. Pound, *Literary Essays*, 298, 301, 329, 332.

61. Ibid., 296.

62. Pound, "Remy de Gourmont" (1919), *Literary Essays*, 339.

63. Pound, *Poems and Translations*, 525.

64. Ibid.

65. Ibid., 526.

66. Ibid.

67. A draft of this poem has the old lady responding, "And I would say that he didn't." Pound, "Moeurs Contemporaines," Beinecke YCAL MSS 43, folder 5213.

68. Pound, "Moeurs Contemporaines," Beinecke YCAL MSS 43, folder 5209; see also *Little Review* 6.1 (May 1918): 31.

69. Background and history of Poole's can be found in Hudson John Powell's *Poole's Myriorama!: A Story of Travelling Panorama Showmen* (Bradford on Avon: ELSP, 2002), esp. 15, 83, and 142.

70. For a complete account of the development of vortography, see Frank Difederico, "Alvin Langdon Coburn and the Genesis of Vortographs," *History of Photography* 11.4 (1987): 265–96. For a focus on Pound's role, see Beasley's "The Modern Public and Vortography" in *Ezra Pound and Referentiality*, ed. Hélène Aji, 177–89.

71. Pound, *Ezra Pound and the Visual Arts*, 154–56.

72. Ibid., 78.

73. Ibid.

74. Pound, *Selected Letters*, 180.

75. Mid-century Pound criticism in particular focused on the identity of the speaker/s in this sequence, such as the debate between Leavis, who interpreted the poem as an autobiography confessing Pound's artistic failure, and Kenner, who read the poem as the utterance of Mauberley, "a poet with whom Mr. Pound is anxious not to be confounded." Leavis, *New Bearings in English Poetry: A Study of the Contemporary Situation*, 3rd ed. (London: Chatto and Windus, 1959), 133–57; Hugh Kenner, *The Poetry of Ezra Pound* (Norfolk: New Directions, 1951), 166. Jo Brantley Berryman's *Circe's Craft: Ezra Pound's Hugh Selwyn Mauberley* (Ann Arbor: UMI Research Press, 1983) summarized and attempted to encompass these debates. In *Shapes of Power*, Bruce Fogelman moved the discussion forward by treating the poem not as a series of personae but as the representation of a "controlling consciousness," but as Scott Hamilton has observed, the poem is less controlled than it is unstable and ambivalent, in particular stemming from Pound's unresolved feelings about French poetry (*Ezra Pound and the Symbolist Inheritance*, 111–30). I think it should be clear by now that those ambivalent feelings extend also to Rossetti and Swinburne, whose earlier and perhaps deeper influence is buried under the references to Gautier. "Yeux Glauques" demonstrates this layering of ambivalent relationships: the poem is about the Rossetti circle, but takes as its title a translation of Gautier's "Caerulei Oculi" from *Émaux et Camées*. Any ambivalence that Pound expresses here toward Gautier's Parnassian Aestheticism is thus also being expressed toward the English branch of the movement, in a mixture of feelings that is impossible to measure with any precision.

76. Coyle, "Hugh Selwyn Mauberley," 432.

77. Pound, *Selected Letters*, 180.

78. Catherine Paul, *Poetry in the Museums of Modernism: Yeats, Pound, Moore, Stein* (Ann Arbor: University of Michigan Press, 2002), 68–69.

79. Mao, *Solid Objects*, 165; Beasley, *Ezra Pound and Visual Culture*, 149.

80. My discussion of Mauberley here is particularly indebted to Mao's observation that "in trying to bring the past closer Pound was struggling against his own persuasion that others, alive or dead, will always in some sense appear as objects impermeable to full knowledge, even against the possibility that the monuments left by the departed are finally no more mute to us than we living are to each other." Mao, *Solid Objects*, 156.

81. Quoted in Upstone, "King Cophetua and the Beggar Maid," 149.

82. Upstone notes that the sitter for *The Beggar Maid* may also have been Frances Graham, the daughter of Burne-Jones's (and Rossetti's) patron, William Graham. Ibid.

83. Pound, *Poems and Translations*, 552.

84. Gautier, *Selected Lyrics*, 68.

85. Craig Hamilton finds a different set of mixed messages in this poem, conflicted over what can or cannot be said in words about a visual image. "Ekphrasis, Repetition, and Pound's 'Yeux Glauques,'" *Imaginaires* 9 (2003): 215–23.

86. Pound, *Poems and Translations*, 562.

87. Ibid., 558, 559, 561.

88. Max Beerbohm, *The Incomparable Max* (London: William Heinemann, 1962), 94.

89. Ibid., 98.

90. Pound, *Poems and Translations*, 561.

91. Ibid., 562.

92. Ibid., 561; Swinburne, *Major Poems and Selected Prose*, 118.

93. Pound, *Poems and Translations*, 561.

94. Ibid., 551, 562.

95. Salomon Reinach, *Apollo: An Illustrated Manual of the History of Art throughout the Ages*, trans. Florence Simmonds (New York: C. Scribner's Sons, 1907), 58.

96. Ibid., 189–91.

6 Pastoral Mode

1. Williams, *I Wanted to Write a Poem*, 21.

2. On pastoral as a mode as opposed to a genre, see Fowler, *Kinds of Literature*, 109–10.

3. John Marsh, "'Thinking/Of the Freezing Poor': The Suburban Counter-Pastoral in William Carlos Williams' Early Poetry," *William Carlos Williams Review* 27.2 (2007): 97–117, 99.

4. Maria Farland, "Modernist Versions of Pastoral: Poetic Inspiration, Scientific Expertise, and the 'Degenerate' Farmer," *American Literary History* 19.4 (2007): 905–37, 912.

5. John Higham's *Strangers in the Land: Patterns of American Nativism 1860–1925* (Westport: Greenwood Press, 1981), the standard study of American Nativism from 1860 to 1925, identifies World War I as the starting point of the movement, which was initially focused on German immigrants until 1917; see chapter 8, "War and Revolution."

6. Walter Benn Michaels, *Our America: Nativism, Modernism, and Pluralism* (Durham: Duke University Press, 1995), 76.

7. Dijkstra's *Hieroglyphics of a New Speech: Cubism, Stieglitz, and the Early Poetry of William Carlos Williams* discusses Stieglitz's leadership in this movement in chapter 4, "The Evangelists of the American Moment."

8. Peter Schmidt, "Some Versions of Modernist Pastoral: Williams and the Precisionists," *Contemporary Literature* 21.3 (1980): 388.

9. For an analysis of Williams's use of oppositions, see Barry Ahearn, *William Carlos Williams and Alterity*, 2.

10. Frank Kermode, *English Pastoral Poetry: From the Beginnings to Marvell* (London: G. G. Harrap, 1952), 14–19; Leo Marx, *The Machine in the Garden: Technology and the Pastoral Ideal in America* (New York: Oxford University Press, 1972), 25; Toliver, *Pastoral Forms and Attitudes* (Berkeley: University of California Press, 1971), 1, 14.

11. Conversation notes by Thirlwall, 16 Oct. 1954; quoted in Williams, *Collected Poems*, 2:489.

12. Spoken remarks from 1956; quoted in Williams, *Collected Poems*, 2:489.

13. Williams, *I Wanted to Write a Poem*, 21.

14. Paul Mariani, *William Carlos Williams: A New World Naked* (New York: McGraw-Hill, 1981), 64–65.

15. Williams did not allow any of *Poems* to be reprinted, but the book is described in Emily Wallace, *A Bibliography of William Carlos Williams* (Middletown: Wesleyan University Press, 1968), 7–8.

16. Marling, *William Carlos Williams and the Painters*, 119.

17. Eileen Gregory discusses Symonds's reputation in *H.D. and Hellenism: Classic Lines* (New York: Cambridge University Press, 1997), 163.

18. Symonds, *Studies of the Greek Poets*, 2:302–3.

19. Lang, *Theocritus, Bion, Moschus*, xxxvi.

20. Ibid., xxii–xxiii.

21. Ibid., xxxiii; J. M. Edmonds, *Greek Bucolic Poets* (New York: Macmillan, 1912), ix. Williams used the Edmonds edition later when translating Theocritus (see *Collected Poems*, 2:489); it may have been the place where he first encountered the poet.

22. Symonds, *Studies of the Greek Poets*, 2:307.

23. Williams, *Collected Poems*, 1:42.

24. Ibid., 1:43.

25. Ibid., 1:81.

26. Ibid., 1:42.

27. Letter to Viola Baxter Jordan, December 24, 1914. Yale Collection of American Literature, Beinecke Rare Book and Manuscript Library YCAL MSS 175, folder 103.

28. Higham, *Strangers in the Land*, 194.

29. Williams, "America, Whitman, and the Art of Poetry," 27.

30. Marling, *William Carlos Williams and the Painters*, 68. As the many studies of Williams's interaction with the art world have shown, the poet retained his artistic independence while staying in touch with contemporary developments in American Modernism. The extent of his contact with the Alfred Stieglitz circle has been debated: Bram Dijkstra's *Hieroglyphics of a New Speech* was the first book-length study of Williams's artistic contacts and strongly argues for a relationship with Stieglitz dating back before 1922 (86–87). Marling disputes this dating, pointing out that Williams writes quite formally to Stieglitz in 1925 (Marling, *William Carlos Williams and the Painters*, 3). MacGowan, too, downplays Williams's association with Stieglitz before the 1920s, emphasizing the influence of Pound during the 1910s (*William Carlos Williams's Early Poetry*, 37). All recognize, however, the centrality of Williams's friendship with Hartley, through whom he was exposed to the ideas of the Stieglitz circle.

31. Lynes, preface to Hole, *Marsden Hartley and the West*, xi.

32. Ibid., xiii.

33. Hartley, *Adventures in the Arts*, 241.

34. Hole, *Marsden Hartley and the West*, 44.

35. Hartley, "Aesthetic Sincerity," 332.

36. Ibid., 333.

37. Hartley, "America as Landscape," 342, 341.

38. Frank, *Our America* (New York: Boni and Liveright, 1919), 4.

39. On the significance of the Kora myth for Williams, see Audrey Rodgers, *Virgin and Whore: The Image of Women in the Poetry of William Carlos Williams* (Jefferson, NC: McFarland, 1987), chapter 2.

40. Williams, letter to Dora Marsden, *Egoist* 4 (Aug. 1917): 111.

41. In *O'Keeffe, Stieglitz, and the Critics*, Barbara Buhler Lynes examines Stieglitz's interpretation and promotion of O'Keeffe's work, showing both the continuities of his interpretation with nineteenth-century conceptions of femininity, but also the relative

lack of misogyny in his particular deployment of the language of nature to describe O'Keeffe's femininity (19–26). Hartley's similar treatment of O'Keeffe can be found in the essay "Some Women Artists in Modern Painting," in *Adventures in the Arts*.

42. Alfred Stieglitz, "Georgia O'Keeffe—C. Duncan—Réné Lafferty," *Camera Work* 48 (Oct. 1916): 12.

43. Quoted in full by Dorothy Norman, *Alfred Stieglitz: An American Seer* (New York: Random House, 1960), 137.

44. Lynes, *O'Keeffe, Stieglitz, and the Critics*, 25.

45. Ibid.

46. Celeste Connor, *Democratic Visions: Art and Theory of the Stieglitz Circle, 1924– 1934* (Berkeley: University of California Press, 2001), 188.

47. See Marling, *William Carlos Williams and the Painters*, 119–35.

48. Williams, *Collected Poems*, 1:95.

49. Ibid., 1:63.

50. Marling, *William Carlos Williams and the Painters*, 128.

51. Williams, *Collected Poems*, 1:66.

52. Ibid., 1:106.

53. Hole, *Marsden Hartley and the West*, 16.

54. For discussions of Kandinsky's influence on Hartley, also see essays in Kornhauser, ed., *Marsden Hartley*, such as Kornhauser's "Marsden Hartley: 'Gaunt Eagle from the Hills of Maine'," Patricia McDonnell's "'Portrait of Berlin': Marsden Hartley and Urban Modernity in Expressionist Berlin" (esp. 43), and Jonathan Weinberg, "Marsden Hartley: Writing on Painting" (esp. 123–24).

55. Kandinsky, "On the Spiritual in Art," as translated in *BLAST* 1: 122.

56. Hartley, "Aesthetic Sincerity," 332.

57. Williams, *Collected Poems*, 1:87.

58. Ibid. Ahearn interprets "the rest of my clothes" to mean that she is wearing something, which she would be willing to take off for the intruder; on the contrary, she has no other "rest" of her clothes, which is why she says she would be cold without the covers. Ahearn, *William Carlos Williams and Alterity*, 75.

59. Williams, *Collected Poems*, 1:87–88.

60. Ibid., 1:90.

61. Ibid., 1:88.

62. Ibid., 1:489.

63. Ibid., 1:99.

64. Williams, *Imaginations*, 24.

65. Ibid., 23–24.

66. Pound, *Pound/Williams: Selected Letters of Ezra Pound and William Carlos Williams*, ed. Hugh Witemeyer (New York: New Directions, 1996), 137.

67. Williams, *Collected Poems*, 1:129, 152, 150, 152, 154.

68. Ibid., 152.

69. W.J.T. Mitchell interprets this poem as an instance of "ekphrastic ambivalence," "the desire to see accompanied by a sense of its prohibition." This ambivalence can be more specifically located, I think, in Williams's conflicted relationship with poetic sources, on whom he depends for meaning yet seeks to do without. The erotic element of the poem is more polemical than ambivalent, however; as a response to what he sees as Demuth's fetishization of European culture, Williams promotes a red-blooded American heterosexuality. *Picture Theory*, 169–70.

70. Williams, *Imaginations*, 27.

71. Allara, "Charles Demuth: Always a Seeker," 86.

72. Ibid.

73. Pater, *Three Major Texts*, 262.

74. Allara, "Charles Demuth: Always a Seeker," 88–89.

75. Ibid.

76. Haskell reads the scene as an interpretation of the relationship of the narrator to Watteau in Pater's story: "The absent gaze that Watteau directs toward the model's shoe suggests the psychological distance that he retained between himself and the adoring narrator" (*Charles Demuth*, 111). Allara reads the gaze at the shoe as an expression of Demuth's disappointment with having not found a satisfying heterosexual relationship ("Charles Demuth: Always a Seeker," 89). Weinberg interprets the shoe as a male fetish object in Freudian terms (*Speaking for Vice*, 88).

77. Donald Posner, "The Swinging Women of Watteau and Fragonard," *Art Bulletin* 64.1 (1982): 86–88.

78. Hartley, *Adventures in the Arts*, 241.

79. Weinberg, *Speaking for Vice*, 88.

80. Mitchell, *Picture Theory*, 169.

81. Williams, *Collected Poems*, 1:129.

82. Hartley, "Aesthetic Sincerity," 333.

Coda

1. Christopher Sawyer-Lauçanno, *E. E. Cummings: A Biography* (Naperville: Sourcebooks, 2004), 50.

2. Milton A. Cohen, *Poet and Painter: The Aesthetics of E. E. Cummings's Early Work* (Detroit: Wayne State University Press, 1987), 43.

3. Cummings, *Tulips & Chimneys* (1922 manuscript), 64.

4. Ibid., 83.

Selected Bibliography

"About Portraits and Portrait-Painting." In *Bentley's Miscellany*, vol. 1, 411–21; 513–25. London: Chapman and Hall, 1861.

Ahearn, Barry. *William Carlos Williams and Alterity: The Early Poetry*. New York: Cambridge University Press, 1994.

Aji, Hélène, ed. *Ezra Pound and Referentiality*. Paris: Presses de l'Université de Paris–Sorbonne, 2003.

Albright, Daniel. *Untwisting the Serpent: Modernism in Music, Literature, and Other Arts*. Chicago: University of Chicago Press, 2000.

Allara, Pamela. "Charles Demuth: Always a Seeker." *Arts Magazine* 50.10 (June 1976): 86–89.

Apollonio, Umbro, ed. *Futurist Manifestos*. Translated by Robert Brain. New York: Viking Press, 1970.

Armstrong, Carol. *Manet Manette*. New Haven: Yale University Press, 2002.

Ayers, David. *Modernism: A Short Introduction*. Oxford: Blackwell Publishing, 2004.

Banerjee, Ron. "Dante through the Looking Glass: Rossetti, Pound and Eliot." *Comparative Literature* 24.2 (1972): 136–49.

Barnstone, Willis. Introduction to *The New Spoon River*. New York: Macmillan, 1968.

Beasley, Rebecca. *Ezra Pound and the Visual Culture of Modernism*. New York: Cambridge University Press, 2007.

———. "Ezra Pound's Whistler." *American Literature* 74.3 (2002): 485–516.

Buchanan, Robert (under pseudonym Thomas Maitland). "The Fleshly School of Poetry: Mr. D. G. Rossetti." *The Contemporary Review* 18 (1871): 334–50. Reproduced in the *Rossetti Archive*, http://www.rossettiarchive.org/docs/ap4.c7.18.rad.html.

Bush, Ronald. *The Genesis of Ezra Pound's Cantos*. Princeton: Princeton University Press, 1976.

Bynner, Witter. *Guest Book*. New York: Alfred A. Knopf, 1935.

———. (as Emmanuel Morgan) *Pins for Wings*. New York: Sunwise Turn, 1920.

Casteras, Susan P. *English Pre-Raphaelitism and Its Reception in America in the Nineteenth Century*. Rutherford: Fairleigh Dickinson University Press, 1990.

Cheeke, Stephen. *Writing for Art: The Aesthetics of Ekphrasis*. New York: Manchester University Press, 2008.

Christ, Carol. *Victorian and Modern Poetics*. Chicago: University of Chicago Press, 1984.

———. "Gender, Voice, and Figuration in T. S. Eliot's Early Poetry." *T. S. Eliot: The Modernist in History*, edited by Ronald Bush, 23–37. New York: Cambridge University Press, 1990.

Colie, Rosalie. *The Resources of Kind: Genre-Theory in the Renaissance*. Berkeley: University of California Press, 1973.

Corbett, David Peters. *The World in Paint: Modern Art and Visuality in England, 1848–1914*. State College: Penn State University Press, 2004.

Cork, Richard. *Vorticism and Abstract Art in the First Machine Age*. Berkeley: University of California Press, 1976.

Coyle, Michael. "Hugh Selwyn Mauberley." In *A Companion to Modernist Literature and Culture*, edited by David Bradshaw, 431–39. Oxford: Wiley-Blackwell, 2006.

Cummings, Edward Estlin. *Tulips & Chimneys: The Original 1922 Manuscript*. Edited by George James Firmage. New York: Liveright, 1976.

Dasenbrock, Reed Way. *The Literary Vorticism of Ezra Pound and Wyndham Lewis: Towards the Condition of Painting*. Baltimore: Johns Hopkins University Press, 1985.

Davidson, Peter. *Ezra Pound and Roman Poetry: A Preliminary Survey*. Atlanta: Rodopi Press, 1995.

Diggory, Terrence. *Yeats and American Poetry: The Tradition of the Self*. Princeton: Princeton University Press, 1983.

Dijkstra, Bram. *Hieroglyphics of a New Speech: Cubism, Stieglitz, and the Early Poetry of William Carlos Williams*. Princeton: Princeton University Press, 1969.

Dorment, Richard, and Margaret MacDonald. *James McNeill Whistler*. London: Harry N. Abrams/Tate Gallery, 1995.

DuPlessis, Rachel Blau. "Propounding Modernist Maleness: How Pound Managed a Muse." *Modernism/Modernity* 9.3 (2002): 389–405.

Edwards, Paul. *Wyndham Lewis: Painter and Writer*. New Haven: Yale University Press, 2000.

Eliot, T. S. *The Complete Poems and Plays*. New York: Harcourt, Brace, 1952.

———. *Inventions of the March Hare: Poems 1909–1917*. Edited by Christopher Ricks. New York: Harcourt Brace, 1996.

———. *Knowledge and Experience in the Philosophy of F. H. Bradley*. London: Faber Straus, 1964.

———. *The Letters of T. S. Eliot*, vol. 1. Edited by Valerie Eliot. New York: Harcourt Brace Jovanovich, 1988.

———. *Poems Written in Early Youth*. New York: Farrar, Straus and Giroux, 1967.

———. *Selected Essays*. New York: Harcourt, Brace, 1932.

Fowler, Alastair. *Kinds of Literature: An Introduction to the Theory of Kinds and Modes*. Cambridge, MA: Harvard University Press, 1992.

Fried, Michael. *Absorption and Theatricality: Painting and Beholder in the Age of Diderot*. Berkeley: University of California Press, 1980.

———. *Courbet's Realism*. Chicago: University of Chicago Press, 1990.

————. *Manet's Modernism, or, The Face of Painting in the 1860s*. Chicago: University of Chicago Press, 1996.

Gautier, Théophile. *Selected Lyrics*. Translated by Norman Shapiro. New Haven: Yale University Press, 2011.

Greenberg, Clement. "Modernist Painting." *Art and Literature* 4 (Spring 1965): 193–201.

Grieve, Thomas F. *Ezra Pound's Early Poetry and Poetics*. Columbia: University of Missouri Press, 1997.

Hagstrum, Jean. *The Sister Arts: The Tradition of Literary Pictorialism and English Poetry from Dryden to Gray*. Chicago: University of Chicago Press, 1958.

Haley, Bruce. *Living Forms: Romantics and the Monumental Figure*. Albany: SUNY Press, 2003.

Hamilton, Rostrevor. *English Verse Epigram*. London: Longmans, Green, and Co., 1965.

Hamilton, Scott. *Ezra Pound and the Symbolist Inheritance*. Princeton: Princeton University Press, 1992.

Hartley, Marsden. *Adventures in the Arts: Informal Chapters on Painters, Vaudeville, and Poets*. New York: Boni and Liveright, 1921.

————. "Aesthetic Sincerity," *El Palacio* 5.20 (Dec. 9, 1918): 332–33.

————. "America as Landscape," *El Palacio* 5.21 (Dec. 21, 1918): 340–42.

Haskell, Barbara. *Charles Demuth*. New York: Whitney Museum of American Art/ H. N. Abrams, 1987.

H.D. *Collected Poems 1912–1944*. Edited by Louis Martz. New York: New Directions, 1983.

————. *End to Torment: A Memoir of Ezra Pound by H.D.* Edited by Norman Holmes Pearson and Michael King. New York: New Directions, 1979.

Heffernan, James. *Museum of Words: The Poetics of Ekphrasis from Homer to Ashbery*. Chicago: University of Chicago Press, 1993.

Helsinger, Elizabeth. *Poetry and the Pre-Raphaelite Arts: Dante Gabriel Rossetti and William Morris*. New Haven: Yale University Press, 2008.

Hole, Heather. *Marsden Hartley and the West: The Search for an American Modernism*. Preface by Barbara Buhler Lynes. New Haven: Yale University Press, 2007.

Hollander, John. *The Gazer's Spirit: Poems Speaking to Silent Works of Art*. Chicago: University of Chicago Press, 1995.

Holmes, John. *Dante Gabriel Rossetti and the Late Victorian Sonnet Sequence: Sexuality, Belief, and the Self*. Farnham: Ashgate Publishing Co., 2005.

Jackson, Thomas. *The Early Poetry of Ezra Pound*. Cambridge, MA: Harvard University Press, 1968.

James, Henry. *The Portrait of a Lady*. Edited by Geoffrey Moore. New York: Penguin Books, 1984.

Kermode, Frank. *The Romantic Image*. New York: Vintage Books, 1964.

Koritz, Amy. *Gendering Bodies/Performing Art: Dance and Literature in Early Twentieth-Century British Culture*. Ann Arbor: University of Michigan Press, 1995.

Kornhauser, Elizabeth Mankin, ed. *Marsden Hartley*. New Haven: Yale University Press, 2002.

Krieger, Murray. *Ekphrasis: The Illusion of the Natural Sign*. Baltimore: Johns Hopkins University Press, 1992.

Laity, Cassandra. *H.D. and the Victorian Fin de Siècle: Gender, Modernism, Decadence*. New York: Cambridge University Press, 1996.

Lang, Andrew. *Theocritus, Bion, Moschus, Rendered into English Prose with an Introductory Essay*. London: Macmillan, 1880.

Langbaum, Robert. *The Poetry of Experience: The Dramatic Monologue in Modern Literary Tradition*. New York: Random House, 1957.

Lewis, Wyndham, ed. *BLAST* 1 (June 1914).

Litz, A. Walton, and Lawrence Rainey. "Ezra Pound." In *The Cambridge History of Literary Criticism*, vol. 7. *Modernism and the New Criticism*, edited by A. Walton Litz, Louis Menand, and Lawrence Rainey, 57–92. New York: Cambridge University Press, 2000.

———. "Pound and Yeats: The Road to Stone Cottage." In *Ezra Pound among the Poets: Homer, Ovid, Li Po, Dante, Whitman, Browning, Yeats, Williams, Eliot*, edited by George Bornstein, 128–48. Chicago: University of Chicago Press, 1985.

Loizeaux, Elizabeth Bergmann. *Twentieth-Century Poetry and the Visual Arts*. New York: Cambridge University Press, 2008.

———. *Yeats and the Visual Arts*. New Brunswick: Rutgers University Press, 1986.

Lowell, Amy. *Complete Poetical Works*. Boston: Houghton Mifflin, 1955.

Lukács, György. *The Theory of the Novel: A Historico-Philosophical Essay on the Forms of Great Epic Literature*. Translated by Anna Bostock. Cambridge, MA: M.I.T. Press, 1971.

Lynes, Barbara Buhler. *O'Keeffe, Stieglitz, and the Critics, 1916–1929*. Ann Arbor: UMI Research Press, 1989.

MacDonald, Nesta. *Diaghilev Observed by Critics in England and the United States, 1911–1929*. New York: Dance Horizons, 1975.

MacGowan, Christopher J. *William Carlos Williams's Early Poetry: The Visual Arts Background*. Ann Arbor: UMI Research Press, 1984.

Mackail, J. W. *Select Epigrams from the Greek Anthology, Edited with a Revised Text, Introduction, Translation and Notes*. London: Longmans, Green, and Co., 1906.

Mao, Douglas. *Solid Objects: Modernism and the Test of Production*. Princeton: Princeton University Press, 1998.

Marling, William. *William Carlos Williams and the Painters, 1909–1923*. Athens: Ohio University Press, 1982.

Masters, Edgar Lee. *The New Spoon River*. Edited and introduced by Willis Barnstone. New York: Macmillan, 1968.

———. *Spoon River Anthology: An Annotated Edition*. Edited and introduction by John E. Hallwas. Urbana: University of Illinois Press, 1992.

Materer, Timothy. *Vortex: Pound, Eliot, and Lewis*. Ithaca: Cornell University Press, 1979.

McGann, Jerome. *Dante Gabriel Rossetti and the Game That Must Be Lost*. New Haven: Yale University Press, 2000.

———. "Medieval versus Victorian versus Modern: Rossetti's Art of Images." *Modernism/Modernity* 2.1 (1995): 97–112.

———. "Pound's Cantos: A Poem Including Bibliography." In *A Poem Containing*

History: Textual Studies in the Cantos, edited by Lawrence Rainey, 33–62. Ann Arbor: University of Michigan Press, 1997.

McPherson, Heather. *The Modern Portrait in Nineteenth-Century France.* New York: Cambridge University Press, 2001.

Mitchell, W. J. T. *Picture Theory: Essays on Verbal and Visual Representation.* Chicago: University of Chicago Press, 1994.

Moretti, Franco. *The Way of the World: The Bildungsroman in European Culture.* Trans. Albert Sbragia. New York: Verso, 2000.

Nagy, Christoph de. *The Poetry of Ezra Pound: The Pre-Imagist Stage.* Bern: Francke Verlag, 1960.

Pater, Walter. *Three Major Texts: The Renaissance, Appreciations, and Imaginary Portraits.* Edited by William Buckler. New York: New York University Press, 1986.

Perloff, Marjorie. *Dance of the Intellect: Studies in the Poetry of the Pound Tradition.* New York: Cambridge University Press, 1985.

———. *The Futurist Moment: Avant-Garde, Avant Guerre, and the Language of Rupture.* Chicago: University of Chicago Press, 1986.

Porter, Roy, ed. *Rewriting the Self: Histories from the Renaissance to the Present.* New York: Routledge, 1997.

Pound, Ezra. *Ezra Pound and the Visual Arts,* ed. Harriet Zinnes. New York: New Directions, 1980.

———. *Ezra Pound's Poetry and Prose: Contributions to Periodicals.* Edited by Lea Baechler, A. Walton Litz, and James Longenbach. 11 vols. New York: Garland Press, 1991.

——— *Ezra Pound and Dorothy Shakespear: Their Letters 1909–1914.* Edited by Omar Pound and A. Walton Litz. New York: New Directions, 1984.

———. *Gaudier-Brzeska: A Memoir.* New York: New Directions, 1970.

———. *The Selected Letters of Ezra Pound, 1907–1941.* Edited by D. D. Paige. New York: New Directions, 1971.

———. *Literary Essays of Ezra Pound.* Edited by T. S. Eliot. Norfolk, CT: New Directions, 1954.

———. "Moeurs Contemporaines," autograph ms and typescript. Beinecke YCAL MSS 43, folders 5209–5213. Beinecke Rare Book Library, Yale University.

———. *Poems and Translations.* Edited by Richard Sieburth. New York: Library of America, 2003.

———. *Poems 1918–1920, Including Three Portraits and Four Cantos.* New York: Boni and Liveright, 1921.

———. "To La Mère Inconnue." Undated manuscript, Beinecke YCAL MSS 43, Folder 4743. Beinecke Rare Book Library, Yale University.

———. *Umbra: The Early Poems of Ezra Pound.* London: Elkin Matthews, 1921.

Powel, Harford, Jr. "Notes on the Life of T. S. Eliot." Brown University master's thesis, 1954.

Prettejohn, Elizabeth, ed. *After the Pre-Raphaelites: Art and Aestheticism in Victorian England.* New Brunswick: Rutgers University Press, 1999.

———. *Art for Art's Sake: Aestheticism in Victorian Painting.* New Haven: Yale University Press, 2003.

———. *Rossetti and His Circle.* London: Tate Gallery, 1997.

Propert, W. A. *The Russian Ballet in Western Europe, 1909–1920.* New York: John Lane, 1921; reissued Benjamin Blom, 1972.

Ramazani, Jahan. *The Poetry of Mourning: The Modern Elegy from Hardy to Heaney.* Chicago: University of Chicago Press, 1994.

Ribeyrol, Charlotte. "Swinburne-Whistler: Correspondances." *Études Anglaises* 57.1 (2004): 63–78.

Riede, David. *Dante Gabriel Rossetti and the Limits of Victorian Vision.* Ithaca: Cornell University Press, 1983.

Robinson, Edwin Arlington. *Collected Poems of Edwin Arlington Robinson.* New York: Macmillan, 1937. American Poetry Full-Text Database.

Roper, Derek. "T. S. Eliot's 'La Figlia Che Piange': A Picture without a Frame." *Essays in Criticism* 52.3 (2002): 222–34.

Rossetti, Dante Gabriel. *The Collected Poetry and Prose.* Edited by Jerome McGann. New Haven: Yale University Press, 2003.

———. *The Complete Writings and Pictures of Dante Gabriel Rossetti: A Hypermedia Archive.* Jerome McGann, general editor. Charlottesville: University of Virginia. http://www.rossettiarchive.org.

———. *The Correspondence of Dante Gabriel Rossetti.* Ed. William Fredeman. 6 vols. Rochester, NY: D. S. Brewer, 2002.

Rubin, William, ed. *Picasso and Portraiture: Representation and Transformation.* New York: Museum of Modern Art, 1996.

Schneidau, Herbert N. *Ezra Pound: The Image and the Real.* Baton Rouge: Louisiana State University Press, 1969.

Schneider, Norbert. *The Art of the Portrait: Masterpieces of European Portrait-Painting, 1420–1670.* Translated by Iain Galbraith. New York: Benedikt Taschen, 1999.

Scodel, Joshua. *The English Poetic Epitaph: Commemoration and Conflict from Jonson to Wordsworth.* Ithaca: Cornell University Press, 1991.

Shefer, Elaine. "A Rossetti Portrait: Variation on a Theme." *Arts in Virginia* 27.1–3 (1987): 2–15.

Smith, William Jay. *The Spectra Hoax.* Middletown: Wesleyan University Press, 1961.

Steiner, Wendy. *Exact Resemblance to Exact Resemblance: The Literary Portraiture of Gertrude Stein.* New Haven: Yale University Press, 1978.

Surtees, Virginia. *The Paintings and Drawings of Dante Gabriel Rossetti (1828–1882): A Catalogue Raisonné.* 2 vols. Oxford: Clarendon Press, 1971.

Swinburne, Algernon Charles. *Major Poems and Selected Prose.* Edited by Jerome McGann. New Haven: Yale University Press, 2004.

———. *The Swinburne Letters,* vol. 1. Edited by Cecil Lang. New Haven: Yale University Press, 1959.

———. *Poems and Ballads: First Series.* London: Chatto and Windus, 1889.

Symonds, John Addington. *Studies of the Greek Poets,* vol. 2. London: Smith, Elder, 1873.

Symons, Arthur. *The Symbolist Movement in Literature.* London: A. Constable, 1908.

Taylor, Charles. *Sources of the Self: The Making of the Modern Identity.* Cambridge, MA: Harvard University Press, 1989.

Treuherz, Julian, Elizabeth Prettejohn, and Edwin Becker. *Dante Gabriel Rossetti*. London: Thames and Hudson, 2003.

Upstone, Robert. "King Cophetua and the Beggar Maid." In *The Age of Rossetti, Burne-Jones and Watts: Symbolism in Britain, 1860–1910*, edited by Andrew Wilton and Robert Upstone, 147–49. London: Tate Gallery Publishing, 1997.

Wagner, Peter, ed. *Icons, Texts, Iconotexts: Essays on Ekphrasis and Intermediality*. New York: de Gruyter, 1996.

Weinberg, Jonathan. *Speaking for Vice: Homosexuality in the Art of Charles Demuth, Marsden Hartley, and the First American Avant-Garde*. New Haven: Yale University Press, 1993.

West, Shearer. *Portraiture*. Oxford: Oxford University Press, 2004.

West, T. Wilson. "D. G. Rossetti and Ezra Pound." *Review of English Studies* 4 (1953): 63–67.

Williams, William Carlos. "America, Whitman, and the Art of Poetry." *Poetry Journal*, 8.1 (1917): 27–36.

———. *The Collected Poems of William Carlos Williams*. 2 vols. Edited by A. Walton Litz and Christopher MacGowan. New York: New Directions, 1991.

———. *Imaginations*. Edited by Webster Schott. New York: New Directions, 1970.

———. *I Wanted to Write a Poem: The Autobiography of the Works of a Poet*. Edited by Edith Heal. Boston: Beacon Press, 1958.

Wollheim, Richard. *Painting as an Art*. Princeton: Princeton University Press, 1987.

Woodall, Joanna, ed. *Portraiture: Facing the Subject*. Manchester: Manchester University Press, 1997.

Yeats, W. B. *Collected Poems of W. B. Yeats*. Edited by Richard J. Finneran. New York: Macmillan, 1989.

Index